EARTHWALK

·ANCHOR·PRESS· ·DOUBLEDAY·

Philip Slater

Earthwalk

ANCHOR BOOKS
ANCHOR PRESS/DOUBLEDAY
Garden City, New York

Earthwalk was originally published in a hardcover edition in 1974 by Anchor Press/Doubleday.

Anchor Books edition: 1974

To Jackie

Contents

Preface

> *The path to joy leads through despair.*
> **Alexander Lowen**

With the mania for classification that taints our cultural heritage, critics tend to dismiss all radical analyses of modern society as pessimistic or optimistic, according to whether or not the virulent diseases diagnosed are accompanied by spontaneous regenerative processes. This leaves the field clear for "practical," "balanced" analyses which argue that nothing is fundamentally wrong with modern society—that its ills can be cured with enough will power, education, liberal values, and a half-dozen proposals for legislative reform.

I have a personal investment in this issue since I have been dismissed into both wastebaskets: called dour for suggesting that our society's difficulties lie at its very root—in its most treasured values, assumptions, and thought patterns—and cannot simply be pruned away; and called a Pollyanna for suggesting that solutions already exist and do not need to be invented or legislated, but only fostered.

Some people will react to the opening chapters of this book as an invitation to despair, but for me real hope begins with the recognition and identification of dilemmas. I see no purpose in refusing to consider the possibility that our society is founded on pathological premises, or that our species itself may not be viable. To evade these possibilities is to rob ourselves of the opportunity to examine the problem in its fullness.

To argue that Western civilization at some point took a wrong turning is not to say that we can retrace our steps. It is simply a recognition that we cannot construct a humane society out of the dominant trends of our present one. A patient in psychotherapy does not literally return to childhood to unlearn the self-destructive pattern he evolved in growing up, although he may engage in much regressive experimentation in order to undo that negative learning. What is essential is that he be able to relinquish his attachment to his pathway—be able to say to himself, "I have wasted X years of my life in a painful and useless pursuit; this is sad, but I now have an opportunity to try another approach."

This is hard for people to do. There is a strong temptation either to rationalize our wrong turnings as a necessary part of our development ("it taught me discipline"), or to deny that we participated fully in them ("that was before I became enlightened"). Giving up these two evasions leads initially to despair, but as Alexander Lowen points out, despair is the only cure for illusion. Without despair we cannot transfer our allegiance to reality—it is a kind of mourning period for our fantasies. Some people do not survive this despair, but no major change within a person can occur without it.

People get trapped in despair when their despair is incomplete —when some thread of illusory hope is still retained. When artificial lights are turned off in a windowed room at night, it takes a little time to become aware that the darkness is not total, and the longer we are bedazzled by the after-image of that artificial light, the longer it takes to perceive the subtle textures of natural light and shadow—to realize that we can, in fact, see.

One of our most familiar illusions, for example, is the idea of progress: the past was barbarous, the present an improvement, the future will be glorious. Gangrene on the body politic is just a stage we are going through and will respond to social antibiotics. Ecological deterioration is a matter of getting the bugs out of technological development. So long as we imagine things are getting better we will never re-examine basic assumptions. The core fallacy of the idea of progress is the notion that it is possible to optimize everything at once. This is a cherished liberal illusion in America, and its collapse leads naturally to apocalyptic visions. Once we realize, however, that the idea of progress is not merely a dream unfulfilled but an inherent absurdity, then its opposite also becomes absurd. It was silly for people to keep saying, as the technocrats do, "*this* autumn will not lead to winter but to something unimaginably wonderful"; but it is just as silly to think winter will not be followed by spring.

Culture, like personality, is merely a pattern, an arrangement of universal but dissonant elements. In a given time and place one arrangement may be more convenient than another, but every culture makes selections maximizing the fulfillment of some human needs and neglecting others. Nothing can be utterly eliminated. Social change is merely a rearrangement of elements, the expression of a preference for one kind of inconsistency over another. Once we relinquish the fantasy that it is possible to combine all good things in one cultural package we are in a position to realize that the cures for our worst social ailments are already present.

Despair is incomplete (and therefore chronic and suicidal) when we still believe in the *possibility* of an illusion such as progress and imagine only that we have failed to achieve it. This is the worst of both worlds—to be committed to an enterprise without the hope of success. Once we recognize that the illusion *itself* is absurd we can invest our energies in the possible. Who would not like to believe, for example, in the possibility of a society that would maximize personal autonomy and relatedness at the same time? But there is no way to guarantee that one man's need to be alone will never coincide with his neighbor's need to be with him. Every society tends to protect one need more than the other in a given situation. Accepting the fact that this issue must always be negotiated between people—that privacy and community are antithetical needs and cannot simultaneously be maximized—leads to full and complete despair, the despair of disillusionment. But it also enables us to notice and build upon our own fulfilling experiences.

A Note on Language

This book discusses certain aspects of a gigantic symbolic conglomerate: usually designated as "Western civilization" when considered as a long event, "industrial society" when discussed as a much shorter event, or "post-industrial society" when discussed as a very short event. The geographical boundaries of the conglomerate are extremely fuzzy even when the temporal boundaries are more clearly specified. Some of what I will have to say applies to Western industrialized countries, some to all urban centers around the globe, some to all of the notable civilizations of history, some merely to the United States. Most of the time, however, I will use the terms "our society" or "our culture" to designate the conglomerate, allowing context to locate it in time and space. For I am describing processes, not entities, and the processes are found throughout the conglomerate, although more sharply concentrated in some areas than others.

A second terminological awkwardness centers around the terms "man" and "mankind," when used to denote humanity. While sensitive to the issues of sexism involved in such usage, I feel it would be equally unjust to talk about "womankind" or "humanity" when referring to the follies of patriarchal history. I have attempted, therefore—I hope successfully—to use the term "human" when referring to events in a humane potential condition, while reserving the term "man" for events in the male-dominated past. To refer to technology as an "extension of woman" would seem to me to miss the very important point that women have not generally displayed the same need to monumentalize themselves all over the environment.

To tell the truth ineptly is to lie. Most arguments about the truth or falseness of concepts, furthermore, are really disagreements as to their importance. Truth is relative to time, place, and person, and an absurd emphasis may be necessary today to make tomorrow's truth available. Thus to talk of disease, as I have done throughout this book, is not, in the long run, a useful way to think about social processes, any more than it is useful in thinking about psychological or physiological processes. It often creates the illusion that there are processes that are simply bad and can be dispensed with—a notion that contributes much to the awkwardness and destructiveness of Western ways. This defect to me seemed outweighed by the value of the parallels that could be drawn, but it is a mode of thinking that I hope will be outgrown as soon as possible.

Many contemporary authors are struggling with some of the same issues I attempt to confront in this book. Those that seem to pluck the strongest chords of recognition in me are Gregory Bateson, Norman Brown, David Bakan, and William Thompson, but there are obviously many others. In the case of Bateson there is a specific debt to acknowledge, since his presence, along with Warren Brodey, at a conference in which I also participated, was an important precipitant of this book.

Parable 1

*Once there was a man who lost his legs and was blinded
in an accident. To compensate for his losses, he developed
great strength and agility in his hands and arms, and
great acuity in hearing. He composed magnificent music and
performed amazing feats. Others were so impressed
with his achievements that they had themselves blinded
and their legs amputated.*

THE EXTENSIONS OF MAN
or
SAY HELLO TO
THE NICE FIST

> *[People] have to make themselves*
> *predictable, because otherwise the*
> *machines get angry and kill them.*
>
> **Gregory Bateson**

> *It looks better out there.*
>
> **R. J. Gatling**

Discussions of technology usually point out that tools and machines are extensions of the human organism: the hammer an extension of the fist, the wheel an extension of the foot, the computer an extension of the brain, and so on. Through these extensions, it is said, humanity gains control over its environment. It is true that there are certain unpleasant side effects. People must be more cautious, they say—plan ahead a bit more. Technology must be controlled: A greater part of technology must be devoted to the problems created by technology, and so on.

If this were a psychological problem instead of a social one, the therapist to whom it was brought might tactfully suggest that the difficulty lay in the way the "patient" defined it. Therapists are not usually hopeful that an obsessional patient will achieve serenity by devoting additional hours each day to ordering his thoughts, or that a paranoid patient will achieve security by taking additional precautions against his pursuers, or that a heroin addict will vanquish his dependence on the drug by taking a particularly large dose. The circularity of all our thinking about technology suggests that we are in some way recreating the problem in our efforts to solve it.

To exercise control over the environment limits its freedom to influence us. We act on it in such a way as to make its influence a product, in part, of our own efforts—that is, we help create the stimulus to which we respond. Control means that we put a bit of us in the environment and then treat it as if it were a wholly independent stimulus.

Control thus dulls and deadens our experience. The more we control our environment the less possible it is to experience novelty, however avidly we seek it and seek to coerce it. For novelty and freshness cannot be coerced—cannot be commissioned or scheduled, like a happening. They are dependent for their very existence on our having no control over them. To pursue them is to destroy them.

The attempt to control and master the environment thus automatically pollutes it, for it decreases that aspect of the environment that renews, refreshes, surprises, and delights us. The purpose of control is to generate predictability, but predictability is boring as well as secure, fatiguing as well as comforting. Each act of mastery replaces a bit of the environment with a mirror, and a house of mirrors is satisfying only to very sick people.

If this were the only form of pollution resulting from our attempts to master the environment, we could probably live with it, and liberal efforts to solve the technology problem with more technology might be endorsed, albeit without much enthusiasm. But the problem is more serious than this.

I observed that control means putting a bit of ourselves in the environment. But which bit? Something good or something bad? Something known or something unknown? Of what is our man-made environment composed? From what parts of ourselves do these choices come?

Norman Brown summarizes psychological thought on this question, and it is not reassuring.

"The self . . . is maintained by constantly absorbing good parts . . . from the outside world and expelling bad parts from the inner world."

If this is true, then pollution is not merely an accident—a function of carelessness or old-fashioned industrialism. Pollution is an inescapable part of humanity's relationship with the environment —*our very identity rests upon psychic pollution*, just as our physical integrity rests upon expelling organic wastes.

But the environment can absorb a man's organic wastes, and even turn them to good use; and as to his psychic pollution, what difference do fantasies make? Let him project his evil-heartedness wherever he likes—what does it matter?

The danger arises when a man's psychic excretions are given material form—when his projections appear as physical objects. We cannot ignore his fantasies of superpotency when they are represented by overpowered automobiles that claim a thousand lives a week; his paranoid fears when they are expressed in bugging devices and security data banks; his hatreds when they appear in the form of a nuclear arsenal capable of eliminating vertebrate life on our planet.

Our psychic excretions, in other words, show an annoying tendency to become part of our real environment, so that we are forced to consume our own psychic wastes in physical form. Instead of being recycled, as they are in emotional exchanges between people—thus keeping the level of psychic poison relatively constant—their materialization leads to increasing poison accumulation. People have known for centuries that any place inhabited in large numbers by humans is not healthy.

Recycling requires an acceptance of the mortality of individual structures, and the technological impulse—that is, the tendency to give material rather than interpersonal form to psychic impulses —is strongly influenced by the need to deny human mortality.

A science-fiction film some years ago dramatized the problem of psychic waste materialization in the following way: Space explorers discovered a planet that had once boasted a civilization of the highest order, the inhabitants of which had found a way to materialize thoughts directly. The explorers could not understand why this civilization had vanished utterly, until gigantic monsters began to appear. They then realized that the planet's inhabitants had neglected to consider that unconscious wishes and fantasies would materialize along with their consciously purposed thoughts, and had been destroyed by this lack of perspicacity.

This drama is a parable for our time. Our own reality differs from the space fantasy primarily in that (1) thought materialization takes a longer time, and (2) there is no separation between conscious and unconscious products. Every technological advance contains within itself a monster, for each one expresses in one form or another man's monstrous narcissism as well as the simple desires of which it appears superficially to be an expression.

Consider the notion of "finger-tip control" or "push-button control" and the way it appeals to fantasies of infantile narcissistic omnipotence: I am the world, it is my body. The infant cries, the breast arrives, the world smiles. This is finger-tip control. Press a button and all wants are met. But how is it that fantasies (and the reality) of finger-tip control seem to lead to the fantasy (and the reality?) of "pressing *the* button"? Why does the dream of narcissistic omnipotence always lead to that of universal destruction? Why is it that the push-button satisfaction of needs does not evoke bliss?

To understand this process we must first remember that the fantasy of infantile omnipotence is delusional. Personal mastery over the environment plays almost no part in gratification at the beginning. The infant is helpless, and its needs are met not because it is omnipotent but because, and only insofar as, someone loves it. Pleasurable gratification is centrally associated with *not having to satisfy one's own needs*—with what Grace Stuart calls "leisure from self-concern." Primitive societies understand this very well, and devote great amounts of energy to reciprocal gift giving, a practice that Western anthropologists and sociologists usually interpret as promoting all sorts of social and economic side effects. But while these by-products are important and interesting, they are not needed to account for the existence of the practice. We would not think of attributing our preference for sexual relations over masturbation to the fact that the former promotes community solidarity by creating a network of social bonds. We merely say that it is more pleasurable, and the same holds for reciprocal gift giving.

Our own culture seems to have lost track of this point and is fully committed to the narcissistic delusion that pleasure can be obtained through mastery. But being able to command pleasure or love has a built-in self-contradiction. The desire lying at the root of the compulsive striving for mastery is that someone will love me without my having to do anything to bring it about, that I shall receive gifts without having to ask, and that pleasure will come to me that I did not expect or seek. The more control one has over the process—the more one can command these bounties —the less gratifying they automatically become. Control and pleasure cannot coexist, for they destroy each other. The quest for security debases the currency of whatever it seeks to ensure.

A vicious circle is now set in motion. Since the more we can control the production of pleasure the less pleasurable it becomes, pleasure is made scarce by our efforts. The more scarce it is, the more we seek to control it—to ensure it—which, in turn, diminishes the gratification value of the pleasure-source, and so on. The decadent tyrant is a familiar symbol of the advanced stages of this process: "Your wish is my command" is all he hears, yet he is bored and dissatisfied. He wants his wishes satisfied because someone spontaneously *wants* to satisfy them, but there is no way to command this. The tyrant also wants someone to love him for himself, but he dares not risk this and mistrusts any love he does receive. "I would give my kingdom for one true friend," he says, but never does. He seeks more and more exotic pleasures, but they always end by boring him. He requires constant diversion, but it takes increasingly sadistic forms as he tries to test the love of those who seek to satisfy him. He sleeps poorly, and experiences a need to act out destructive fantasies, to risk death and loss.

This is how push-button control leads to fantasies of pushing the nuclear button. The unloving, ungiving, unsatisfying world must be destroyed, along with the worthless, unlovable self. The ceaseless quest, the unbearable tension must be brought to an end. It is the ultimate command, seeking the ultimate satisfaction. It is also the ultimate challenge to the world, containing as it does the secret hope that an even more powerful but loving being will finally come to the rescue at the last minute and gratify the wish to be relieved of the responsibility of self-nurturance.

Humans are the only malevolent animals. They kill for sport and have impulses that cannot be extinguished. Their extensions create an environment that is correspondingly malevolent and unmanageable. Historians have long observed that war is the prime progenitor of technological development. From the materialization of a need to coerce, what else can come but discord and destruction? And when war, cold or hot, is not available to stimulate technological growth, competitive greed seems to be the major spur. Technology, in other words, is an extension of the scarcity-oriented, security-minded, control-oriented side of man's nature, expressed vis-à-vis a world perceived as unloving, ungiving, and unsatisfying.

It is absurd, therefore, to talk of using technology for good or evil, just as it is absurd to talk of using a bomb constructively. The impulse that goes into designing, building, and dropping a bomb is inherently destructive, and the technological impulse by the same token is inherently suspicious, coercive, and life hating.

This has been the theme of science-fiction and monster films for decades, and while it is easy to disdain the simple-minded science-is-dangerous message of such films, perhaps we should not too abruptly dismiss a warning repeated so often, even from so humble a source.

The typical film of this type features a scientist who discovers a secret that confers a special power of some kind. The scientist is usually extremely vain and ambitious. Through his discovery he either creates a monster, becomes one himself, or in some other way lets loose a terrible force on the land, by which he is ultimately destroyed, along with many others. The rather stupid but good-natured folk who oppose him survive the calamity, and the malevolent force is by some (usually rather unconvincing) means destroyed. The last scene often shows the discovery itself being destroyed—the laboratory exploding in flames, the notebook consigned to the living-room grate.

Perhaps through this crude formula we are trying to tell ourselves something. For men in pursuit of personal fame and glory *have* created monsters that are destroying us. The formula film is simply a dramatization of the past century.

Scientists, inventors, engineers (as well as many other prominent persons who fortunately have a less concrete impact—

writers, artists, musicians, and so on) are rather too frequently people who have failed to draw love and admiration from those around them by their intrinsic qualities and have, therefore, turned to the non-human environment in an attempt to extract these responses through their personal accomplishments. When we talk about the extensions of man, then, we should recognize that what is being extended into the environment is not joy and the fullness of life, but jealousy, bitterness, frustration, and revenge. It is very little wonder that when we look at the man-made world around us it contains so much that is ugly and life hating, and forces us to flee to some relatively untouched bit of countryside.

Our mastery of the world has proceeded to the point where the parts of ourselves that we have extruded into it keep backing up and flooding the personality with its own rejected components. This also happens in the interpersonal sphere, where we again have more control over our environment than is beneficial for us. In small, stable communities you can pick your closest friends, but not your total social environment—it is given. Everyone knows everyone and must interact with everyone to some extent. This guarantees a certain balance of interpersonal styles and expressive patterns. Everyone is obliged to have a balanced interpersonal diet as it were.

But urban and suburban Americans do not live in communities, they live in networks. A network is an address book—a list of people who may have little in common besides oneself. Each network has only one reference point that defines it. No two people have the same precise network. This means that everyone controls her own social milieu, and if she likes can subsist entirely on interpersonal candy bars. The persons in her network do not all know each other, so she is never forced to integrate the disparate sides of herself but can compartmentalize them in disconnected relationships. This is one reason why people so often experience anxiety upon entering encounter groups—the exposure of compartmentalized aspects of themselves to different people at the same time makes them feel their whole personality is on the line. On the other hand, this anxiety is accompanied by feelings of excitement, risk, and vitality.

The network system forecloses the possibility of novelty—one tends simply to repeat the same experience in successive encounters. One may have different types of friends but is never forced to experience new combinations of types, while many types are selectively excluded altogether. No true community (one in which everyone interacts with everyone else) is entirely balanced, of course—there are always gaps and limitations. But a true community *maximizes* the utilization of whatever human resources exist in it—that is to say, all possible combinations tend to be realized in the communication system—while networks *minimize* such utilization, since it is limited by each individual's capacity to absorb unsettling stimuli (new combinations).

A true community is like an ecological system where one species' waste is another species' sustenance, like the oxygen-carbon dioxide exchange between plants and animals. What one extrudes, another seeks. The full range of human emotionality and behavior can thus be realized in some form or another. In a network, however, we create closed circuits in which we continually re-encounter what we have dumped. As Ross Speck has shown, intervening in a network in such a way as to make it more like a true community tends to have profound reverberating impacts on the individuals involved. It also produces a general group effect—a heightening of feelings of aliveness, emotional availability, and compassion. This heightening is like the effect of breathing fresh air after a long period indoors inhaling one's own exhalations.

People in our society are indoctrinated from birth with the notion that personal choice is an unqualified boon to humankind —that all our ills derive from the persistence of obstacles to its fullest realization. Yet rats, faced with the choice between a healthy diet and saccharine will select the latter and starve to death, and the frantic buying activity that Americans exhibit is perhaps the same phenomenon.

Choice tends to be liberating and exciting when it is dualistic —when one can either accept what appears to be one's fate or reject it. This is the situation facing those who first leave a stable community. But the life-space of most middle-class Westerners —in which any number of possibilities can, in fact, be realized —is considerably less joyous. If all options are equally pleasurable and there are more than two choices, then on a purely mathematical basis more would be lost than gained with each decision. Nor is this merely mathematical frivolity: Kiyo Morimoto of the Harvard Bureau of Study Counsel writes poignantly of the sense of depression and loss that seems to accompany choices made by students for whom almost anything is possible.

There is probably no arena in which free personal choice is more universally valued than that of marital selection, and certainly much misery and horror resulted from the imposition of cultural norms and parental wishes on reluctant brides and bridegrooms. At the same time it would be difficult to maintain that free choice has brought any substantial increase in marital bliss throughout the land. What was lost when people began to choose their own mates was serendipity. When the choice was made on purely practical, social, or economic grounds there was an even chance that one might marry a person whose personality and interpersonal style would necessitate a restructuring of one's own neurotic patterns. The compulsive tendency people now have to reproduce their childhood experiences in their marriages is jarred in such a system by the reality of the other person. While I would never advocate a return to the older system, we should be alert to its advantages as well as its more familiar drawbacks.

Much of our current pathology is based on an unfortunate human tendency to seek autarchy. If the species turns out to be a flop, it will probably owe its demise to this urge. By autarchy I mean self-sufficiency—the ultimate high tariff system in which nothing goes in and nothing goes out. But lack of exchange is death—living systems are in constant physical interchange with their environments. What makes humans seek quiescence so avidly?

Humanity achieved its present dominance through prolonging infantile dependency. The human infant is the most helpless cub on earth, assaulted from within and without by stimuli over which it has no control. But every thrust has its counterthrust, and when the species took this terrible risk it simultaneously developed a fierce longing for security and self-sufficiency. We may feel most alive and thrilled when we allow ourselves to re-create our early vulnerability, but few humans can tolerate it for any length of time.

Yet security is death just as surely as life is vulnerability. Never to risk terrible hurt and suffering is not to be alive. "Life is problems," decides the hero of Chayefsky's film, *Middle of the Night,* in opting for a troublesome but lively future, and Norman Brown argues that "to be is to be vulnerable." Security mechanisms mimic death and bring one closer to it. Life is gaining all and losing all; security is gaining nothing and losing nothing. Insurance is death on the installment plan.

Autarchy emphasizes not only security, but also the importance of individual boundaries—of identity. And this identity is also a dead thing—only individuated organisms are mortal. Human individuality begins with mausoleums—pharaohs and rajahs invented it. Life is merging and flux and movement: That which has no identity lives forever. To announce oneself is to announce one's death.

Individuality began with kings because they were the first to be set apart and seduced into the fantasy of autarchy. Kings, and authoritarian systems generally, arose only when small organic social units collided, were disrupted or uprooted by involuntary migration, or fell victim to hypertrophy as a result of prosperity, and had somehow to be welded together in oversized units. The loss of a sense of a total and manageable relatedness to the personal and physical environment generated both dependent longings and the quest for autarchy, the first of which was directed toward, and the second projected upon, the king.

But consciousness of self with its illusion of self-sufficiency engendered in kings the fear of death. When men lose awareness of their connectedness they are afraid to die. They wish to live a long time and to immortalize themselves through children or monuments ("Great king, live forever!"). This need to extend oneself in a linear way into the environment is called narcissism and is no longer the exclusive province of kings. It constitutes the single greatest threat to our species. The result of men's fear that dying is ultimate loneliness is an increased likelihood that all humanity will die together.

The West lives amidst the advanced stages of the disease. Millionaires try to add to their wealth, or seek to have their names put on piles of stone. A few people even want their corpses frozen so they can be revived when the cure for their illness is found (the first act of any vital society would be to pull the plug on these refrigerated mummies). Yet all this extraordinary behavior is regarded as perfect sanity by most Americans. Western culture is a kind of Maginot Line of the mind.

Now it may be objected that this gloomy picture rests upon a limited and biased notion of technology—that what I have described reflects merely the mechanical *weltanschauung* of the early industrial revolution, ignoring the more holistic and sophisticated vision of the electronic or cybernetic revolution. Yet if the technological impulse is fueled by the kinds of needs I have described, the role played by technology in human affairs will remain the same, regardless of how sophisticated that technology becomes in its imitation of life. In the original *Frankenstein,* the tormented doctor tries to undo the mischief caused by his first creation by making a second, but at the last minute—realizing that generating a whole race of monsters is a dubious solution to the problems created by a single one—destroys his new Eve. Unfortunately, no technocrat since has shown the same intelligence, possibly because *Frankenstein* was written by a woman.

To make my point clearer, I would like to look ahead to the *third* technological revolution—that which will soon be ushered in by our ability to manipulate genetic codes. Before many decades have passed most existing technology will have been rendered obsolete by the ability to program living matter. Who will bother with anything as clumsy and rigid as a machine when living monsters with specialized adaptations can be created to do the same tasks? Once the genetic code is completely mastered we can create living beings of inordinate strength, or fantastic intelligence, or huge or tiny size, or abundant nurturance, or docility, or sensuality. Hands, eyes, and ears can be modified in a hundred ways for a hundred tasks—the horse's hoof is just a big fingernail, after all. Not only will these monsters be more flexible and adaptable than machines, but also more interesting—sexier, if you will—because they fit more closely our fantasies of power. Also they will reduce, in the short run, the pollution of the environment, since they will be biodegradable and will require only biodegradable energy fuel. The ancient metaphor that opposes greenness and metal will no longer be relevant to ecological issues if, indeed, it ever was.

Science-fiction writers have been playing with the idea of such "androids" for years. Usually they are portrayed rather unimaginatively as a sort of servant class created on a rigid human model and carrying out routine domestic tasks—as if there would be any point in bothering with the whole idea unless one created an infinite variety of new species. In some stories there is a revolt, in which the androids take over and destroy their makers, following the example of their mechanical and electronic predecessors.

My point is that even this genetic form does not and cannot avoid the basic dilemma of technology—*that it facilitates the replacement of real (bilaterally determined) relationships with fantasied (unilaterally determined) ones.* Indeed, the problem is actually heightened, since the difference between a truly separate being and a being programmed by oneself will become more difficult to ascertain. In this new era everyone can be a Pygmalion, constructing lovers, friends, parents, protectors, sex objects, slaves, disciples, and twins. Indeed, bilateral reproduction may disappear altogether when people are faced with the tempting process of reconstituting themselves in an exact genetic likeness. An individual, as Wiener points out, is fundamentally a message, and being able to transmit this message over time is even more likely to titillate immortality freaks than the refrigeration of corpses. Androids, just like machines, can outdistance their creators, conquer, and reinfluence them. But they cannot transcend the vanity and fatuity of their makers without destroying them, since their existence is in itself an expression of the human false-self system. One of the most hopeful possibilities for the human species has been its inability to control the genetic process, thus allowing for an occasional curative dose of serendipity. The loss of that degree of freedom will probably sound the death knell for humanity—whether for good or evil I cannot say.

Alvin Toffler anticipates that people will soon be able to "fill the world with twins of themselves," create human beings with gills for living under water, increase the life span indefinitely, and keep alive disembodied brains: "The human body will come to be seen as modular." While he permits himself an uncharacteristic twinge of discomfort over these developments, the assumptions on which they are based are not questioned. First, technology and the demands of engineering are the master, human beings the servant. For Toffler, who represents a kind of Neville Chamberlain in humanity's relation to technology, the human body is simply an object to be manipulated for mechanical ends. If a gibbon is better adapted to space travel than a human, we will construct humans built like gibbons. If tails are useful, we will graft tails onto people. If legs are superfluous, we will chop them off. One can hardly object to these brutalities since they differ only in degree from the callousness with which humans ordinarily treat their bodies. Whatever is "needed"—that is, whatever someone's arbitrary blueprint calls for—humanity will adapt itself. The feelings aroused by these forced adaptations are of secondary importance, to be dumped on the towering slag heaps of accumulated human misery that encircle every technological enterprise.

Second, power is the only legitimate human motive. One of the most common words in Toffler's book, besides "will" (referring to the inevitable "progress" of science and technology) and "must" (referring to the required human adaptation to this juggernaut), is "able." Human beings will be *able* to live at the bottom of the sea, *able* to miniaturize themselves, *able* to create other humans in the laboratory, *able* to construct machines to make everyday decisions for them. To live at the bottom of the sea, under the ground, on the surface of the moon, or in a space capsule is undoubtedly a great accomplishment—like being able to fart "Annie Laurie" through a keyhole—but one wonders why anyone would bother to do it except to show off. When we look at these "ables" more closely, moreover, a lot of them turn out to be "musts" as well. Because we are "able" to keep more people alive some of us "must" live at the bottom of the sea, some in Antarctica, some on Mars. And if we seek to discover why we should want to be "able" to keep embryos living *ex utero,* we find that it is a matter of economy: The weight of full-grown humans in a space capsule bound for Mars would require more fuel! Thus, to the absurdity of having one's existence determined by some government bureau's arbitrary decision to colonize Mars, would be added the absurdity of having the *form* of that existence determined by the agency's desire to stay within its budget. Leaders of alien civilizations in space fantasies often have motives that seem hilariously trivial, but the joke is on us since those fantasies are simply projections of our own culture. It is in *our* culture that people's lives are threatened or destroyed because some unknown person is consumed with dispassionate scientific curiosity, or mechanically carrying out some bureaucratic procedure, or obeying an order whose premises have been forgotten.

Third, the body is viewed, in accordance with Western medical thinking, as a machine rather than an organism. This machine has replaceable parts which are thoroughly understood, but the whole is of little interest and comparatively unknown. The problem-solving part is most highly valued and the fantasy of separating it from the rest is extremely popular. The conviction of many schizophrenics that the brain could function better if only the annoying body in which it is embedded could be lopped off, is now shared, not surprisingly, by scientists. "Better" means that it could pursue its own logic without distracting feedback from the real world. Since the troubles that currently surround us are largely a product of such disembodied thought, however, perhaps this assumption, too, needs to be re-examined.

When man invented the machine, for which there is no external model in nature, he invented it in his own image. The machine does not come from nowhere—it mirrors man's mechanical head. The human is the only animal programmed to ignore the very feedback that it is simultaneously programmed to utilize, which is why only a human can make an animal, or another human, neurotic or crazy. As Weston La Barre points out, reality alone cannot make an animal neurotic—it takes the mechanical application of some twisted symbolic system to wreck an animal's responsivity. This is perhaps why autistic children are usually the offspring of intellectuals. Psychopathology is an inherent by-product of the ability to generate symbols, which is always presented, in renditions of the comedy of evolution, as humanity's unique strength. But attached to this strength is a fatal flaw, built into the species at the start—a capacity to disregard significant feedback in favor of inner symbolic circuitry.

Freud once commented on the widespread fear of automata, and in the same context suggested that uncanny (*unheimlich*) sensations were activated by familiar (*heimlich*) but repressed visions. Putting these two ideas together I would argue that what is *heimlich* and *unheimlich* about automata is that they reflect a quality repulsively and uniquely human. Our fear of robot-like creatures that move in mechanical disregard of external consequences is a fear of the human head. The heroine in a horror film pleads for mercy but the monster is oblivious. "It is in-human," she shrieks, but she is wrong. Humanity is the only species that disregards its own surrender signals. Human beings are "freed" from the instinctual necessity of inhibiting aggression when a cospecific yields. A machine is free from everything but its program. A blind man is free from the blinding sun, a deaf man from the deafening thunder. Much of the time when we talk of freedom we mean freedom from messages—the ability to pay attention only to interior conceptual patterns. This schizoid freedom—the capacity to operate solely in response to internal logic, to ignore feedback—is what makes mass killing possible. Hiroshima, Dresden, Auschwitz, Vietnam—all rest on this liberation—this ability to proceed according to a set of systematic principles, mechanically, bureaucratically, rigorously.

But horror is not the only reaction to automaton behavior. Henri Bergson pointed out long ago that "mechanical inelasticity," or the presentation of "something mechanical encrusted upon the living" was an important source of humor, and inspirational narratives of a patriotic or religious nature also draw heavily on the capacity to ignore feedback. Following an internal script regardless of external information is comic, horrifying, or heroic, depending on how the culture defines the situation. The mechanical monster that frightens us, the clown who sits on a non-existent chair, and the thin red line of soldiers marching bravely to their death merely represent different attitudes toward the same phenomenon.

In the past the tendency to ignore feedback, both from the gut and from the external world, was called "courage" and highly valued. Courage has always been carefully distinguished from mere valor or recklessness—to be courageous you had to be able to recognize your mortal peril and at the same time disregard both the danger and your life-preserving instincts. There is no such thing as a courageous animal: if it does not run when in danger, it is either because (a) it is trapped, or (b) it is more angry than afraid. When fear outstrips anger it will run if it can.

A machinelike response in the face of danger had no real value until men began to make war on each other—it was of no use either in hunting or in surviving other predators. The most mechanical peoples won over those less so, so that a profound cultural selection took place. Evolution is full of such mistakes.

If this process is not reversible, our species will destroy the planet—hopefully before it has an opportunity to excrete any colonists. When human beings were freed from dependence upon instinct for communication, they were also freed from having to communicate about their instincts at all, or having to respond to such communications. This means simply that we who share space on the same little planet must try to get our needs met in the face of our "freedom" to misrepresent those needs to each other and our "ability" to disregard the needs of others, whether misrepresented or not.

Many of the most treasured virtues of the past several thousand years no longer have survival value. From an ecological viewpoint virtues such as courage and perseverance are simply bad habits. We should consider the possibility of giving medals for cowardice, for a coward is responsive to the environment and to the bodily needs of at least one human being. The virtue of being able to complete a task might also be examined with more suspicion. What is distractibility but responsiveness and sensitivity pejoratively defined? From the viewpoint of a horse with blinders, horses without blinders are distractible. Western culture looks at its "undeveloped" (i.e., no blinders) contemporaries in the same way, disdaining their slight tendency to be distracted by the relationship of a single innovation to everything else in their lives. To be distractible is to be aware of the indissoluble interconnectedness of living matter—clearly no way to get things done.

To exemplify this issue, let me quote from a letter written by a Moroccan graduate student:

". . . Every single little act becomes a very complicated interaction. I live in the old Arab city where there are not many phones. I need a phone to contact the people I am to interview and who happen to be the bourgeois modernized élite who will be choked if I drop by as we traditionally do. I went to the public phone which is not an automatic one. I gave my list of numbers to the operator who happens to have known me since ages. He wanted to know why I want to call all these people. I explained briefly that I was doing a sort of sociological survey. He wanted more details. I told him that it will take us about an hour, and that by then the post office will have to close. He took it as an insult and asked me to wait until he called me. I did. He called me to say that the numbers were either busy or not answering, and that in any case I should not try to monopolize a public phone by calling so many people. I then told him I was sorry

I was so worried about the time, and that I was ready to tell him what I was doing. I did. He wanted to know how can 10 or 20 people, very special and particular, be representative of hundreds and thousands, who only have some things in common with them. So I proceeded to explain '*la théorie de la probabilité.*' He then disagreed and rejected the theory as being junk. I told him that it was his right to reject it, that that was the normal destiny of a theory—some accept it and some reject it. He did not like my attitude and said that I was avoiding discussing the matter with him, because I think in my head that he is not worth discussing with because he did not have my chance to carry on his studies and ended up doing a stupid job, etc. I tried to convince him of the opposite. It took me two more sessions and three days to get to use the phone.

"The famous 'anesthésie' which bothered me so much in Cambridge is in fact what allows you to be efficient there, and its absence leaves you completely immersed in an environment you can't control because you are so emotionally involved and at such a passionate level."

A traditional culture is full of distractions. One cannot deal impersonally with the environment, or follow out an internal program in the mechanical, linear way we are used to doing in the West. One is caught in an intricate web of ties that pull one back and demand an examination of how every new act interrelates with everything else. Relationships are primary, taking precedence over the pursuit of knowledge or personal achievement.

The ecological problems we face today are not possible so long as this kind of thinking persists; the absorption in interrelationships prevents one from even contemplating the kind of mechanical response that leads to ecological imbalances. One is not allowed to postpone (indefinitely) dealing with the "social" or "human" consequences of some narcissistic pursuit. Until the foundations of a traditional society have been shattered, the development of such grotesqueries as nuclear weapons and sociological surveys are out of the question, even if the technical knowledge were available. Their value, *weighed against everything else in the society,* would have to be established *prior* to embarking on the enterprise, rather than being asserted by a public relations department after it was a *fait accompli,* as is the practice in our own society. Americans delight in the ease with which they can get things done, but we owe it all to the simple device of having abolished every social mechanism for weighing actions in advance. This is done largely through absolutistic slogans like free enterprise, scientific freedom, freedom of choice, and so on. These slogans have been marketed so successfully that most civilized peoples, confronted daily with the disastrous consequences of the removal of social balancing mechanisms, feel that the price is worth paying.

Virtues such as courage, perseverance, and personal achievement are fundamentally disconnectors. They rip the individual or group out of the social and ecological fabric in which they are embedded and set them on autonomous linear courses, looking neither right nor left. If you remove part of the forebrain of a fish, it loses its schooling response, and presumably, if enough other parts were removed as well, it would ignore its environment altogether and swim right around the world, following a course as true as that of a human navigator. As things are, it must be admitted, fish never get anywhere. Nature, in her primitiveness, has arranged that all they ever do is hover uselessly, like butterflies, around their food supply, their breeding grounds, and each other.

All of the disconnector virtues—courage, perseverance, rectitude, chastity, ambition, honor, dutifulness, self-discipline, temperance, purity, self-reliance, impartiality, incorruptibility, dependability, conscientiousness, sobriety, asceticism, spirituality —are ecologically unsound. All express the same arrogant assumption about the importance of the single individual in society and the importance of humanity in the universe. To imagine that it matters (except to those in immediate contact with him) whether or not a man is righteous, holy, or self-actualized is the height of pomposity.

The opposite qualities—cowardice, distractibility, sensuality, inability to complete tasks or resist temptations, partiality, dependency, inconsistency, corruptibility, and so on—are humble virtues. They express humanity's embeddedness in a larger organic system—a system that has its own laws and justice. As such they ultimately have higher survival value than the disciplines since they serve to reconnect the individual with his or her environment. This is not to say that the arrogant virtues should be extirpated from the human repertory. We need only recognize the *price* of the disconnector virtues.

Anglo-Saxons, for example, have always aimed a good bit of mockery, tinged with envy, at the *"mañana* mentality" of Latin proletarians. In most cases, however, saying *"mañana"* is simply a matter of putting first things first—of being unwilling to sacrifice joy and good relationships in the service of the get-rich-quick schemes of industrial hustlers. As we discover increasingly that much of what the poor Latin has been unable to get done would have been better left undone in our own society, we begin to develop more respect for his priority system.

Yet few peoples have been able to hold out against the assault of Western ideology. Seduced by the promise of a little affluence and a longer life, they have deserted in droves. Is this not an indication of the superiority of our achievement-oriented culture? Our own ancestors presumably lived in some kind of stable, present-oriented culture and apparently were dissatisfied with it. Since there is no going back, in any case, and since most peoples seem to have rejected it when they had a choice, what is the point of these invidious comparisons?

There is enormous variety among cultures that are present-oriented or traditional or "primitive," so let me state what I am lumping together in making comparisons with the industrial West. I call a "simple community" one in which people live in a small village or band; are rarely exposed in a lifetime to a place lying outside their village, hunting territory, or nomadic circuit; will gain few new relationships in a lifetime except through births, and lose few except through deaths; live largely in the present; and feel themselves to be an organic and undetachable part of their immediate social and natural environment. Half the population of the world still lives under conditions that approximate this type in many respects, but their numbers are decreasing with great rapidity.

I do not wish to hold up the simple community as a utopia. People raised in an industrial society are unfitted for life under such conditions and would be miserable if they tried. Furthermore, the simple community has one enormous weakness—it is highly vulnerable to conquest. Nor should we be so naïve as to posit some sort of primeval bliss in the simple community. Even among those uncontaminated by Western contact, many are plagued by oppressive social mores, and if the joys of such living appear to be far more intense, so are the miseries. Life, furthermore, although emotionally richer, is also shorter. Westerners would also find it dull, if only because of their own blunted senses and flattened emotionality—necessary for life under conditions of urban chaos.

I dwell on the simple community only because the relation between what we lost when we gave it up and our present crisis is so poorly understood. Our cultural history tends to be presented either as an uninterrupted ascension into paradise (not quite yet achieved, but just around the corner) or as a brave venturing forth from comfortable dependency to lonely but admirable freedom. Occasionally someone suggests, with bleak nostalgia, that the entire enterprise was an unmitigated disaster—like Napoleon's invasion of Russia or the Vietnam War—but they are usually dismissed as nervous Nellies.

My purpose is not to condemn Western culture or idealize the past. I want only to correct the balance a little. The vituperation that writers like Toffler heap upon those who reflect with any affection upon the past betrays a stubborn unwillingness to make the radical changes necessary to extricate ourselves from our present difficulties. If we take the position that every move Western humanity has made thus far was necessary and desirable we are unlikely to come up with any new thinking on the matter.

Let me return, then, to the simple community and the reasons for its rejection. First of all, it is incorrect to say that such communities have always chosen "progress" when given a choice. Our own country contains many Amerindian tribes who have clung desperately, against absurd odds, to their own way of life, and others may be found in every part of the world. Again and again individuals in "primitive" societies have made lucid and articulate comparisons between their own and Western culture, showing a clear understanding of the latter and what they found wanting in it. Indeed, their criticisms are substantially the same as those made by Westerners themselves.

Furthermore, what is glossed over as "choosing" Western culture often turns out to be more a matter of having it jammed down one's throat. Decimated by armed slaughter and Western diseases, flooded with Western artifacts, and with their own institutions overthrown by violence, it has become a matter of adopting Western ways or having no coherent culture at all. In South Vietnam we have created a whole nation of displaced persons, many of whom will undoubtedly "choose" Western patterns.

But even in the case of those who have freely chosen Western culture, we need to look at what it is they are choosing. What impresses non-Western peoples most about our culture is its power. Guns, bombs, bulldozers, helicopters—all express the power of the colonialist. There is no question of Western culture providing more pleasure, more wisdom, better relationships between people or with the environment—only power. Few people would argue seriously that a volcano is better than a flower, but humans have always been more inclined to worship volcanoes than flowers. When someone comes and repeatedly hits you with a club, you respect and envy his club and his power to get away with that hitting, and try to emulate it, if for no other reason than self-protection.

Co-operative assumptions always give way to competitive ones when one powerful body begins to play by its own competitive rules. This is all it takes to destroy trust and give rise to a competitive system. The history of the West is simply the progressive dissemination of this infection: A dominant society brutalizes a simple one, which ultimately overwhelms its oppressor and becomes itself an oppressor.

To say that Western peoples became dissatisfied with primitive life and moved beyond it is therefore misleading. It would be more accurate to say that cultural selection has populated the world with dissatified people—people incapable of enjoying the world around them as it is. This is hardly surprising—dissatisfied people make better fighters. But it is ultimately destructive to life on the planet to have an ecological whole dominated by those who are so alienated from it as to have lost the capacity to perceive it. If we are not content with our planet, we should perhaps commit suicide and leave it to those who are. But in any case the conditions that gave competitiveness survival value have long since evaporated, as many observers have pointed out, and we are looking now to the losers to see how the ultimate victory may be gained.

The difference between the two modes of thinking is nicely exemplified in the area of health. It has taken more than a century for Western medicine to rediscover what witch doctors and shamans have known all along: (1) that a disease occurs in a whole organism, not, as in a machine, in one defective part; and (2) that every organism is organically related to others, and to the total environment, and hence any "cure" that does not take account of these relationships is likely to be ephemeral. What we stigmatize as magic is scientific inasmuch as it teaches the wholeness and interconnectedness of living forms. Scientific medicine, on the other hand, is irrational in that it treats the organism as if it were a machine, disconnected from its surroundings and internally disconnectable. As Bateson observes, medicine is a science "whose structure is essentially that of a bag of tricks," with "extraordinarily little knowledge" of the body as a "systematically cybernetically organized self-corrective system. Its internal interdependencies are minimally understood."

Doctors are fond of saying things like "your body needs fuel, just like your car," or more ambiguously, "your body is the only machine that improves with use." The technique of the Western doctor is essentially that of the plumber or mechanic—to locate the problem in a specific site and then deal with that part as if it were independently malfunctioning—consider the fascination with transplants, for example. Once the problem is localized the automobile model is again employed in "fixing" it. The faulty part is removed or replaced, or its functioning improved through the use of chemicals. The patient's capacity to verbalize her distress is given the same weight as a mechanic would give to remarks coming over a car radio. The answer to "I hurt" is a series of tests. The doctor listens to the motor, checks the pressure in the tires. While the witch doctor responds to the patient's own message and to his or her life situation and relationships, the Western doctor responds to his own equipment. Doctors frequently will ignore a confusing complaint from a patient in favor of treating a "disease" (revealed by tests) of which the patient is unaware and from which he or she does not suffer. This fragmented and invasive approach to the organism threatens the individual's psychic boundaries and hence generates anxiety, which produces more symptoms to be treated in the same fragmented way, so that the physician is constantly trying to cure the effects of his own bad medicine.

Western medicine exemplifies strikingly our alienation from

the body—viewing it as a machine that doesn't belong to us, and which we are willing to ply with poisons at a moment's notice in order to chastise those parts not "working" in a way that allows *us* to work. Even when someone comes along to point out our neglect of the body, it is usually to say that "it" will work better if "its" needs are catered to: "relaxing will give you renewed energy for work," or "paying attention to your natural body rhythms will make you more efficient." Nothing could provide a more chilling example of schizoid detachment from the body than such phrases, yet they appear daily in the media. It has been suggested, for example, that pills will soon be developed to cure jet lag—a beautiful example of our willingness to brutalize the body in the service of technology, and one that typifies the manner in which technology "solves" the problems it creates. A human need is sacrificed to further some instrumental task. But since a scorned body tends to take its own revenge, a problem is created for the task-minded: days off from tasks will be required to adjust the body to the shock. To save more time (since this is why we have jets in the first place) a pill is designed to obviate the necessity of such adjustment. The side effects of such a pill may well require another pill to offset it—for such chain reactions are the bread-and-butter of pharmacology in America, where a large proportion of all disease is drug-produced. This may hasten the emergence of cold-turkey health retreats where people will go for a period of time to unravel the multiple interactive effects of all the pills they take, under cautious medical supervision. And so another industry will have been spawned by the classic American technique of proliferating disharmony. The striking increase in cancer in the United States is hardly surprising: A disintegral medicine is merely reflected in a disease of bodily disunion.

But aside from these peripheral follies, hasn't Western medicine generally been a success? Is it fair to put the Western physician down in comparison with the witch doctor, when, in fact, he has achieved far more with his supposedly inadequate theory than the witch doctor has?

No one could deny that the Western doctor has "achieved" more—that, after all, is what Western civilization is all about. Whether he has cured more people of what troubles them is far more doubtful—it depends, as usual, on which criterion we use.

Western medicine always uses that of longevity—a revealing choice given the role of immortality yearnings in forming the technological impulse—and there is no question of the extraordinary power of Western doctors to keep people alive, even against their will and the welfare of the species.

But if we use the criterion of healthiness per capita, the much-touted triumph of Western medicine begins to look like a pyrrhic victory. What we appear to have bought is a longer life but a more sickly one. Doctors who have had an opportunity to examine "primitive" peoples living under stable but rigorous conditions, protected from Western contact, and not grossly malnourished, have been impressed with their healthiness by contrast with Westerners. This good health, it is true, owes more to the absence of change, stress, and urban confusion than it does to the occasional ministrations of the witch doctor, whose principal contribution may be his adherence to Hippocrates' cardinal rule—so consistently and grossly flouted by those who are taught it. René Dubos emphasizes the importance of unchanging conditions for health, and cites, as does Toffler, the overwhelming evidence that environmental change tends to foster disease.

But it would be foolish to rest this argument on a few unspoiled Edens. For every one of these islands of health there is an equally "primitive" tribe debilitated by poor nutrition and parasitic infestation. Western medicine could make it on the healthiness criterion if it could show that Western populations were by and large free of disease a majority of the time.

Unfortunately, this is not the case. Recent efforts to assess the health of the population at large have suggested that almost everyone is diseased at least to the point of "requiring" medical attention. This might be dismissed as an effort to whomp up more business for doctors, but other studies have found that in a 24–36 hour period, from 50 per cent to 80 per cent of the entire population takes at least one medical drug. Whether or not the United States is a sick society, it certainly *thinks* it is. With all the brilliant medical achievements of the past two hundred years, it appears that the average person on an average day feels, if anything, a little worse than before.

But the "advances" of medicine were only secondarily motivated by a desire to increase health. Their primary motive, as in the case of other technological and scientific achievements, was to gain and display power. Western physicians have always been more enthusiastic about conquering the body than curing it. The old joke about the operation being a success although the patient died still expresses the fundamental disparity between the goals of the patient and those of her supposed healer, but it seems a little off center today, since the major non-pecuniary goal of the profession seems to be to display its godlike power over death. Consider the fanatical zeal with which moribund patients are kept alive with tubes, wires, and chemicals. For whom is this heroic effort made? For the patient, who is unconscious? Had she been asked (and of course she never is—her body belongs to the institution, it would seem), she would probably have expressed a desire to leave this inhuman environment and die at home among her loved ones. For the relatives, who are going into bankruptcy to pay for this magnificent achievement, and are unable either to mourn or to carry on their lives? Hardly. It is for the doctor himself and his profession. He has "done all he could" (note the narrow assumption on which that phrase is based—his role is to keep a body alive, not to minister to the health of the living, which might require letting the dead die), and the medical priesthood has celebrated its famous victory dance over death for a time.

Boosters of technological progress have always emphasized the joys of mastery. Yet it is interesting that the word "accomplishment" means to fill up, to complete. But what is lacking? No one on earth seems to feel as incomplete as the Western man. Has he made a hole in himself just to fill it up? Could there be any relationship between his stubborn insistence on perceiving the world as a series of disconnected parts and his inability to feel whole? And could the frantic and ceaseless energy output of Western man, as well as the bewildering proliferation of information, artifacts, and enterprises, all come from trying desperately to create the missing whole by the futile procedure of adding more disconnected parts?

These questions must be postponed for now. For the present I want merely to point out that the inability to perceive wholes usually goes by the name "rationalism," for some reason. The strategy is a simple one. If you operate with quantitative criteria, as rationalists always do, then it is more important to be right about details than about totalities, since there are far more parts than there are wholes. Now science, medicine, and technology have shown a masterful accuracy about countless details and a trained incapacity to grasp a total organic system—an incapacity they have passed on to all of us, however much we may struggle against it. This adds up, quantitatively, to a pretty good record, and is the basis of all of our arrogance in relation to primitive magicians and medicine men, who tend to be correct about totalities and absurd about many details, and thus do far worse on a purely quantitative basis.

But even granting all of the above, the argument is often made (usually with ill-concealed pride) that "technology cannot be stopped." If this means that legislation "forbidding" technological innovation is unlikely to be passed, or if passed, enforced, I would agree. I can't think of anything more absurd, offhand, except perhaps the notion, shared by Toffler and most observers, that technological growth will just continue in the same linear, accelerative path it has followed thus far. Both notions share a misconception about how social change occurs, a question I would like to postpone until a later chapter. Technological growth will sag drastically when the motivational pathology that drives it dries up, and there are signs that this has already begun to happen. On the other hand, if it does not happen soon, the current impetus of technology is sufficient to destroy the planet in thirty years, and this also has begun to happen. Which will happen first is a matter of guesswork, but the drying up of the technological impulse depends in part upon the diffusion of uncharacteristic thought patterns, a largely spontaneous phenomenon of which this book is a slightly self-conscious example.

Parable 2

A girl from Berkeley told a story about People's Park.
When people were fixing up the park some of them took shovels
and just started digging a hole. They had not really talked
about why they were digging the hole, but every day they
continued. Other people would also stop and dig for a while,
and the hole got deeper and deeper. They did not recognize
any kind of leadership. At first they thought they should make
a fountain, but the hole was getting too big for a fountain.
So then they thought a wading pool for kids would be the
thing, but the hole was getting too big for a wading pool.
Then they thought a swimming pool would be nice, but that
would be dangerous without lifeguards or a fence around it. But
they kept digging anyway.

One day a guy came up, picked up a shovel and started
shoveling dirt back into the hole. "Hey, what do you think
you're doing?" someone shoveling the dirt out shouted angrily.

"You feel like shoveling dirt out of the hole, I feel like
shoveling dirt into the hole. I'm doing my own thing, just like
you."

(Glenda Cimino, from *Venceremos Brigade*)

SOCIAL METASTASIS
or
SPREADING THE WORD

> *If we would have pure knowledge of
> anything we must be quit of the body.*
> **Plato**

> *Apart from the body, life is an illusion.*
> **Alexander Lowen**

> *Freedom's just another word for nothing
> left to lose.*
> **Kristofferson and Foster**

Dirt has been defined as matter in the wrong place. Similarly, a poison can be defined as a substance ingested in too great a quantity over too short a time.

We are just beginning to awaken from a kind of madness, under the influence of which it was believed that growth was a magic quality not subject to this definition. No amount was considered harmful, no speed too great. The importance of balance and harmony, which peoples around the globe had hitherto recognized with reverence and wonder, was forgotten during these centuries of delirium. Western man instead worshipped imbalance and hypertrophy. "Maximal" and "optimal" became interchangeable terms. Growth was regarded as an unmixed blessing to such a degree that the term was even applied to improvements in personal character. To "change and grow" became an imperative of the American leisure class, raising the specter of a race of psychic behemoths.

In the organic world hypertrophy is pathology. Growth is regarded as healthy only when the rate of change is in the long run decelerative—an accelerative rate of growth is usually deemed malignant. A human child, for example, grows more in the first year of life than in any other. If it grew at a higher rate each year the monstrosity would collapse from gravitational stress before it reached school age. Yet the growth of technological change and its correlates: science, knowledge, the production of material artifacts, legislation, population, and so on, is viewed as healthy even when constant or accelerative.

The kind of growth Western culture has experienced over the past three hundred years would be considered a sign of gross malfunction in any other context. Healthy growth is paced differently—it does not absorb or destroy everything living around it. It is cancerous cells that grow and reproduce rapidly in total disregard of their connection with surrounding cells. From this viewpoint technology would have to be regarded as a cancer on human culture, Western culture a cancer on the human species, and the human species as a cancer on terrestrial life—a cancer that may in the end be treated by radiation and radical surgery at the same time.

Let us hope another cure can be found. The problem has at least been diagnosed in the report of the Club of Rome called *The Limits to Growth,* in which it was finally recognized that the only conceivable outcome of the present philosophy of constant economic growth is ecological catastrophe. Our task here is to understand the origin of the growth delusion, how it took hold of us so violently, how it ramifies through our thought processes, and how to eradicate it.

We are used to hearing pathological growth figures cited with pride and awe, only recently tinged with alarm: that scientific knowledge doubles every ten years, that half of all the energy consumed in the last two millennia has been consumed in the last century, that the tempo of human evolution is 100,000 times as rapid as that of prehuman evolution, that the earth's urban population will double in eleven years, that a civilized teen-ager is surrounded by twice as many newly manufactured goods as she was as an infant, that 90 per cent of all the scientists who ever lived are now alive, and so on. But *why* are humans consuming all that energy, for example? What is the motive behind such frenzied activity? When animals become this restless we assume they are under some kind of stress.

In these three chapters I will try to trace some of the factors responsible for this pathological growth. At times my remarks may seem to imply that the species was doomed from the very start. Yet for hundreds of thousands of years humans were only potentially destructive. One might say that the disease was present, but only in the same sense that harmful bacteria are always present in the body. René Dubos observes that "the severity of a microbial or toxic disease is determined as much by the intensity of the body response as it is by the characteristics of the microbe or toxin involved." Similarly, David Bakan, following Selye and Freud, sees the organism as in more danger from its adaptive reactions than from external agencies.

We are in the acute phase of a virulent disease, and while it is of some value to trace its ultimate sources, it is more important to look at how it got out of hand. Our species has always been vulnerable to the disease. Yet only a portion of humankind fell victim to it, while others are still resisting it, although with rapidly decreasing success. The vulnerability is depressing, but the existence of healthy tissue is encouraging. We need to understand both our intrinsic vulnerability to the disease and the nature of the forces that facilitate or resist it in its acute form.

I find I make frequent use of the cancer metaphor in discussing our society. It is difficult to see the recent technological explosion, with its extraordinary proliferative irrelevance, as anything but a neoplasm. But the analogue is deeper than that: "It has been demonstrated that when normal tissues are grown on a glass surface, the cells stop growing when they touch each other. But cancer cells similarly grown on a glass surface continue to grow, unimpeded by cellular contact." (Bakan) Studies of cancer cells seem to suggest that some kind of mutually limiting communication present between normal cells is weak or absent between cancer cells. It is as if cancer cells had been heavily indoctrinated with the ideology of individualism and personal achievement.

Imagine a mass of cancerous tissue, the cells of which enjoyed consciousness. Would they not be full of self-congratulatory sentiments at their independence, their more advanced level of development, their rapid rate of growth? Would they not sneer at their more primitive cousins who were bound into a static and unfree existence, with limited aspirations, subject to heavy group constraint, and obviously "going nowhere"? Would they not rejoice in their control over their own destiny, and cheer the conversion of more and more normal cells as convincing proof of the validity of their own way of life? Would they not, in fact, feel increasingly triumphant right up to the moment the organism on which they fed expired?

Yet it would be a mistake to imagine that our tendency to embrace our disease ever more fervently is merely a matter of arrogance. There is a spiral effect that comes from the fact that our disease is continually being externalized. The more we create a diseased environment the more frantic we become in our efforts to escape it. And each motion in the service of escape carries us farther and farther from the state of health to which we are so desperately seeking to return. Toffler, for example, sees more clearly than anyone the devastating impact of our frantic change pattern, yet demands that we increase our adaptability to change, thus insuring that change will further accelerate. He wants to "free" human beings from those spontaneous reactions that tend to slow down or interfere with the rate of change. He wants us, in other words, to adapt to a bad environment.

Now adaptation to a bad environment not only provides positive feedback for that environment, but also reduces one's ability to respond to a good one. The small child left for weeks in a hospital remains in a psychically healthy state just so long as it continues to cry bitterly for its parents. Psychic damage begins from the moment it settles down to a peaceful indifference, making what pleased hospital personnel call a "good adjustment." The consequences of prolonged adaptation to that impersonal and somewhat inhuman environment are an emotional shallowness, an inability to form lasting attachments, and chronic depressiveness. Similarly, recent studies of schizophrenia show that the patient's illness can be considered a reasonable adaptation to a grossly malfunctioning family communication system. In fact it would not be far from the mark to say that all disease—psychological, physiological, societal—is adaptation to a bad environment. If this is true, then the difficulty in recovering health when a disease is externalized becomes clear. The environment cannot improve since the disease is continually fed back into it. Further adaptation yields further disease which worsens the environment, necessitating a more exaggerated adaptation, and so on. The most obvious examples of this process would include such fatuities as adapting to overpopulation by learning to live under the sea, or adapting to the surplus of cars by building more roads.

But there are other examples that I personally find more painful. The search for social justice over the past century has rested in large part on principles of consistency, objectivity, equality, fairness, and so on. In the fight against oppression and exploitation a major weapon has been to expose the fact that two individuals from different backgrounds are not treated the same before the law, or that they have unequal opportunities, or that they receive different responses for the same behavior. Another is to demonstrate that a value embraced in the abstract is notably flouted in some specific instance.

Our society is riddled with oppression, and not to utilize these weapons would be a crime of omission against humanity. Yet we need to recognize the degree to which objectivity is a symptom of our cultural disease, and consistency the mechanism of its metastasis. The assumption that progress is achieved by trading the brutalities of a personal slaveowner for those of an impersonal one needs to be examined.

In the simple community, objectivity as we understand it scarcely exists. Almost all acts, decisions, and rewards are based on particular relationships and positions within the community. There is inequality, there is inequity, even a modest degree of exploitation. There is certainly scapegoating and personal misery. Still, everyone is recognized as having some sort of value, and some sort of meaningful connection with everyone else. No one dies unnoticed or unmourned. When, with increasing size, this form breaks down and authoritarianism takes its place, we begin to encounter exploitation and brutality on a scale and in a form familiar to us. Here for the first time rewards and decisions tend to be based on a kind of crude principle: the closer to the center of power, the more rewards. The distribution of rewards can now be predicted by an outsider without knowing the entire network of relationships and customs in the community. And as power becomes more centralized and less hedged with legitimacies, anyone can achieve material success simply by managing to please the tyrant. Social mobility begins with autocracy.

But with further increases in size and complexity, authoritarianism itself breaks down. The personal limitations of despots give rise to demands for objective, mechanized systems for distributing rewards. People begin to feel that personal relationships should play no part in arriving at political or economic decisions. Power increasingly lies in impersonal mechanisms, although those who reside at the center of the machinery are paid off so handsomely in counterfeit rewards for the stress they endure that they imagine themselves to be the masters of it—a fantasy endorsed by those at the periphery.

As the system becomes more and more objective and depersonalized, any remaining tendency toward corruption or exploitation becomes grossly magnified; and as the web of personal relatedness becomes further shattered by the emphasis on universal and objective criteria, the consequences of exploitation become more vicious. The possibility of appeal through personal channels is lost and whole categories of individuals can simply be forgotten. The unimportant individual in a simple community has rights, merely by virtue of his being a relative and neighbor of everyone in the system, that his counterpart in a society like ours can never achieve. In the most corruption-free bureaucratized society the individual can appeal only to a series of abstract principles which may not apply to her and which ignore her personal condition. Exploitation and oppression tend to assume a form that is massive and impersonal. The system is unwieldy and has high inertia: Anything moving is hard to stop and vice versa. In a personalized system, on the other hand, while there is much movement, nothing can go too far in any direction without corrective forces coming into play.

We respond to this unwieldiness by adapting to the principles on which it is based, accepting and trying to expand them. But striving for more consistency and fairness exaggerates the unwieldiness and inertia of the system still further. In a simple community everyone is treated differently because her position in it is unique. Since in most of the business of everyday life we *have* no relationship with those with whom we deal, we seek ways to be more fair, to make sure that everyone is treated alike, to apply abstract criteria that ignore particularities. The brutalities of judges, doctors, and administrators in our society derive less from their failure to apply equitable principles than from their total ignorance of the people affected by their decisions.

Organic networks are full of inconsistency. They arrive at some sort of balance through spontaneous blundering toward multiple accommodation. The application of abstract principle destroys this balance irrevocably, and the efforts to re-establish that balance on a mathematical basis are a little like trying to balance a ball on the point of a sword by firing bullets at it whenever it starts to lean. The demand for consistency treats the disease by seeking to extend it to the entire organism.

Since I feel somewhat uneasy about putting this argument into the hands of conservatives, I want to add a word of clarification. No significant radical social movement in America today derives its validity and meaning from these principles, although all radical movements use them as political arguments. While such movements begin with the rhetoric of equality, fairness, and consistency, they tend to shift—in response to radicalization and continual social analysis—to a conviction of the particularized superiority of their own constituents. Women, blacks, Indians, and third-world nations still lay considerable stress on equality, but their more militant representatives have come to recognize that the dominant Western white-male society needs them a great deal more than they need it, independent of all issues of fairness and justice. The dominant forces in society tend not to perceive this distinction, since it is far more comfortable to assume that someone merely wants a share of your pie than to acknowledge yourself a prisoner in a diseased and moribund system.

Linearity and Principle

Much of what I have said seems to cast a suspicious eye on the use of abstract concepts and principles in human affairs— even though I have not hesitated to employ my own. Now since the first (usually the only) three skills taught to intellectuals are

(a) how to classify an argument without listening to it, (b) how to find internal contradictions in it, and (c) how to turn it against its author, it is clear that I have strayed into troubled waters.

Perhaps I need to stress that I am not interested in eliminating any human qualities but only in assessing their cost. Had anyone fully understood, at the time, the social cost we would have to pay for the privilege of riding around in a machine on rubber wheels, the automobile might not have been marketed. Or it might simply have been approached very differently. Even qualities like individualism that have become poisonous through exaggeration are in some more minute proportion indispensable. My wish is not to expunge, but to rebalance and reintegrate. But the reader must not expect this desire to be clothed in the garb of serenity in a world where the very idea of harmony only arouses impatience and irritability.

Harmony lacks a sense of movement, and this produces a caged feeling in people under severe stress. Western civilization is a man running with increasing speed through an air-sealed tunnel in search of additional oxygen. You can quite reasonably tell him he will survive longer if he slows down, but he is not likely to do it. Without detracting in any way from the importance of McLuhan's contribution, it must be said that linearity in human culture is more than a stylistic orientation derived from sensory ratios. The sense of unimpeded motion in linearity expresses a desperate need for headlong flight that a mosaic pattern completely frustrates.

Straight lines are something of a rarity in nature—the sight of one usually suggests a civilized human presence. And when humans have departed or allowed nature to reassert herself the straight lines are rounded out. The beauty of fallen snow is that it restores to even the most rectilinear city an appearance of organicity. A flight of steps becomes a rippled sand dune shaped by a set of forces that are in some kind of playful balance with one another, rather than by a single ruthless and domineering concept. The sense of some frantic and insatiable human need— always suggested by the straight line—is muted and softened.

Perhaps there are no straight lines in nature—our most certain candidates keep turning out to be curved in the long run. Perhaps the straight line is merely a human figment—a fantasy of utter independence and irresistibility. Ultimately everything reveals itself to be interconnected and subject to external influence, but the dearest wish of the thoroughly indoctrinated individualist is that he might pursue a life devoid of negative feedback—that he would be "right on" eternally, never deflected from his rigid and purely self-perpetuating course.

In brief, the existence of linearity betrays the absence of negative (that is, corrective) feedback, and the inability to receive negative feedback is ultimately calamitous. Nothing, for example, has contributed more than the myth of pure science to the grotesqueness of its applications. If the concept of pathology has any utility at all, linearity is pathological.

The problem remaining for this chapter is to examine the form and nature of that pathology at its most elementary level. We cannot begin all over again, nor will anything be gained by trusting to a spontaneity that no longer exists in an organic system that is severely damaged. But it may be useful to understand how we got here—to assess the soft spots in the psychosocial equipment of the species. Every human virtue contains an evil, and we need to understand the price paid for the qualities we hold dear and deem essential.

The Schizoid Mammal

In *The Divided Self* Ronald Laing describes schizoid techniques for obtaining security in a psychically dangerous environment. Although intended as a psychological description it might also serve as a metaphor for the evolution of Western culture. As such, it points up a serious flaw in the species and suggests the hazards of cultural as compared with biological evolution. Of most acute relevance is the schizoid quest for autarchy, which reproduces with some precision the changing relation between the individual and her environment produced by the technological revolution.

The schizoid process begins by detaching a piece of oneself from connectedness with the environment. This piece, which is regarded as the inner or "real" self, is thus disengaged, unresponsive to feedback, unembodied. It observes everything that happens to the rest of the organism (from sexual gratification to beatings) with dispassionate detachment. All transactions with the environment are unreal, since the "real" self is not involved. Yet because nothing real is coming into the self nothing real can go out of it, and hence it experiences even itself as increasingly unreal, dead, and meaningless. The search for safety through detachment proves ultimately unsafe, for as the self becomes progressively emptied of life it becomes more vulnerable to engulfment by others, who are real, and to implosion from real external stimuli. The sense of freedom and autonomy that this autarchy provides is illusory, since it is exercised in a vacuum, and that which is free is continually diminished and made lifeless. The sense of identity requires the existence of another by whom one is known, and in relation to whom one's existence finds expression. Gregory Bateson once remarked on the folly of trying to delimit something by cutting the pathways that are the definitions of its being.

What Laing describes is a defensive posture available to the entire species. The schizoid defense becomes possible with the emergence of the capacity to generate, manipulate, and relate symbols. Once that ability exists it is possible for the organism to withdraw from the complex network of mutual feedback in which it is embedded and respond to its inner circuitry alone. Nature and the body no longer rule the organism.

This is one way to interpret the Garden of Eden myth. Originally, the harmony of the planet was maintained by a balancing of forces in which all species participated unwittingly, each organism ruled by its efforts to avoid discomfort or seek pleasure. Humanity alone opted out of the system, forswearing pleasure and uncertainty in order to be "free."

In the biblical story the first symptom of the disturbance is a sudden loss of comfort with the body—a tendency to feel detached from it and be ashamed of it. "The [schizoid] individual's being is cleft in two, producing a disembodied self and a body that is a thing that the self looks at, regarding it at times as though it were just another thing in the world." (Laing) When Adam and Eve cease to be *in* their bodies they cease to be capable of living in Paradise and are driven out. Having taken the schizoid route, they must now toil endlessly to approximate the equilibrium they have forsaken.

The source of the fall is vanity: "You will be like God, knowing good and evil," and the illusion that a man can "rise above" his body has led to history's most impressive atrocities. The source of the illusion is the peculiar petulance many humans exhibit when confronted with the fact that all specific organic structures are temporary—indeed, more or less irrelevant. They cling to the notion of personal continuation the way a pedant does to a concept or a bureaucrat to a procedure. It is as if a particular configuration in a game of Cat's Cradle, say a passably executed Jacob's Ladder, wished to preserve itself eternally in stone—that *particular* child, that *particular* string, and that *particular* mediocre representative of the form. The child knows she can do it again, probably better. The technique, after all, like the genetic message, transcends the moment. But the particular trial exists only in that time, and must be content with the fact that it will *always* exist in that moment—that it is located in time, that it has a place. But humans have difficulty accepting that limitation, and in their frantic efforts to spread themselves over a larger temporal area they have often ended by scarcely existing at all. Like the man who wants to be everywhere at once and ends by being nowhere, the man who seeks immortality ends by not being present in his own time. Yet no matter how much people rejoice in the changing seasons, in the sunset and sunrise, and in birth—the passing of their own configuration is distressful.

The desire to borrow more time is the sign of an unlived life. The man who most wants a party to last longer is the one who has spent the evening not approaching a girl he is attracted to, out of fear of rejection. Furthermore, this sense of temporal scarcity, like all such scarcity, is contagious. The man who invades posterity's time dilutes the lives of his descendants, and leads them also to seek immortality, just as the horde that invades another's country motivates those invaded to invade others.

The connection between narcissism and the longing for immortality explains why the serpent and Eve receive all the blame in the Eden myth. Early humans envied the serpent because it sloughed its skin and hence was imagined to be immortal. And men have always envied women because they can visibly reproduce themselves. Eve is, in fact, punished for this: childbearing is made painful. But the myth is really about Adam's fall: The idea that he was tempted by Eve is merely the oppressor's way of saying that he became envious of her. "Temptation" is to Adam what "provocation" is to a big country that wants to attack a little one. As C. S. Lewis remarks, "We think the lamb gentle because its wool is soft to our hands: men call a woman voluptuous when she arouses voluptuous feelings in them." Since men are in poorer touch with their feelings than women, they tend to blame women whenever their own feelings get out of hand. But it is men who have most enthusiastically opted for disembodiment and the quest for spiritual immortality.

But I realize that I am presuming upon a sympathy the reader may not feel. Wasn't the "Fall" in fact a great victory, in which humanity was freed from dependence on impulse? Hasn't it brought us all the benefits we now enjoy and allowed us to control our own destiny, unlike other species whose spontaneity has permitted us to extinguish them?

It is certainly true that the withdrawal into inner circuitry has had a certain survival value in the short run, and I would advise anyone concerned with longevity against seeking a return to the paradisiacal condition so long as there are any beings like us in the immediate neighborhood. As to the relative advantages of a short flavorful life and a long unfeeling one, we must all weigh this for ourselves. And as to the benefits of civilization, they are unquestionably, each and every one, a product of man's schizoid proclivities, as are all the cruelties of civilized life. There is absolutely no way to keep the goodies and toss away the evils —it's a package deal and we will make no headway whatsoever so long as we try to evade this fact. You cannot hang a Rembrandt on a palm tree. People talk, for example, of the Peloponnesian War or World War I as putting an end to the Golden Ages that preceded them—ages in which arts and sciences flourished with particular abandon. This is nonsense, for in both cases the wars were as true an expression of the age as any work of art, and indeed, great art and major wars proceed from the same grandiose impulse. There is no way to retain great art without the narcissism that makes war inevitable. If we wish to moderate the conditions that give rise to war, we must settle for a more modest level of individualistic achievement in other spheres.

But it is the issues of freedom from impulse and control of one's own destiny that need most clarification. No word has ever done heavier labor in the service of mystification than "freedom" (in America one of the most popular euphemisms for rejecting a lover is, "I'm going to set you free"). No one who has become alienated from his body is in control of his destiny, however much he may be able to throw his dissociated weight around in the external environment. To whatever degree we take refuge in inner circuitry and break communication with bodily and outer circuitry, the freedom we achieve is illusory and temporary, as in the term "free fall" in sky diving.

For a living organism there is no such thing as full autonomy. There is only variability in the pathways through which its parasitical dependency can be exercised. A fish is not autonomous in relation to water at the moment it is gasping its life out in the bottom of a boat. Nor is an astronaut in relation to the atmosphere or the earth when he is shut up in a metal ball a hundred thousand miles out, sucking oxygen and responding to messages from someone he cannot see, while relying on the construction skills of men he may not have known. Whether one is aware of being controlled by bodily needs and impulses, by one's own cultural norms and values, by neurotic aspirations, or by some set of ideological vanities from some other culture makes very little difference. Our existence is in fact defined by all of these things—only the proportions change, and that much less than we like to imagine. Without air we die, without love we turn nasty, without feedback we go crazy. We are born with energy, matter, and information going in and out of us, and we continue in this way until we die. Too great a deviation from the normal degree of inflow and outflow is disturbing to our sense of our own boundaries, which means that *too little influence, stimulation, control, or whatever, from outside is just as likely to be experienced as an invasion of our being as too much, even though we have been trained not to perceive it.* The notion that people begin as separate individuals, who then march out and connect themselves with others, is one of the most dazzling bits of self-mystification in the history of the species. Through this mystification we make ourselves vulnerable to manipulation by essentially mechanical forces: technological systems, bureaucratic regulations, ideological consistencies. The paranoid who imagines himself to be controlled electronically is in better shape than most of us—he at least has some sense of where his self-mystification has led him.

Weston La Barre summarizes humanity's much-touted freedom from instinct by pointing out that a man, through his dependence on learning, "meets reality very largely via the not disinterested individuals that make up his immediate family and society. He adjusts perforce to their mistakes . . . not to nature itself . . . as a man he will be whatever outlandish domesticate his parents unconsciously prefer or unwittingly shape." Freedom from instinct, then, means a transfer of dependence from something that cannot make you psychotic to something that can. Freedom from instinct is the freedom to have reality falsified for you. Freedom from instinct is the beginning of psychic pollution. As La Barre says, man is unique among animals in "his practiced ability to know things that are not so."

This is, of course, a one-sided view. If you can imagine what is not, you can behave in such a way as to bring it about, instead of merely searching aimlessly until a stimulus fits your yearning. The price paid is that while you are imagining, you are not experiencing what is—which may be even nicer. And by the time the imagined blessing is brought into being you may have lost the capacity to experience *it*, and will already be imagining some other non-existing state.

Now a pimple is a long way from a terminal cancer, just as smoking dope or chewing gum is a long way from shooting heroin. The first time a man killed something that he didn't eat and that wasn't trying to eat him, a channel was opened that made Hiroshima possible, but it certainly didn't make it inevitable. By the same token, the capacity to create and manipulate symbols, while it opens the door to a schizoid process, doesn't make it universal and mandatory. When men take to the sea they create for the first time the possibility that they will drown. But when an epidemic of drownings occurs we begin to look for other reasons, like faulty boats. It is enough to suggest at this point that the capacity to symbolize contains a danger, like boating, and requires safeguards that have as yet been insufficiently stressed.

Another channel is opened with the emergence of culture. If humanity is a schizoid animal, culture is a schizoid approach to evolution. As La Barre observes, schizophrenics are only exaggeratedly human individuals, since "qualitatively there is no discernible difference in content between a culture and a psychosis." The only difference is quantitative—if many people share a symbol-system it is a culture, if only one does, it is a psychosis. Both are independent of reality and both provide specious solutions to security problems, but as La Barre points out, a culture has the advantage that if many people believe a lie, its power to allay anxiety is immensely heightened thereby. Furthermore, if a whole group of people are behaving as if some social fiction were true, it tends to acquire a degree of reality—one which at the very least will help prevent the truth from emerging in that setting. Children, for example, can be warped in a great variety of ways, and if some breed is believed to be superior or inferior or lazy or aggressive or brittle or stupid or tempestuous, they will tend, in fact, to exaggerate those traits. A paranoid person is likely sooner or later to get himself persecuted, hence confirming his view of reality, but with a culture likelihood approaches inevitability. Sociology, economics, and political science are to a large extent studies of the materialization of schizoid process.

Culture, then, frees humanity still further from reality, for as La Barre points out, there is no natural selection among ideas and beliefs; millions can believe the same falsehood for thousands of years. This is not in itself harmful—many delusions are after all innocuous. But there is danger in the shift away from being deeply in touch with the external environment and one's own bodily sensations. Once lost, that tactile immediacy, that groundedness in experience, can never be entirely recaptured. A connection is broken, a balance wheel lost, and the system becomes capable of exponential growth, of robot-like movement, of running amok.

Yet clearly this doesn't happen immediately. All cultures, even very simple ones, seduce their adherents into commitment to outlandish and absurdly inconvenient beliefs and practices, but not all of these take people far out of contact with their bodies and their natural environment. Some of those beliefs and practices that seem most irrational to Westerners are in fact expressions of that sense of closeness. Several further steps are necessary before the danger becomes acute.

Giving a name to an experience detaches us a little from the experience itself, as many people have pointed out. Combining those names into some sort of conceptual system detaches us a good bit further, since we begin to seek our sense of coherence from the conceptual system rather than from reality itself and our embeddedness in it. But as long as the system is merely a kind of rough contour map that reflects the relative emotional or practical significance of various features in the environment, its capacity to pull us out of the world and into inner circuitry is limited. It is when we begin to manipulate that system as an end in itself—rationalizing it, ordering it, applying principles of logic and consistency to it—that the void begins to yawn beneath us. At this point it has become an inner world capable of detaching us from our tactile world. This is not to say that such a system may not be an excellent guide for grasping certain aspects of the real world and manipulating it in specific directions. But we are no longer *in* it—we think of ourselves as *outside* (usually *above*) the world looking at it. Furthermore, *since we have detached ourselves from the rest of the totality, totality is the one thing we cannot see.* As Bateson observes, "consciousness is, almost of necessity, blinded to the systemic nature of the man himself. Purposive consciousness pulls out, from the total mind, sequences which do not have the loop structure which is characteristic of the whole systemic structure." *It is "objectivity," in other words, that prevents us from seeing the totality of which we are a part.*

Mechanistic knowledge of the physiology of the body, for example, is an excellent device for blunting awareness of one's own bodily responses and their relation to environmental stimuli. Treating the body as an object takes one *out* of the body and hence out of the environment. This enables someone in an anxiety-laden setting to take a pill instead of yelling or running out of the room, but this in turn increases the possibility that whatever is amiss in that room will not be corrected, thus requiring further anesthesia. Our society is built up of millions of such small choices, and this necessitates an enormous amount of anesthesia for its participants.

What I am saying is that abstract concepts facilitate self-objectification, which in turn tends to deprive our man-made environment of the negative feedback necessary to prevent it from behaving inhumanly. An architect who treats his own bodily needs and emotional responses as an annoying impediment to rapid completion of his task is unlikely to design a building that is pleasurable to live in, and the same may be said of planners, executives, technologists, teachers, parents, and so on. We cannot live without conceptual systems, but we must be alive to the dangers to which they expose us.

The capacity of conceptual systems to suck us into their own machinery and detach us from our organic connections is a familiar topic for humor, pathos, and satire: the army officer who treats his son "just like any other soldier," the rule-bound bureaucrat, the ideologue whose belief system deprives him of simple pleasures. Perhaps the most classic example is our tendency to lose contact with our own emotional needs in the face of economic logic—as in the phrase, "it's so cheap you can't afford not to buy it." It is the power of such purely economic considerations to overwhelm the imagination that lends truth to the notion that "money can't buy happiness." In principle, money can buy happiness or anything else—if it doesn't, it is because people don't use it that way. The kind of commitment necessary to accumulate money often seduces people into responding to economic rather than emotional yardsticks—"It's overpriced," instead of, "I want it that much," or "It's a giveaway," instead of, "I don't want it in my life." People abandon homes to which they have devoted decades of love and energy because they are "too expensive to keep up," and spend years in deep depression or even die in response to the loss of familiar and loved surroundings. The reasoning behind such an act is that money will thereby become available for many more reasonably priced goods and services which are not nourishing to the soul, however enjoyable or even necessary they may seem to be. This is called being "sensible" about money, i.e., accepting external criteria of value—using money primarily to buy more money. The opposite tendency, using money primarily to buy happiness or satisfy deep internal needs is usually called being "capricious," "inconsistent," or "irrational" about money.

Mechanical Responsivity

Although organic responsivity is lost through the evolution of formal structures and logical principles, the capacity of human beings to respond to influence is not. The illusions of individualism blind us to the fact that a single human being is born as a *part* of an interaction system—he is not and cannot ever be a complete and self-sufficient entity. Part of the genetic message of a human being is a complex pattern of receptivity to influence, especially from other humans. The individual is like a template requiring some external message to complete it. It is programmed to imitate and accommodate, however much we may detest these words. When organic responsivity is deadened, the readiness to react to external messages still remains. In the absence of the original channel others will be used. Authoritarian submission is one such channel, with symbolic authorities (traffic lights, signs, written instructions) being increasingly substituted for personal ones as the anesthesia progresses. Another channel is ideology: that is, a general instruction which has been internalized and from which specific rules for behavior and attitude can be logically deduced.

The problem with these impersonal channels of conformity—which I have grouped under the term mechanical responsivity —is that they lack fine tuning. Logical systems tend to be a bit simple. A substantial proportion of bureaucratic rule making, for example, consists of efforts to prevent a single unfortunate event from recurring by the crude device of eliminating some category to which it belongs. A public scandal or threatened lawsuit will almost guarantee the promulgation of new regulations (each of which erodes the vitality of the organization) to ensure against an event whose probability of recurring is infinitesimal. If a scandal occurs in a particular room, that room will be declared off limits henceforward; if it occurs after hours, doors will be locked and time checks instituted. If an embezzler uses green ink, green ink will be banned. Security is sedulously pursued by the futile device of using bigger and bigger conceptual nets to catch smaller and smaller particularized fish. No one in the history of the world has ever succeeded in finding a general formula that would ensure happiness or avoid evil in any given context, but the search goes on, so great is the desire for freedom from the ambiguity of daily living.

But there is a more serious problem with the rule of law as compared with more personal and informal modes of social control. The objectification of morality makes it possible for an individual to feel moral or assuage guilt by conforming to a set of abstract rules even in the process of committing all sorts of viciousness. For there is no behavior so cruel or outlandish that it cannot be justified in terms of some perfectly reasonable principle, just as there is no place on the globe so "out of the way" that it cannot be reached by flying in a straight line in some direction.

Unfortunately, the kind of social control that exists in simple communities cannot be reproduced on a large scale, while a return to complete localization would simply start the whole historical process all over again. Even the simplest communities have some abstract rules, so we know the seeds are already there. We are stuck with size and we are stuck with abstract principles. But we need to be more clearly aware of the dangers they pose —humans have a horrible weakness for making virtues out of ugly necessities, thereby allowing them to become more ghoulish in their impact than need be.

The ideology of individualism exemplifies this weakness. No one could have done more than the popular social critics of the 1950s (Fromm, Riesman, Whyte, et al.) to convince people of the virtues of disconnectedness and smooth the path of mechanical responsivity. By raising the specter of immersion in group life —of losing one's narcissistic consciousness—they frightened and shamed people into an ever more frantic pursuit of autonomy and self-sufficiency. Thus disconnected, more and more of the population became available for attachment to the impersonal machinery of modern life. Americans can be so easily manipulated by advertising *because* they are individualistic. Ripped out of their social fabric their social responses are constantly seeking a missing stimulus to which they can attach themselves. A flock of ducklings deprived of their mother became "imprinted" on Konrad Lorenz whom they then followed about. Humans deprived of community can become, in a sense, "imprinted" on rules, machines, ideologies, and bureaucratic structures. The anti-conformity critics, therefore, helped create precisely what they were attacking. By heaping scorn on social responses fundamental to humankind, they helped further the process of disconnection in the society, thus making the population ever more vulnerable to authoritarian and impersonal manipulation. For the forms in which conformity and authoritarianism appear in modern society are a *product* of the ideology of freedom and individualism—desperate and shamefaced efforts to fill the hole left by the every-man-should-strive-to-be-a-lonely-genius-head-and-shoulders-above-the-worthless-gregarious-dependent-masses guilt trip. The illusion that the individual is an independent entity threatens the *internal* integrity of the organism, which is rooted in interdependence. The individual is an arrangement of ways of relating. Without any object for these relational responses, she must either hallucinate or crumble, just as a victim of sensory deprivation must. (The hermit, for example, relates to fantasy objects—parent figures, gods, the entire community, or whatever, sometimes disguised as parts of the self.) Detachment, in other words, is as likely to produce internal disintegration as overinvolvement.

This tendency to see the individual organism as an entity rather than a process, a terminal rather than a conduit, has led to some odd cultural norms, such as the high value placed on the capacity to be alone—the psychic equivalent of the ability to hold one's breath, or go without sleep, or twist oneself into a pretzel, or otherwise torture an alienated body in the service of vanity. To praise the ability of a social animal to trash its biological equipment is a little like saying that the most virtuous bird is the one that can tunnel through the earth. Fritz Perls, the father of Gestalt therapy, maintained that "to grow up means to be alone," which he apparently did not recognize as a violation of his view that therapy should not consist in bringing about adjustment to a sick society. Yet this is precisely what Gestalt therapy does most effectively. In a society founded on unstable, fragmentary, transient, competitive, and unco-ordinated relationships the Gestalt approach is a survival kit, although it also contributes to and fosters the *status quo*. There is something a little eerie about the sight of 200 million people slavishly adhering in the same unhappy way to a norm of personal independence and uniqueness.

Our era has been inundated with literary, cinematic, and video fantasies of overintegrated societies. In our present condition they seem a little comic, like the fantasies of an overcontrolled man that his rage, if it ever broke through, would be homicidal or world destroying. There is a grain of truth in such fantasies; namely, that control exaggerates the longing it suppresses. But there is also a grain of deceit in that the fantasy of exaggerated strength can encourage continued suppression of a perfectly ordinary impulse. In our bogey-books about overintegrated societies (*1984, Brave New World, We, Fahrenheit 451*) that impulse is the longing to abandon one's isolated autonomy and become a part of something. Marcia Millman shows how underneath the surface horror of these fantasies lies a hidden conviction that happiness lies in loss of self. The societies are portrayed in such grotesque forms (all of them are sociological anomalies, containing many traits that could only arise in an individualistic society) in order to frighten us out of realizing that need even in the mildest form.

Drama and Detachment

Drama has also contributed to this process, serving both as a substitute for, and a vehicle for the erosion of, community life. Drama as we know it begins when community street life ends—when a person cannot assume that she will run into the people she wants to see in the normal course of a day.

The most powerful source of drama is the family—the great tragedies are mostly family affairs. In a simple community when a family crisis occurs people run into the street and the community gathers around to mediate, nourish, and absorb. As a community becomes larger and less integrated the capacity of the family to generate drama does not change, but it can no longer be shared. The community becomes privatized, the family isolated, the streets empty. It is at this point that drama in the form familiar to us begins to emerge—as if people had to have some place to go with their collective responsivity. Into the hole left when the family retires inside the dwelling a dramatic scene is poured, enacted by performers.

We can see this transition most clearly in Greek tragedies, which are generally set in the street outside the family home. Indeed, the killings and mutilations usually take place *inside* the home, offstage, and then are reported to the chorus, just as if they, and the audience, were villagers gathered in the street. Athens, in the period when Greek drama was at its peak, had witnessed a rapid urbanization, with shrinking and isolation of the family unit, not unlike what we have experienced during the past century.

Occasionally performers have tried to ply their trade in communities that have not lost their social responsivity, with unfortunate results. The simple people forget the artificiality of the setting and are prone to enter the action. A villain risks his life in such a setting. We smile condescendingly at this behavior, but it is this responsivity and sense of interconnectedness that make such communities nourishing social environments. It is not that the people are childish or stupid, only that their social impulses are still working in an intense and automatic way, whereas ours have atrophied. Supposedly we have substituted rational and judicious behavior for this responsivity, but how poorly it works can be seen at a glance. Referral agencies, mental hospitals, prisons, and nursing homes are a few of the tardy, impersonal, inhumane, and generally rather dilapidated mechanisms we have evolved to replace this naïve responsivity.

The drama—live, on film, or on video—is one of the ways we deaden this response. We are conditioned very early to look on passively while people are being beaten and killed, or suffering in every conceivable way. The success of the drama in anesthetizing our social impulses is apparent on any city street corner. The theater helps train us in non-responsiveness so that the formal institutions that depend for their existence on our social narcosis can survive.

It is the theater itself that has begun to develop an antidote to this condition, not without considerable resistance from its case-hardened audiences. Environmental theater seems almost to pinpoint this issue—not only in its efforts to engage the audience in action, but in its impulse to return to the street.

Freedom and Will

The more closely we examine the search for freedom, the more suspiciously it looks like a search for interpersonal security—for a predictable, no-risk human environment. What the freedom addict seeks is control and order through the blocking of constraining or disturbing feedback. Freedom means maximizing the extent to which one controls one's own input, which is another way of saying that I am most "free" when the form and content of what I encounter as stimulus is myself. Freedom is thus inherently illusory since one cannot in fact alter the interdependence of living matter—indeed of all energy—one can only alter one's perception of it. This, as David Bakan observes, is the paradox of mastery: "In order to master, the ego rules things out of existence. Yet it is often what is ruled out that arises and asserts itself, so there is no mastery precisely where mastery was sought." Freedom, in short, is what Kitty Genovese enjoyed: the freedom to be leisurely stabbed to death in a New York street for an hour without some small-town busybody poking his nose in her private affairs.

The capacity to symbolize is often described as having freed humanity from the instinctual prison in which all other animals are forever pent. This freedom is a freedom of the mind—the freedom that allows a man to starve amid plenty and glut himself on dreams—the freedom manifest in the term "freeway." The mechanism that enabled humanity to leap beyond all other species in the evolution fairy tale ("thus man evolved from the hominids and lived happily ever after") is the same that Laing describes as the root of the schizoid process. It is the capacity to ignore information coming from the body or the environment in favor of conceptual circuitry. But he who frees himself in this way from a friend is chained to his own need, loss, and pain, while he who frees himself in this way from an enemy is bound to uncertainty, fear, and paranoia.

I have suggested that the human capacity to create and manipulate symbols opened the door to pathology, and that this was heightened by the evolution of culture and the ability to organize symbols into hierarchies of abstraction. Thus far we seem to be dealing with irreversible and perhaps essential attainments. Given these dangers it seems vital for the survival of the species that it foster an avid commitment to maintaining awareness of organic interconnectedness, since it is forever in acute peril of losing this awareness. Grounding the individual in the here-and-now—in concrete, immediate reality—is the antidote to schizoid collapse, and the same holds at the cultural level. Given our unavoidable susceptibility to schizoid responses, we need to guard against gratuitous encouragements. The mind-body dualism that has dominated Western thought (and much Eastern thought as well) is clearly one of these; few ideas provide a more fertile context for schizoid development than the notion that the spirit is independent of the flesh. Another, even more potent, is the emergence of cultural patterns that encourage the hypertrophy of will.

As Alexander Lowen points out, will is an emergency mechanism. Under ordinary conditions the controlling principle of an organism is pleasure. Bodily pleasure not only integrates the organism itself but maintains harmony in the organism-environment system. Behavior that is based on pleasure, Lowen observes, seems co-ordinated and effortless, whereas behavior based on will tends to be jerky, rigid, and mechanical. The schizoid individual, whose entire life tends to be governed by will, not only inhibits impulses, but in order to achieve this inhibition shuts off the information channels along which they normally travel, so that he has difficulty knowing what he wants and tends to base all his behavior on principles. "Normally, one eats when one is hungry, but in the schizoid state one has lunch because it is twelve o'clock. . . . The schizoid individual engages in sports . . . to improve his control over his body and not for the pleasure of the activity or the movement."

As an emergency mechanism will power is useful as a biological short cut when all other means have failed. Normal desires for pleasure and safety are circumvented so that the unnatural can be accomplished. We might view this mechanism as a way of bringing the organism back into synchrony with its environment when it has for some reason fallen out. Persistent use of will, however, takes one *out* of synchrony and tends to encourage its further use in an increasingly self-defeating effort to re-establish synchrony. This use of will power in normal, routine activities is diagnostic of a schizoid condition: "When the will becomes the primary mechanism of action, displacing the normal motivating force of pleasure, the individual is functioning in a schizoid manner." (Lowen) Since in our society this tendency is the rule rather than the exception, it becomes reasonable to speak of it as a schizoid society.

The futile effort to achieve synchrony is to some extent responsible for our efforts to "live by the clock." Unfortunately, we are out of phase with the rest of the ecological system—not because we are too slow, but because we are too fast, which is why efforts to "catch up" are self-defeating.

Living by the clock is, for all its absurdity, a genuine effort to maintain connectedness. What it overlooks is that connectedness between organisms and between organism and environment already exists. This is a characteristic schizoid maneuver: to lose awareness of a real connection and attempt desperately to construct a conceptual one to replace it. Thus mechanical clocks take the place of biological clocks. Thus the schizoid character cannot understand how his body can keep working all by itself, without his willing it. And thus the politician believes that no social change will occur without legislation.

Freud once said that civilization is a process of exchanging joy for security, and Lowen seems to be making the same point when he contrasts the primitive sense of unity with the linear cause-effect thinking of Western peoples. The latter view provides security against the vicissitudes of experience, Lowen argues, but at the expense of a feeling of harmony with nature and body. But cultural patterns that exaggerate will and ego controls go far beyond the effects of citification in creating the kinds of problems we now face.

Lowen sees the evolution of the human ego as following the typical course of the heroic leader brought in to protect the people, who then usurps power and becomes a tyrant. He points out that while the alleged function of the ego is to *test* reality, in actuality it is largely engaged in *dictating* reality. "The ego creates the discontinuities which it then attempts to bridge with knowledge and words." Life becomes an exercise in power, control, and self-deception instead of a pleasurable interplay of interdependent organisms. While ideally the ego is held in check—bodily sensation balancing ego imagery, feelings balancing ideas, pleasure needs balancing power needs, and so on—these checks and balances collapse in a "culture which values knowledge above feeling, power above pleasure, and the mind above the body."

The evolution of culture parallels this process. Among lower animals culture is limited to a small amount of acquired and transmitted knowledge about poisons, and so on, and some patterning of learned relationships. At this level culture merely mediates between the organism and reality in a useful way. But at the human level, culture, like the ego, assumes the function of defining and dictating reality so that delusions can be widely shared.

Culture also tends to reinforce the tyrannical proclivities of the ego through surplus negative feedback. Nature responds to exploratory behavior in a neutral manner: correct motions yield success, incorrect ones yield failure. Failure, in other words, is its own punishment. The exploring individual is not subjected to any additional punishment for her incorrect behavior.

Cultures, however, are not so kind. An individual who makes a cultural blunder, a social error, is shamed, humiliated, frightened, or made to feel guilty. The reason for this is obvious: since cultural knowledge has no intrinsic validity it cannot rest on intrinsic reward and punishment. Cultural laws are arbitrary and must, therefore, be reinforced by surplus negative feedback to ensure learning. No one needs to be ridiculed or humiliated in order to learn the futility of trying to start a fire with wet leaves or use a piece of loose shale as a tool. Such errors are self-punishing through failure—an error in etiquette is not.

The effect of punishing an individual for making an error is obviously to discourage exploratory behavior and to reward conceptualization. Conceptualization is a kind of security mechanism —a device for anticipating outcomes and reducing risks. This, in turn, facilitates the emergence of the kind of automatically self-validating conceptual systems of which Lowen speaks.

Technological Culture

Still another threshold is crossed when the schizoid processes described above are combined with an ability to give concrete form to one's conceptual imagery—permitting, in Laing's terms, the organization of a false-self system around a material reality. The development of an unembodied inner self is greatly facilitated by the presence of an externally embodied false self.

There is much confusion about this issue in contemporary thought. The United States, for example, is described as a "materialistic" culture, apparently because it is deluged with material artifacts. Yet there has probably never been a people with less emotion invested in specific material possessions. Americans as a rule are Platonists when it comes to possessions—it is the *idea* or *form* of a house, car, chair, or bowl to which they are attached rather than the specific object. One has only to observe the care, devotion, and human meaning invested in some possessions by people in less "developed" societies to realize just how shallow our supposed materialism really is. In part, of course, this is simply a matter of numbers. The maternal instinct in animals is an inverse function of litter size, and, similarly, one cannot be as intensely involved with a hundred objects as with two or three. Equally important, however, is our utilitarian orientation to objects, and their replaceability. Mass production is based upon, and in turn encourages, a conceptual attitude toward objects. It is more difficult to particularize and love a house, shirt, or car that is virtually identical with many others and will be abandoned for a replacement before long. The value we attach to possessions tends to be based on quantitative criteria (money, status) which reduce all differences to a single standard. This in turn facilitates an attitude in which objects have no independent reality but are merely manifestations of our own conceptual processes.

The self, says Laing, "seeks by being unembodied to transcend the world and hence to be safe. But a self is liable to develop which feels it is outside all experience and activity. It becomes a vacuum. Everything is there, outside; nothing is here, inside." But what if the only part of the external world in which the self participates consists of embodied fantasy images? Will not the same vacuum occur? Since one is continually breathing one's own exhaust the same impoverishment must result, although, since the person appears to be fully engaged with his environment, the illusion of normality can be somewhat more easily maintained.

Laing says that in the schizoid condition, "the self can relate itself with immediacy to an object which is an object of its own imagination or memory but not to a real person." This provides an illusory sense of freedom, since one cannot be hurt by an image; but of course one cannot be gratified either. "The self's relationship to the other is always at one remove." But insofar as technology has provided us with highly tangible images that predefine most of our relationships we are all living in the schizoid condition, since it is virtually impossible to experience an adult relationship that has not been previewed and rehearsed in the media. The media mediate our interpersonal encounters. Furthermore, what communications technology does symbolically, other technologies do in actuality. Laing points out that in the non-schizoid person only a certain number of his or her actions are mechanical. But Western culture has progressively expanded this mechanical domain to the point where average citizens of a technological society can feel, in schizoid fashion, that they are being lived *by* their mechanical actions rather than the reverse. They eat, sleep, awaken, work, and stop work when mechanical contrivances tell them it is time to do so. They even eat laxative foods to keep their eliminative processes "on schedule." And should all this become so painful to them that they seek psychiatric assistance, they will find that even their therapeutic encounters are occasioned, not by the intensity of their distress, nor by their readiness to confront their problems and work, but according to a mechanically preset schedule.

Technological culture, in other words, helps generate a false-self system even in the absence of individual pathology. The same search for security and freedom that motivates the schizoid character in Laing's analysis has produced in modern culture the same kind of personal autarchy, the same internal atrophy, the same robot-like behavior, the same feelings of inner deadness, falseness, and unreality. There is the same longing for intimacy, experience, stimulation, life, and the same fear that any genuine feelingful encounter would implode the personality. David Bakan observes that "much of the contemporary hunger for meaningfulness is based on the monotonousness of what the ego will allow and the deep but unacknowledged fear of what is not acknowledged."

This ambivalent urge to make contact with reality is reflected in the attempts of the media to borrow reality from dramatic events. Laing's description of one of his patients could be applied with very little strain to network television: "If anyone said anything to her which she classified as 'real,' she would say to herself, 'I'll think that'; and she would keep repeating the word or phrase over and over again to herself in the hope that some of the realness of the expression would rub off on her."

The failure of all these devices is as visible in the rigidification and disintegration of our own society as it is in the frankly psychotic individual. "The tragic irony is that even finally no anxiety is avoided"—for technology has created worse dangers than those it has removed. "In the escape from the risk of being killed, [the self] becomes dead"—our society sees threat as coming from without, yet is in danger of being destroyed by its own defensive system. In a technological society everyone "is related primarily to objects of [their] own fantasies."

If the dynamic that Laing describes can be applied to technological culture, we may expect the following developments:

(1) The technological system will become more extensive and autonomous;

(2) Those enmeshed in it will be "charged with hatred in [their] envy of the rich, vivid, abundant life which is always elsewhere; always there, never here";

(3) Since, however, this life is too frightening to be grasped, and the longing for it too acute to be denied, they will attempt "to destroy the world by reducing it to dust and ashes, without assimilating it";

(4) Reality will be courted by sadistic and masochistic means —proving one's reality by the distressful effects one is able to produce in others (I bomb, therefore I am) or by subjecting oneself to pain and terrifying risks.

In the individual this process culminates in a psychotic explosion, which Laing sees as a revolution in the mind—the dissolution of a decayed structure into the ocean of boundless possibility. Sometimes a new, richer, and more flexible structure emerges from the plunge; sometimes the individual drowns. So, too, Western culture may undergo chaos, confusion, and cataclysm before a new and viable system emerges, if, indeed, it emerges at all.

Only those fascinated with *Gotterdammerung* fantasies would actively seek such an outcome, which might well reduce Spaceship Earth to a wandering cinder. While there is still time to change, it seems absurd not to try. And if it turns out we must die as a species, we will at least have a better idea why.

We know that by detaching ourselves from the rest of the organic system of which we are a part and retreating within our technologically-insulated schizoid security turret we have "beaten" nature, much the way our teeth defeat us when they bite our tongue. Whether a species could ever evolve with a knowledge of *things* (as opposed to an understanding of *relationships*) equal to ours without following the same course is uncertain. In any case this line of "progress" has reached a dead end—the most sophisticated thinkers in all fields are busy trying to mimic the relational thought processes of primitive peoples. We must simply accept the proneness to schizoid ideation that is part of the human condition and try to isolate those patterns that engender the kind of full-blown pathological eruption in which we now live.

We can look back on our own childhood or youth and say, "I was sick in such-and-such a year and almost died." But a social illness may span many lifetimes, even in its acute phase, and hence cannot be distinguished from normality by those who live in it, for it is all they know. This makes our task more difficult, but also more necessary, lest we adapt still further to the pathology in which we find ourselves.

Parable 3

A man went crazy and started running down the street,
claiming that people were pursuing him, trying to kill him.
The bystanders were mightily impressed by his energy and
speed. "How is it you are able to run so fast?" they asked.
"I am running for my life, you fools!" he gasped. His terror
spread panic among the bystanders and all began
to run. More and more people joined the swelling group
of runners, half in admiration, half in fear, until it had become
an enormous crowd that ultimately poured over a cliff
into the sea.

THE UGLY SWAN
or
CURBING THE
PROPHET MOTIVE

> *Exterminate the sage, discard the wise,*
> *And the people will benefit a hundredfold;*
> *Exterminate benevolence, discard rectitude,*
> *And the people will again be filial;*
> *Exterminate ingenuity, discard profit,*
> *And there will be no more thieves and bandits.*
> **Lao Tzu**

> *It is only those who are not working in the*
> *fields who have time to wonder about*
> *grain. It is they, too, who have no right to*
> *do so, for they have not tasted it, nor*
> *are they working towards the production*
> *of flour for the people.*
> **Idries Shah**

There is a cybernetic law that states that the more probable a message is, the less information it provides. The information contained in a message, for example, decreases with its repetition. This creates a curious dilemma for any group: the longer its members are together, the less they have to say to each other—at least about the group's own relational structure. Since the circuitry of the group is known to everyone, the information value of what is being communicated is going downhill all the time. The more effectively a group communicates about itself and its constituents, the more quickly it will stagnate in the absence of inputs from outside.

Even *with* outside inputs information will tend to decrease, since the structure itself acts as a filter for screening out jarring information which it interprets as noise. Only stimuli that affect the group's circuitry are at issue here—those that affect relationships within the group.

Those participants most central to the group—those most invested in the structure (most "influential," therefore)—must protect it from such disturbing stimuli. They are like sense organs for the group—letting in what will help preserve it, but keeping out (for our senses keep out far more than they let in) anything that challenges its circuitry. If they fail to do this, the group will lose its integrity. If they succeed, it may stagnate or become oppressive.

A system, in other words, needs occasionally to achieve a perception of the universe, including itself, through eyes other than its own, since its sense organs are designed to exclude most information from awareness. The only way to achieve this is to extrude a bit of circuitry which will evolve a perceptual apparatus different from the parent circuit and hence inhale a different vision. But at this point the parent circuit can no longer "understand" the extruded segment except with reference to residual similarities between the segment's present and original circuitries. In other words, the more information the segment acquires the less able the parent circuit will be to absorb it. The process must therefore be repeated. A prophet is extruded into the desert, obtains a vision, and returns. He is then either rejected or his vision absorbed and a new circuitry evolved in the parent system. A new prophet is extruded, and so on. Clumsily the parent system hunches along, like an inchworm, on the information provided by its extruded members—toward an ever-receding and unattainable goal of total, perfect, and conscious circuitry.

What the prophet sees in his vision is of trivial significance—it is *how* he sees that is important. He is not merely a scout exploring unknown territory, he is the territory—not the experimenter but the experiment. What he innovates is his own internal structure. Most of these innovations, like most mutations, turn out to be pointless and grotesque: The prophet returns from the wilderness with seven toes on each foot and a ring in his nose, proclaiming that life is a waterfall. He is scorned and discarded, for prophets are highly expendable.

But occasionally the prophet actually evolves an inner circuitry that would confer a boon on the parent circuit if it were reintegrated with it. At this point a dilemma arises: How can a system absorb an external modification which came into being through a procedure premised on the system's inability to tolerate such a modification? It is a little like the socially ambitious parents who send their child to an elitist school so that the child will evolve a life-style uncorrupted by their own crudities. They want the child to be "better" than they are, but when the child returns they are dismayed and say, "Who are you? I can't relate to you. How can you snub your own parents who gave you everything?" Parent and child will be able to maintain a close bond only to the degree that the child's attempted metamorphosis was unsuccessful.

In the case of the social climber, the problem can be handled to some extent by compartmentalization: The child can maintain two identities, one for the parents and one for the rest of the world. So long as the two worlds never come into contact, everyone will be spared embarrassment and conflict. But in that case the parents will be unable to share in the child's life, and their own system will remain uninfluenced.

Or imagine that an organism needs, for survival, to alter the composition of its bloodstream. Since it is not possible to do this within the context of its own programming, it extrudes a small quantity of blood, which, freed from the constraints of the total organism, manages, with the aid of external influences, to achieve the desired change. The moment the changed blood is reintroduced, however, the entire organism will be mobilized to destroy the intruder utterly.

At the cultural level this dilemma is solved by an interesting mechanism. The extruded circuit is attacked and often destroyed, while its message—the *form* of its newly evolved circuitry—is absorbed and incorporated. In this way, the parent system is able to preserve intact its boundary-maintaining and sensory-screening apparatus while it alters its internal circuitry. This is why the first step in the acceptance of a totally alien idea is to attack it, to show all the reasons why it is wrong, illogical, inappropriate— that is, in conflict with existing circuitry. If the attack is at all intelligent, in the sense that the idea is accurately shown to be non-derivable from accepted premises, then the idea has in fact become part of the culture, albeit an unabsorbed part. All that remains is to simplify the circuitry of the culture by modifying its premises—that is, by developing a higher synthesis that embraces the new idea (this is usually called co-optation). The circuitry of the idea itself has already been taken in, although with a minus sign attached to each node that connects to the old circuitry.

This is why the "truth squad" approach to propaganda is so self-defeating. To attack an idea tellingly is to understand it and internalize it. An irrelevant and stupid attack is effective as long as it can be sustained, but is vulnerable to counterattack, thus provoking the attacker to a more telling follow-up. The only way to resist an alien idea is to ignore it.

Weston La Barre suggests that psychotics are potential culture heroes who have not been successful in communicating with their peers. Successful communication, however, is no guarantee against incarceration or destruction. A prophet is simply a tool of the larger system and what happens to his personal being is of no importance. Success and failure are terms that only have meaning in relation to the message he carries. He may survive the attack on him and be honored in his own time, if not in his own country. What is honored, however, is (like what is attacked) his status as carrier of the message, not his own personality. The visible personality of the prophet, even in the absence of public relations specialists, is an artificial construct—a creation of the recipients of the message in co-operation with the prophet himself in the fulfillment of his role. This is why all public figures and famous personages seem so much alike. Furthermore, the half-dozen character types available for adoption by the famous are, although stereotypical, powerful in their impact upon the inner person when reinforced by constant interaction with others. It is extremely difficult to protect the private inner person from complete absorption by the stereotypic public personality. Those who succeed are able to do so only by rigorously avoiding interaction with strangers—that is, with those who know them as prophets. They must instead surround themselves with people who "knew them when"—that is, as persons rather than message carriers. Even this is difficult, for they are likely to find themselves playing out the role of shy, modest, and still-humble prophet—even in the privacy of their own homes. And while friends and relatives may be able to reinforce the private person by behaving as if the public one did not exist, this will require the prophet to renounce the needs for respect and esteem that led him to accept induction into the prophet role in the first place. Most prophets are strangers, seeking either in a strange land, or by returning with a visibly transformed personality, to achieve the respect they were denied in the first place by their community. Their need for respect not only makes them vulnerable to induction but also makes them susceptible to the belief that the new circuitry they evolved while in the state of extrusion was a conscious and deliberate act of personal creation on their part.

This individualistic delusion arises in part from the circumstances surrounding the prophet's extrusion and in part from those associated with his return. The prophet always returns as a stranger. Often his return is indirect, in the sense that he goes to another country. If his message is accepted there, it will later reach, by diffusion or conquest, the circuit from which he was extruded. "A prophet is not without honour, save in his own country . . ." That is to say, the parent circuit is often the last to know that its effort to transcend itself has been successful.

Should the prophet return directly to the parent system he must be conspicuously changed. Otherwise his former associates will recognize and relate to him in the old way ("It's just old Henry being silly"). His first task as message carrier is to convince everyone that something significant has happened to him—that he is not the same person. It is easy to see, then, why the prophet has such a hard time retaining any sense of personal integrity and continuity apart from his role as message carrier. His existence as a person is so fragile, so dependent upon the response of those around him, that he is sorely tempted to comfort himself with the delusion that he is self-made.

Most of the narcissism of the prophet, however, comes from the conditions surrounding his extrusion. If the extruded segment is to be in a position to evolve new circuitry, it must be cut off in some way from the parent circuit and assigned a degree of autonomy and independence. This is facilitated if the prophet is poorly connected in the first place, as is usually the case. The prophet is expected, at the time of his extrusion, to withdraw his emotional investment from all his relationships and invest it instead in the map of that circuitry that he carries within himself. Gestaltists refer to this process as "taking back one's projections."

Freud once said that the individual ego was merely a precipitate of past relationships; the Gestaltists argue the reverse—that an individual's relationships are merely a stage on which her internal conflicts are acted out. The parent circuitry, when it extrudes a prophet, adopts the Gestalt viewpoint. The prophet is expected to dissolve as many complementarities as possible and rediscover all that variety within. This is not outlandish, for the potentiality for all human traits is within everyone. Every human being knows all the roles that exist in any human drama and can play them, once her revulsion is overcome. In this respect the Gestaltists are utterly correct.

The prophet, then, is forced to cease and desist from allowing other persons to play out aspects of himself. He must develop autonomy, totipotentiality, self-sufficiency—and will inevitably do so to some extent merely by virtue of his extrusion. This creates a strong likelihood that new patterns will evolve—just as a colony that must survive on its own without help from the mother country is likely to evolve a somewhat variant culture.

An unfortunate result of all this is that the prophet comes to imagine that his extrusion was his own doing, and that the new circuitry evolved during his isolation (exile, vigil, peak experience, or whatever) was a personal achievement instead of an almost inevitable result of the situation in which he was placed. This is a natural hazard of the process. The prophet is, after all, a throwaway. Most are flops. From such a miserable condition one must take what comforts are available, and these are unavoidably narcissistic and delusional.

This was harmless enough so long as each extruded segment remained in temporal and spatial isolation. A serious problem emerged, however, when humans began to record their history, thus allowing a culture of prophets to emerge. Not only did this teach future extruded segments how to behave (a useful feature on the whole), but it also made available to them the comforting fantasy that they were not expendable castoffs, but chosen heroes. Once this vision of the prophet became widely broadcast, what was originally a mere analgesic became a way of life, and people began actually to seek out the once-shunned role.

What we see around us now is a social system whose highest priority is given over to the manufacture of mutations. This is essentially what the concept of individualism is all about—the elevation of the peripheral instance to a position of centrality. For the past two centuries Western culture has been moving rapidly toward a system in which every single individual would be socialized to be a heroic castoff—a prophet-mutation for a core system which would thereby have ceased to exist. Like the mechanism of will, discussed in the last chapter, this everyone-a-mutation pattern is an emergency function run amok. It is one thing for a system to throw off a few oddments from time to time as a hedge against the unexpected—a recognition that the circuitry it has evolved, while viable and elegant, is limited and vulnerable to changing conditions. It is quite different for a system to treat the unexpected as an inevitable commonplace and throw off its entire circuitry fragment by fragment. This is a self-perpetuating disease, since the system that continually fragments and expends itself can scarcely claim a workable core. The more castoffs it extrudes the more prophets it can reasonably claim to need, until it reaches total dissolution.

Heroizing the castoff role in our society has reached a point close to this. It is no longer merely the deviant who is socialized to disregard his connectedness with others. Even the ordinary pillars of the community are trained to think for themselves in every conceivable sense of that phrase. If it were only a matter of our being afflicted with thousands of third-rate artists of various kinds, each imagining himself to be the founder of a new creative dynasty, we could survive the influx. The civilized world has never lacked for pomposity. But the spread of the heroic mutation principle has also helped to give us the kind of scientists and physicians we have.

Americans are trained from infancy for mutationhood. They are taught to ignore their connectedness with others and to imagine that whatever successes or failures they experience in life are a function of their own dissociated agency. They are taught to destroy continuity, to adapt mechanically and slavishly to change, and to regard relationships as having no meaning apart from the achievement of instrumental goals. This has produced certain gains: There has never been a people or species better equipped to survive and adjust to some cataclysmic change in the environment. On the other hand, there is a certain futility in living one's entire life around anticipated disaster. It tempts one to produce a disaster just to give the whole thing meaning. Furthermore, readiness for change tends to create change, and our preparedness has led us into a condition in which as a people we are under chronic severe stress from perpetual novelty, as Toffler has shown. Our capacity to deal with this distress, meanwhile, is sapped by our ideology, which tells us that change is necessary and good. A politician who stood up and argued that change of any kind (backward or forward) was usually pernicious would achieve a reputational ranking in our society somewhat below Adolf Hitler. Finally, since changes occur at different rates and since they occur at such a speed that one process is not completed before another begins, the experience of equilibration and integration is now virtually unknown. The proliferation of disharmony is self-generating.

As a result of their socialization, Americans as a group are addicted to the romantic image of the lonely castoff hero who forges his (it is largely a male image) own destiny and changes the parent circuit by his own unique efforts. Children are indoctrinated with this idea early in life by means of fairy tales in which the rejected youth triumphs over the rejecting group; their later childhood years are filled with biographies, both real and fictional, of lonely or scorned adults who achieve pre-eminence through creative achievements. All of these tales indoctrinate the child with the notion that these "successes" were attributable *solely* to individual art and *in spite of* the group in which the individual was embedded. The fact that in reality the individual can achieve nothing without a social context is lost to vision amid the glories of egoistic triumph.

The fantasy of individualistic detachment leads many people to confuse living in organic relation to others with being imprisoned in some sort of authoritarian system. If one begins with the illusion of autonomy all forms of connectedness seem alike, and equally oppressive. Western culture has for two centuries been engaged in a very gradual shift, institution by institution, and with many relapses, from authoritarian to "democratic" modes of organization. This shift has been a pervasive image in Western minds for so long that it is very difficult for us to view social change in ways uncolored by that process. Yet it is, after all, only a brief episode in human cultural history, and must be placed in context. The implication that authoritarianism is an ancient or primeval form of social organization is quite simply false. Authoritarianism as a social form has not even completed the process of diffusing itself throughout the world, even while it is being supplanted in the most urbanized parts of Western society. Western peoples, particularly Americans, have been caught up in the democratization drama for so long that they tend to view the entire past as one long homogeneous era of authoritarianism. Toffler, for example, talks about life in simple communities as "tightly regimented" and restrictive. But this "imprisonment of the past" that seems to dismay him so greatly is not characteristic of the simple community but of the authoritarian forms that overwhelmed, absorbed, and superseded it. The bulk of human history has been taken up with *increasing* individual powerlessness in human societies rather than decreasing it. This is not to say that the more recent push toward democratization (confused and ambivalent as it is) is in any way a return to an ancient form. Mass democracy and the simple community both bear more resemblance to authoritarianism than they do to each other.

The organic social form of the simple community gives way to authoritarianism with increasing size and complexity. The simple community is not centralized and communication is both intense and evenly distributed. (Leaders, after all, are only necessary when a group is too large or too new to act organically.) Much of the collective behavior of the community appears to the outsider as spontaneous, unplanned, almost organismic—as if communication were extrasensory. In fact it is simply automatic —things are "understood," and collective needs are experienced with the intensity that we experience personal ones.

The delicate multiple attunement of such a community cannot altogether survive fusion with an alien tribe. The wars of small tribes usually involve a lot of scuffling, very little killing, and few territorial changes. But when, with large-scale disruptions and movements of peoples, groups engage in conquest and absorption of other groups, we begin to find (a) centralization of power and communication, and (b) hierarchy. That is to say, there comes into being a chief or king, and nobles and commoners.

William Stephens discusses this transition in a cross-cultural analysis of family patterns, finding the most authoritarian forms at an intermediate level of cultural sophistication, with "democratic" patterns at both extremes. He calls the authoritarian form a *kingdom,* defined as having a centralized organ of political control with coercive armed power, a single hereditary ruler, at least two social classes, and economic exploitation. By contrast the *tribe* (equivalent to the simple community) has no centralized power, no chiefs or nobles, no exploitation, no cities, no civilization. Stephens suggests that the authoritarian formula was invented to enable conquering groups to maintain control of a subjugated people and its territory. He finds that son-to-father deference and wife-to-husband deference is low in tribes, high in kingdoms, and low again when the kingdom evolves into a democratic state, and he argues that these authoritarian family forms are simply a by-product of the authoritarian state.

Authoritarianism, however, is an awkward and rigid social form. In times of rapid change it tends either to ossify and shatter or to dissolve into democratic forms that have more flexibility. This is in no way a return to simplicity or to greater organicity. On the contrary, democratization usually carries further the process of disconnection that authoritarianism began—the conversion of organic units into masses of unrelated atoms.

These three stages are in fact an illustration of the prophet dynamic—the idea that change occurs in living systems by the extrusion of particles that are reingested when they have evolved new circuitry. The movement from the simple community to mass democracy is neither a straight line nor a mere oscillation. It is a pulsating movement in which change is brought about by an initial concentration and a subsequent diffusion. Relatively innocuous microorganisms, isolated in a biological warfare laboratory, can be mutated into virulent strains that will, when reintroduced into human organisms, spread rapidly and destroy them. In such a case the microorganism—originally a comfortable parasite—is the prophet, the laboratory the desert, the message death. In the case of the transition from simple community to mass democracy, the prophet is the chief or king, the desert is authoritarianism, and the messages are linearity, individuation, and inhibition.

The simple community is not held together by principle. This is not to say that categories do not exist: Kinship categories are probably of great importance, even allowing for the inherent bias of Western ethnographers trained to assume that all people relate to one another in terms of the categories to which they belong. But kinship categories are bounded and static—they do not lead very far in the direction of more abstract generalization. While they do tend to blunt organicity to some extent, they also form a barrier against the emergence of other kinds of mechanistic order.

In any case, the individual holds a fixed position in the community, one which alters only gradually and very predictably through the life cycle. She is defined by her relationships—if we attempted to examine her in isolation, tabulating individual attributes on IBM cards, we would learn very little about her that would predict her behavior. She is a *part* of something to a much greater extent than a Westerner, for whom such a tabulation would tell us a great deal.

With the centralization of power this begins to change. Initially, power is fixed and hereditary, but the more power the king or chief holds the more dynamic the power variable tends to become. Initially viewed as a representation of powerful environmental forces, kings are hedged about with constraints and restrictions. But over time, by virtue of the power concentrated in them, their individual preferences, whims, and needs weaken and erode the fixed and hereditary limitations. As Henry V says, "Nice customs courtesy to great kings." Modernism begins with despotism.

Kings, then, are the first individualists. They are encouraged, as their power increases, to develop narcissistic and non-interdependent attitudes. They are the prophets of individualism. The people, cut adrift from their social moorings by the collision of alien cultures and increasing size and complexity, have formed an unstated contract with the ruler: He will create an order, they will accord him deference; he will gratify their dependency needs, they will gratify his narcissism. In the simple community both of these needs are almost automatically gratified: Everyone has a place, is embedded in nourishing relationships, perceives order and meaning, and is relatively unselfconscious. Interdependency *exists*, so dependency is highly muted. Narcissism is almost irrelevant since no one views herself as an isolated entity, but only as part of a whole. Authoritarianism restores to the uprooted a facsimile of wholeness and belonging. Dependency needs are now gratified while narcissistic needs remain irrelevant. But for the king this is less true. He is made aware of his separateness and uniqueness, and hence must be flattered and petted to compensate him for his isolation.

This is a gradual process. The court of the ruler is a laboratory or desert in which individualism may take centuries to evolve. When it does the stage is set for the next development—the diffusion of individualism to the masses. This is the process we call democratization. It is often accompanied by an attack on the prophet (king) according to the mechanism described earlier. The king is dethroned, but his narcissism is devoured and absorbed by all the people. The contented social indifference of a Nicholas and Alexandra becomes the cozy callousness of the entire middle class. This is the process that Freud's myth of the primal horde attempted to portray.

The process is the same for linearity. The king, isolated in the laboratory of centralized power, learns to pursue a concept in an unbounded "logical" fashion—to ignore feedback. This, too, is internalized by the masses during the democratization or diffusion phase. Technological culture is simply the internalization of tyranny by the masses. Relationships *within* such a society take on the same chaotic, competitive form that previously characterized relations *between* warring kingdoms.

Finally, authoritarianism is the first step in the development of internalized inhibition of impulse and feeling—the capacity to postpone gratification in the service of narcissistic goals. Stephens observes that kingdoms have more sharply segregated sex roles, and suggests that they are generally more inhibited and restrained than tribes. He cites Rattray Taylor's discussion of the "patrist" syndrome: sexual restrictions, derogation of women, political authoritarianism, fear of spontaneity and pleasure, and so on. Other studies confirm this association between authoritarianism, patriarchy, and sexual repressiveness, when simple communities are compared with kingdoms, although it is not at all clear that sexual constraints diminish immediately in response to democratization. In any case, the inhibition that takes place in kingdoms is external and coercive. The king may be forced by his responsibilities and position to become a specialist in inhibition and gratification postponement (a "bad" ruler is one who fails too conspicuously to do this—he is usually replaced, at least *de facto,* by someone who can—a prime minister or usurper). But the individual citizen is not expected to restrain her *own* impulses in the absence of outside pressure.

We have for two centuries or so been in the second phase of this process, in which the mass attacks the prophet and devours his message. The mass throws off the force and inhibits itself. The entire population begins to exhibit an ethic of control, achievement, and inhibition. Max Weber describes how the kind of asceticism originally consigned to monastic specialists (another group of prophets) was later diffused through the population during the Reformation, and the diffusion of achievement motivation seems to have taken the same form.

One can also see this process at work in the diffusion of earnestness and pomposity. Kings and queens used to play children's games when at leisure. During the nineteenth century this disappeared altogether. By now, as a result of Little Leagues, educational toys, and other forms of adult invasion of the world of children, the children themselves can scarcely play games. I have often been struck by the relative inability of college students (in comparison with their elders) to respond to the invitation to engage in pretending or ritualized play of any kind.

Two points need to be made about this dynamic before leaving the topic of authoritarianism. First, I want to underline the fact that all three of these trends—individualism, linearity, and inhibition—are only partially present under authoritarianism. The most important characteristic of authoritarianism is its compartmentalism. One mode of behavior operates in the court, another in the villages. This is another way of saying that in a stable authoritarian system the simple community remains largely intact all around the edges of the society. Generalizations about the social forms of kingdoms tend in actuality to be about the court and the noble class. The culture of the commoners often remains essentially unchanged. From the point of view of the masses the court really *is* an extruded segment—one that may impinge disastrously upon individuals from time to time but does not immediately affect their culture. True, unbearable taxation, passing armies, or widespread conscription may eventually erode or completely obliterate the organicity of villages, leading to dislocation, wandering, banditry, and urbanization, but by and large the disappearance of the simple community occurs with democratization—with the diffusion of the prophet-king's message.

The second point has to do with our tendency to confuse the organic connectedness of the simple community with the coerciveness of authoritarianism. We have so little experience of prolonged and stable group life that we tend to imagine any intensification of relationship as if it involved being fettered and manipulated. But there is a difference between being a leaf on a tree and a pawn on a chessboard. Being a non-autonomous part of a whole in no way requires being subject to an alien individual's conscious will. Authoritarianism arises when the whole no longer functions spontaneously and intuitively as a unit. Despots and edicts emerge as substitutes, *faute de mieux*. In an organic group no will is necessary to cement the group. But that degree of collective attunement requires long periods of stable relatedness unimpinged upon by outside forces—it is a delicate balance that could not exist in our own society. Hence we have difficulty in conceiving of any intense collectivity not dominated by some form of conscious will—a despot or oligarchy.

But the major flaw in this perception is that it looks at relatedness unilaterally. Americans see "freedom" as the absence of being influenced or controlled, *but it is also the loss of influence and control over others*. The condition that Toffler slanders as "regimented" is simply one in which people are highly responsive to one another. One is more subject to the demands of others (an American nightmare) but one can also count on others being there to meet one's own demands. Individualism is a shell game that distracts us from the rigors of mutuality—from the fact that in a society in which I am powerless to affect you, you are also powerless to affect me. The powerlessness endemic in modern society is produced by the simple device of disconnecting us.

One reason Americans are so prone to fall for this shell game is that they tend to place value on themselves only as *actors*, not as *responders* or *feelers*. (I suspect this is less true of women than of men, wherein lies some hope for the future.) If I only attach importance to what I and others *do*, and not what we *feel*, then close relationships will seem dangerous, since they will seem to impede my action, while their potential for satisfying my needs and desires is less salient in my consciousness.

Specialization and the Household Prophets

The division of labor in society is based upon the odd assumption that the efficiency of the part is more important than the efficiency of the whole. The history of human culture has included an increasingly vigorous commitment to this point of view, despite the considerable cost in human pleasure. Toffler, for example, touts the advantages of "modular" or segmented relationships, to which each individual commits only a fragment of her personal involvement. He points out, quite correctly, that "freedom" and fragmentation go together and chastises modern social critics for not recognizing this. Since freedom, like motherhood and apple pie, is an unquestioned good in American society, he feels he has disposed of the issue. But partial involvement means partial fulfillment: A person who is never more than fragmentarily in the here-and-now is only minimally alive.

Activities that are shared on an undifferentiated basis (everyone doing the same thing together) are more enjoyable but take longer than tasks that are parceled out on a differentiated basis. The time that is saved is meaningful only if the activity is unpleasant, but insofar as it is done collectively it usually is not. Furthermore the efficiency gained by each person acquiring skill at his or her differentiated task is often dissipated through the ravages of boredom, and usually lost in any case through the problems of co-ordinating the differentiated tasks. In our modern sophistication we are supposed to know this—to know that communication and co-ordination are far more important than mere mechanical exactitude in some functioning part. We are also supposed to know that compartmentalization is destructive of the integrity of the person, who cannot be altogether squeezed into some limited function. Yet these apparently obvious truths have had very little impact on the progressive "modularization" of social organization in the West.

Why is this so? How did competence at part tasks come to be valued more highly than co-ordination and integration of the whole? The notion that anything beyond short-range and narrow-gauge efficiency can be achieved in this way is a patent absurdity. Are we then to assume that humanity is simply idiotic?

And what of nature itself? Are we to assume that the blind forces that produced plant and animal organisms are also misguided? Such an assumption—that nature could systematically and consistently err—would throw all knowledge into chaos, and while the possibility is not to be utterly excluded, it would be frivolous to embrace it without exhausting less horrendous alternatives.

One obvious difficulty is that we are using integration as the ultimate criterion, thus implying that an integrated organism is absolutely more viable than one that is not. But we saw at the beginning of this chapter that integration contains its own dilemmas. The division of labor is useful not because (as some social theorists have implied) it leads to integration but precisely because it does not. The communicational difficulties it creates provide opportunity for change and movement.

The usual metaphor for specialization of function is the finely-articulated machine in which everything goes "like clockwork," but this is misleading. The value of the division of labor is that it introduces a bit of chaos into the system. A part that has a specialized function has achieved an autonomy of meaning. This is usually obscured by the fact that physical autonomy is thereby lost. Physical autonomy depends on uniformity: If an organism composed of identical parts is broken up, the parts can survive because they are self-sufficient—each contains some of everything that was present in the whole. If, however, the organism is composed of differentiated parts, they will perish apart from the whole—this is what is meant by interdependence.

In what sense, then, does a differentiated part possess autonomy? I have called it an autonomy of meaning, and by this I intend something rather simple and obvious. Two identical parts, when separated, are independent of each other, but they experience the world (that is, it impinges upon them) in the same way. Two differentiated parts, while dependent upon each other for survival, have an entirely different experience of their environment. The hand does not encounter the world in the way the eye does. The receptors and categories of the one are not available to the other.

This issue is usually passed over by noting that the hand and eye can exist only in conjunction with the total organism, and that their differentiated information is co-ordinated at a higher level. What is overlooked is the fact that such higher level co-ordination is possible only by proceeding to a higher level of abstraction. That is to say, only that information is available to the brain which is translatable from one system to the other. *This means that the eye (or the hand) "knows" much that the brain cannot know because its language is too abstract.* The brain has a kind of international *lingua franca* which does not deign to concern itself with the trivialities of local dialects.

Now, as we have seen, an identical segment can change only if it is isolated from the whole and placed in an altered environment. A specialized segment, on the other hand, can change *without* separation from the whole. Its internal "language" creates slippage, disorder, a lack of full articulation with the total system, and the possibility of independent evolution within itself. The increasing chaotic quality of the system yields increasing flexibility. The system must work harder to maintain its integrity under these conditions, and this will take the form of attempting to extend the range of its abstract language system, or to restrict the independent movement of the subsystems.

Our conceptualization of the prophet dynamic must therefore be elaborated into three different forms. The first and simplest is that already described: A homogeneous system detaches an undifferentiated segment of itself; in an altered environment the segment evolves a new structure, and if this is of value to the parent system, it reincorporates the modified segment and thereby has its own structure modified.

The second form involves a differentiated system. Here a specialized segment is extruded, and the altered environment is unnecessary since the segment is already different from the totality. To survive, however, the specialized segment must complete itself—must evolve ways of meeting needs originally met by other specialized segments. If it should succeed in becoming whole, it will only partly resemble the parent system, since the articulation of the various segments will necessarily differ according to the special circumstances of its own history, its original specialization, the nature of its private language, the conditions of its self-generalization.

The third form is the division of labor itself, even when extrusion and reincorporation do not occur. Every segment of a differentiated system is in effect a prophet, but the desert is inside—a product of its linguistic diversity. In the division of labor each segment stands with its head in the void and its feet firmly planted in the parent system. The latter occasionally allows the kind of meta-information that would revise its circuiting to penetrate it, but this is rare. By and large, change is forced on the parent system by its efforts to maintain integrity in the face of the chaos generated by the evolution of its specialized components.

The division of labor, then, is a kind of compromise formation in which everyone is a prophet but the prophets are kept at home. In the undifferentiated system adaptive flexibility is sacrificed to integrity. That is to say, adaptation is made problematic while integrity is taken for granted. With the division of labor the reverse obtains: Adaptation is taken for granted and integrity becomes problematic.

It would be pleasant to say that what we are experiencing today is merely a state in which the division of labor has become highly elaborated at the expense of integrity, and that it is beginning to correct itself. But the problem is more complicated than this. In our system everyone is a prophet, but the prophets are not kept at home. That is to say, it is not merely the prophet *function* that has been generalized but also the prophet *mentality*. The division of labor minimizes the physical autonomy of prophets while maximizing their number. In our system number, physical autonomy and meaning autonomy are *all* maximized. It is as if, in the diffusion or democratization phase of the prophet dynamic, not only the message was incorporated but the process itself. What was sought was not the new circuitry evolved by each prophet, but his special status.

The Patriarchal Revolution

This state of affairs owes much to what might be called the patriarchal revolution: the emergence of a complex cultural system, exerting controlling power over a society, from the day-to-day operation of which women are largely excluded.

There are those who actually argue that the present (decaying) system of male dominance over women is "natural." Since it certainly is not universal among individuals, nor among human societies, nor among other species, such an assertion is patently ridiculous. One can find examples of almost anything in nature, and anyone who tries to bolster his position by pointing to the way baboons manage relations between the sexes must be prepared to listen to discussions of the praying mantis and black widow spider or, at the very least, the less sexist gibbon.

The fact is, there *is* no natural relation. Across individual couples, societies, and species a great variety of arrangements can be found, all of which have benefits and costs, and all of which fit comfortably into some larger pattern of functions. If I talk about a patriarchal revolution, then, this is not meant to imply that patriarchy as I have defined it is "unnatural"—only that it is, in the history of the species, a relatively recent phenomenon.

I also want to avoid any implication that the condition prior to this revolution was some sort of matriarchy. All social forms become fragile as they become extreme, and all exaggerated patriarchies have been plagued by a pervasive terror of feminine power. Through such eyes the relative sexual equality of a neighboring or conquered tribe tends to take on sinister overtones. The most educated guess we can make is that the typical primeval condition was one of rough equality. While some extremely "primitive" tribes today exclude women from much of the ritual life, real discrepancies in power require a rather high subsistence level. Finally, the term "revolution" is a bit misleading, implying a rapid transition of some kind. The revolving in this case was extremely gradual, occurring over a period of many centuries.

Patriarchy, which appears throughout the world in many forms, was a cultural invention of some importance, with obvious benefits and even more obvious drawbacks. Giving power to a group of specialists means that some needed traits will be heightened while others will atrophy.

The development of a high degree of specialization requires a certain amount of leisure. H. R. Hays points out that in very simple societies women show a great deal of creative energy, but that as soon as a society reaches the point where some function, such as pottery, can be given over to specialists, it is taken over by men. In other words, it is not that women in such societies are uncreative, but rather that they do not have the leisure to specialize. Men have taken over one field after another from women as soon as it became clear that status and prestige could be derived from superior specialized performance. We can see this in our own society, in which men have become chefs and obstetricians. Even without the time and energy and fame-hunger to make a full-time specialty of it, it is quite possible that the best cooks and potters in history were all women who died unknown and unrecognized outside of their families and neighbors. It is also quite possible that none of them felt any need for recognition from people with whom they had no personal connection, however much they may have felt disadvantaged and oppressed in their role as women. By and large it has been men who have felt driven to push any sort of skill into a specialized occupation from which glory could be extracted.

The patriarchal revolution did not "cause" specialization, but was a by-product of it. In the preservation of the species men play a less elemental role than women, and such peripherality tends to be a great advantage in social evolution. As has been suggested elsewhere it is the uncommitted who are in the best position to take advantage of changing conditions or cultural innovations. Being less tied to essential maintenance functions, men in some primitive societies had the leisure and uninvolvement to specialize, to invent, to create further leisure for themselves. The dominance that emerged in the patriarchal revolution was based on unimportance.

Indeed, women are now beginning to achieve power for the very same reason. Just as men became dominant because they were less committed to (and important in) the ongoing everyday functions of primitive life, so women today are less committed to and important in the mechanized culture that men have created. It is women who are in the best position to take up the reins in the more pleasure-prone, aesthetically absorbed, and love-oriented culture that lies ahead. Men may be ideologues of our future culture, but as a group they are too imbued with work and machismo ethics to enjoy anything very thoroughly. Furthermore, those that have attempted to make a career out of hedonism have divorced themselves from any kind of maintenance function and become parasitic. It is women who have best retained the primeval sense of balance, and who are best capable of combining an orientation toward love and pleasure with the optimal performance of necessary maintenance functions.

The particular form of specialization that men adopted is of interest because it reproduces the universal contract between those of differing social status. In relation to women, men have taken the stance assumed by the warrior-aristocrat toward the peasant: "If you will feed me, I will protect you." Before long, of course, every protection contract becomes a protection racket: "Give me what I want and I will protect you against me."

But it is with the results of the patriarchal revolution that we are primarily concerned here. If men were the prophets, what was the message? Men have evolved many bits of new circuitry, most notably the warrior ethos and industrial civilization. In both cases they achieved their innovations by the schizoid device of deadening themselves to their own feelings and substituting the emergency will mechanism for spontaneous bodily responsivity. The cultural contribution of male specialists was the detachment of libido from emotional relationships and bodily pleasure, and the investment of this libido in narcissistic pursuits, achievements, work, power, glory.

No social invention, unfortunately, is without its costs, despite our progress mythology. This male commitment to narcissistic pursuits was purchased at the price of a lowered capacity to tolerate pleasurable stimulation. Pleasure for males became increasingly a matter of tension release: loving, touching, caressing, all became heavily subordinated to an exaggerated emphasis on orgasm. By making a heavy investment in ego pursuits men became sensually crippled relative to women. Rather than attempting to redress this inferiority, however, or accepting it as an unfortunate price paid for their cultural ambitions, they have sought to cripple women as well. Their sexual inferiority was disturbing, not merely because of the reduction in their pleasure capacity, but because of the narcissistic wound formed by *any* sensed inferiority. The history of sexual mores has been one long series of ingenious efforts to reduce women to a condition in which this wound would not be experienced. From enforced chastity to the inculcation of bizarre beliefs about their own bodies to criticism of their inability to abbreviate their pleasure as much as men do, women have been led a most unmerry chase in the service of assuaging this self-inflicted wound to male vanity.

Changes in sexual mores are primarily changes in what is considered acceptable for *women* to do—variations in sexual restrictions on males are relatively miniscule. Sexual rules are by and large made by men and enforced on women, even though women have frequently shared in the enforcing, with the self-destructive enthusiasm characteristic of oppressed groups. But women often become mothers, and whatever cultural poisons they are forced to endure are passed on to their male offspring with talionic precision. The cultural impact of sexual restrictions, therefore, is multiple and cyclical.

But leaving aside these costs, there are others directly attached to the benefits themselves. The cultural innovations derived from male specialization in ego-aggrandizement and bleached-out rationalism exhibit the limitations of that specialization. Only a male-dominated culture, for example, could have invented the jackhammer, with its brutal assault on the senses, in order to save time digging a hole in the ground—an invention only needed in the first place because other males decreed that the earth should be covered with macadam and concrete, depriving the feet of texture, the world of life and color, and the air of oxygen. Men are fond of saying that women have emasculated the modern male, but this is mere projection. If modern man is emasculated, he managed it quite by himself through his own emotional self-castration and the resultant profusion of grotesque machines and mammoth organizations that have constantly diminished him while feeding his narcissistic dreams.

Male specialization in the exercise of will is facilitated by their freedom from the experience of childbirth. Bateson suggests that the alcoholic, when sober, suffers from the delusion that he is master of his fate, a psychic malady that is cured the moment he takes his first drink. Women are less vulnerable to such ecological innocence, since a woman who has experienced childbirth knows what it is like to have one's own body completely taken over by an internal force over which conscious will has no control. It is therefore of great importance that in the advanced stages of our cultural degradation men attempted to gain willful control over the childbirth process, seeing that it took place in impersonal and unemotional male-dominated environments, that the mothers were rendered insensible during the process so that the male obstetrician could "deliver" the baby—thus acting out a ritual pretense of conscious masculine will—and that the baby was instantly deprived of the kind of warm human tactile contact that would help it evolve into a sensitive, sensual, and responsive human being.

Furthermore, from the middle of the eighteenth century through World War II, male doctors and educators leveled a consistent attack on maternal behavior, appointing themselves rationalistic experts in a field that had been a feminine preserve for millions of years. The thrust of this attack was that touching, affection, warmth, cuddling, nursing, body contact, reassurance, protection, soothing, and the spontaneous exercise of bodily functions were all pernicious and should be suppressed as much as possible. A type of maternal behavior that had previously been the prerogative, *faute de mieux*, of the destitute, the indifferent, the sadistic, and the psychotic, was now enjoined on the entire population—even on the wealthy, affectionate, healthy, and well-disposed.

The culmination of this attack came toward the end of the last century, when doctors attempted to eliminate the use of the cradle and, indeed, to persuade mothers that holding or rocking a baby to sleep was "vicious" and "habit forming." For the sheltering, enclosed, and moving cradle was substituted the open, stationary, prisonlike crib. A decade or two later the behaviorists moved in to insist that any show of love or physical contact made the child too dependent. Infants were to be fed by the mechanical clock rather than by their own biological ones, and were generally regarded as little machines to be wound up properly and otherwise left alone. Maternal impulses to love and care for them were to be squelched manfully.

Civilized Western infants are still treated in a highly impersonal manner relative to those elsewhere in the world—born in hospitals, separated from their mothers at birth, given minimal body contact in their early years, weaned early, isolated a great deal, and so on. Fronted by the glamour of Western medicine, furthermore, these barbarities are rapidly being diffused to other cultures.

The future of all this is highly confusing. The schizoid circuitry of the male prophets is every day being diffused more and more widely. Women in Western societies are increasingly caught up in it, and for most men it simply represents normality. But at the same time a new process has begun, as *women* have become prophets evolving (at times) an antithetical system. These two streams are in utter collision at present, forming a cultural whirlpool from which almost any social phenomenon might conceivably emerge.

The Duckling Delusion

The exaggerated spirit of competitiveness spawned by the patriarchal revolution, and the increasing domination of childbirth and child rearing processes by males, has played some part in the evolution of a major mythical theme in our society—that of the ugly duckling. In this myth (Rudolph the Red-nosed Reindeer is one of dozens of examples) an individual, shunned by his fellows by virtue of some defect, demonstrates that the defect is actually a virtue and proves that his alienation from others is due to superiority rather than inferiority.

The function of the myth of the ugly duckling is to hide an ugly reality. The reality is that ugly ducklings usually turn out to be ugly ducks. Even the rare misplaced swan is likely to be pretty ugly on the inside by the time he finds his proper milieu. Mutation is a tragedy for the individuals concerned no matter how the issue turns out for the species. *The Ugly Duckling* is a mutation fairy tale that attempts to hide this tragedy.

The myth also serves to justify past crimes committed in the name of individualism. No one amasses a grossly disproportionate share of wealth or power as a reward for intrinsic virtues. All great fortunes were initially stolen from the people, directly or indirectly. One important function of the police—subsidiary to their primary role of maintaining order and predictability—is to prevent any of the people from stealing it back. The reason radicals are a greater threat to law and order than ordinary criminals is that they wish to steal it back collectively rather than individualistically (the way it was stolen in the first place). Criminal theft does not threaten the structure of our system—it is a technical *faux pas,* a faulty and risk-laden method utilized by those who lack the knowledge and skills to steal without risk.

Once a man has stolen his fortune he must find some way of keeping it. Sometimes naked power suffices, but ultimately, in a stable society, his act must be ratified in some way. In the past this has usually taken some time—at least a generation. The rule is that anyone who inherits a stolen fortune is entitled to it, and after it has been peacefully transmitted from parent to child for a few generations the family that has succeeded in hoarding their ill-gotten gains is regarded as a superior breed of persons. Some of the money is expended on educational, cultural, and status-linked accouterments which serve to nourish this impression, but by and large the mere fact of having been able to retain the money is proof enough. To view social inequality as anything other than deserved would threaten the very foundation of social order, and people are quite reasonably willing to put up with almost anything rather than have their everyday world plunged into chaos, unpredictability, and confused violence.

This mode of ratification, however, is paced too slowly for modern society. Today we more often utilize the myth of personal achievement—the notion that one individual can stand so far above others that he or she *merits* receiving far more rewards. We pay lip service to the notion that any success is a collective effort (Academy Award presentations abound in this sort of thing), but no one really wants to believe such statements even though they are true.

The duckling myth plays an important role in buttressing the individualistic justification of social inequality. In it an individual overcomes the low opinion and expectations of his group and proves in the end to be their superior. Furthermore, he does this without any help from them—indeed, over their scornful resistance. In ancient hero myths the hero received many magical gifts, blessings, or useful information from those around him. In the legends of Perseus and Jason, for example, the hero is merely a representative of powerful forces; like the private eye or secret agent of many adventure stories and films, his only special virtue seems to be an ability to expose himself to danger and be in the right place at the right time. In the scorned-outcast genre, however, the hero is presented as utterly isolated and autonomous. That for which he is scorned turns out to be a saving virtue—a valued mutation, such as Rudolph's nose.

This theme is not restricted to fairy tales, however. It also dominates the simplified biographies of "great" men that are designed for children. Whether inventors, artists, or robber barons, they tend to be shown as "self-made." They are usually poor, educated with difficulty or not at all, rejected by their peers, and surrounded with obstacles. Whatever education they receive is portrayed as useless—everything derives from the skills they develop alone, in their study or workshop, whither they have withdrawn from the insensitivity of the clods that surround them. One always wonders, in stories of this genre, why the hero is so anxious to coerce the love of such despicable persons, but one should not look for reasonableness where wounded narcissism is at issue. In *The Ugly Duckling* itself, the hero finds himself a superior group to which he truly belongs, but the more typical outcome is that the group who rejected the hero now sings his praises.

The special message of these stories is that a defect can be made into a virtue through the exercise of will, and that love can be forcibly extracted from others through successful individualistic achievement. The worthlessness of any love founded on impersonal fame ("spread some of that on me, please") is slyly concealed in these little pep talks—much as the difficulties inherent in intense and exclusive dyadic relationships are masked in the phrase "they lived happily ever after."

This vision of life, wherein the most warped shall ultimately be worshipped by those who initially scorn them, is imbibed by middle-class Americans with their jarred baby foods. It contributes not a little to the monotony of American culture, which mass-produces goods and services for those who fancy themselves to be the "saving remnant." But this bit of self-deception is harmless enough. The real impact of the duckling delusion lies in the way it detaches individual consciousness from its human, bodily, and environmental contexts so that it becomes autarchic and mechanical. The individual's intrinsic connectedness with others is denied—the only dimension of relation that is recognized or valued is superiority-inferiority. The winner of the competition—*any* competition will do—is portrayed as having all needs met, even those that were sacrificed to the achievement of superiority. Mechanical responsivity in the Western World owes much to the duckling myth.

Jonathan Livingston Strangelove

Nothing could demonstrate more dramatically the vitality of the duckling myth in American society than the extraordinary popularity of the best-selling book, *Jonathan Livingston Seagull*—a kind of Christian Science Dawn Patrol rendering of the Rudolph story. Even humanists, radicals, and counterculture freaks were entranced by the story—a puerile tale that glorifies overweening narcissism, compulsive striving, and schizoid alienation from the body. *Jonathan Livingston Seagull* epitomizes the American dream. It reveals the same victory-at-any-price mentality described so poignantly by Gary Shaw in connection with college football, and satirized so brilliantly by Philip Roth in connection with the President of the United States.

The hero of the story is a sort of avian Charles Atlas or self-made entrepreneur—his whole life given over to ambition, mastery, and "self-betterment." While the other gulls are simply grooving on life, he is absorbed in the seagull equivalent of practicing body-building exercises in front of a mirror, or studying the intricacies of the stock market. His control needs are uncontrollable, and he is the helpless servant of his need for mastery. As a result—like the old captains of industry—he is both admired by the masses and viewed as a menace to the community.

This he very shortly proves to be. In his frantic pursuit of speed and glory he almost kills some of his fellow gulls and is therefore banished by the elders of his tribe, who have failed to appreciate that he is a superior being. The book is in fact full of elitism. Jonathan is guiltless for breaking a self-made promise, since "such promises are only for the gulls that accept the ordinary" whereas Jonathan is "a one-in-a-million bird." When he achieves a higher state there is a long discussion as to the desirability of returning to the flock to teach the benighted savages he left behind, before he finally decides that one or two might be worthy to receive the white man's message.

The callous indifference to the lives of those deemed inferior ("The Gull of Fortune smiled upon him this once, and no one was killed") is reminiscent of American pilots in Vietnam: since Jonathan is a superior being, the welfare of the plodding masses (read "gooks" or "niggers") is beneath notice. The difference is merely one of scale, and the scale itself (a B-52 raid, for example) comes from precisely the mastery-power neurosis that Jonathan epitomizes. If you want to know how we got to Vietnam read *Jonathan Livingston Seagull*.

Also of interest is the basis for this superiority. Jonathan wastes no time in idle concern for the near death of his friends, for he has achieved a new speed record: *"two hundred fourteen miles per hour!* It was a breakthrough, the greatest single moment in the history of the Flock"* (his italics). Later, furthermore, he flies "the first aerobatics of any seagull on earth," and feels that thereby he has found a "reason to life." It would be difficult to find a better illustration of the deep inner emptiness of Americans, who so often seem incapable of finding joy in living, but must fill up their days with frantic striving after mastery—either inner or outer. Even when he reaches a kind of heaven, as he shortly does, it turns out to be simply another gym, where the Superbirds spend "hour after hour every day practicing flight, testing advanced aeronautics." Speed, power, and striving are all that this new world has to offer, but he is pleased with it for he has a new body. I am reminded of a magazine ad that began, "Don't Be Caught in Last Year's Body If You Want To Be a This-Year Girl!" Jonathan has traded in his old model for a new one, and his response sounds so much like an automobile commercial that we realize at once why the book was so popular: "With half the effort, he thought, I'll get twice the speed, twice the performance of my best days on Earth!" Ultimately, he pushes this alienation from the body one step further, and becomes "not bone and feather but a perfect idea of freedom and flight, limited by nothing at all."

Other themes we would expect to find are all here: the yearning for immortality (Jonathan is a Methuselah among gulls and he and his disciples ultimately transcend death altogether), the demand for linearity, for total absence of feedback ("Heaven is being perfect," "perfection doesn't have limits," "In heaven . . . there should be no limits," and "whatever stands against that freedom must be set aside, be it ritual or superstition or limitation in any form"), and a view of the body as merely the servant of the will (when Jonathan encounters a gull with a broken wing he comes on like a coach in a Pat O'Brien football movie—telling him he can fly if he wants to, which, this being a narcissistic fantasy, he of course does). All of these express the same impatience with the realities of interdependence and corporeality —an impatience that betrays a deep sense of helplessness and impotence. The organism that cannot cope with limitation is one that is incapable of nourishing itself. It is as if the burden of having to deal with the reality of another person would cause the ego to collapse altogether. The demand for infinite space springs from terror at the prospect of having to confront another, or meet her needs. It is the infant at the breast who cannot tolerate limitation—this is the closest that humans ever come to being without limits.

The rest of the story follows the duckling pattern closely. The outcast finds a group of superior beings to which he truly belongs ("Here were gulls who thought as he thought"), thus proving that his banishment was a result of the elders' inferiority, not his. As is probably obvious by now, there is a heavy undercurrent of racism in the duckling myth, and *Jonathan Livingston Seagull* is no exception. The compulsive need to establish one's superiority, which is what the story is all about, requires the definition of some group of beings as constitutionally inferior.

Finally, as if this weren't enough, Jonathan must return to his original, inferior flock, and show off his superior attainments to the amazed crowd—his enormous speed, his transcendance of death. He and his disciples live happily forever after, thus ending the most recent contribution to the culture of prophets, ecological illiteracy, and the Emotional Plague.

The Well-meant Disaster

The sources of the duckling myth's pre-eminence in modern society are complex. It might have something to do with the frequency with which academics and other high-achievers started as teacher's pets—resented and scorned by their peers. In the United States it may result from having a population of migrants: in animal societies, and generally among humans, it is the losers who are forced to migrate—the United States is thus a nation composed of losers who made it rich in exile. But perhaps the most important factor in popularizing the duckling myth has been the success of Western medicine in keeping alive children who would otherwise die from lack of love and care. Their fantasies and destructiveness have become the myth of our age.

It may seem cruel to engage in speculations of this kind, but should this hypothesis prove correct there are solutions available to us more humane than letting the unloved die. We might find ways of giving them love, for example, instead of merely feeding medical narcissism. And in the meantime we are breeding, every day, more misery, pain, and hatred.

There is by now ample evidence, from both human and animal studies, that inadequate loving and too little tactile contact in infancy lowers the organism's resistance to infection, slows down recuperative powers, and produces chronic depression. In the nineteenth century half of all children born died in the first year. As late as the second decade of the twentieth century, moreover, the death rate for children under one year in *institutions* was 100 per cent. Now, while Western medicine has not succeeded altogether in eliminating this effect, it prides itself on having kept alive large numbers of children who would have died without medical intervention. For this many loving parents have been grateful. We have, of course, no way of knowing which of these children would have rallied without such assistance, nor which parents may have generously extended gratitude to doctors that might more appropriately have been directed toward themselves for having fostered a strong, healthy, and well-beloved child and for tending her lovingly when she was under stress. What we do know is that statistically the medical claim is just: many who would have perished did not.

Eugenics enthusiasts have long pointed out that while this was good for the individual (although the high suicide rate in medically sophisticated countries throws even this assertion in doubt), it was bad for the species. Their arguments tend to be dismissed as callous and elitist, as indeed they often are—full of a rather archaic Darwinian concern about the necessity of "eliminating the weak and unfit" before they reproduce.

But this is not the real issue. Our species will not soon disappear through weakness and genetic dilution, but it may rapidly vanish through its homicidal proclivities, its mad race to destroy its own environment, its burgeoning mechanical malevolence. It is not a genetic flaw that is spreading like an epidemic among us, but a cultural one. Keeping the unloved alive has loosed an infectious emotional disease—the origin, perhaps, of what Wilhelm Reich called the Emotional Plague.

Love is contagious. So is its lack. Those who are truly loved are recognizable by their lovingness, generosity, beauty, strength, health, responsivity, and joyousness. The unloved can be recognized by their misery, malevolence, ugliness, rigidity, and spite. The unloved cannot love, and hence spread the disease to their children. Since unloved children are highly susceptible to infection and sickness, the great epidemics of history tended periodically to purge the species of its potentially most destructive members. This is not to say that only the unloved died— Nature is statistical and careless of individuals. But one must assume that the unloved died in disproportionate numbers. Plagues like the Black Death selected out the most-loved individuals to procreate and raise children—a selection, in other words, that was cultural as much as genetic. Any purificatory effects were probably offset by the horrendous social dislocations involved—Nature's brutalities thus prove to be as inefficient as those of humans. At best, a kind of balance was maintained.

Western medicine, however, has managed to keep alive vast numbers of the unloved to wreak havoc and spread misery through the world. For Nature's callous slovenliness is now substituted Man's perfectionistic perversity.

Love cannot be faked. Yet in our culture it is assumed that all parents will love their children. If there are several children in a family most parents pretend to love all equally, even though the children themselves and outside observers have little trouble deciphering their preferences. Some parents are perfunctory in their love, some are guilty, overprotective, or smothering. The kind of love that really nourishes is not as common as we like to imagine. In task-oriented America, parents often assume that if they behave according to certain precepts laid down by child rearing experts, they will turn out a desirable product, but no technique has ever been a successful counterfeit for love to a child, who needs it to survive.

Western thought is highly combative. It tends to view all conflict as a war of extinction rather than a source of balance. It is only our mad individualism, for example, that makes us see species as competitive because they prey on each other. *Natural selection does not operate to give one species victory over another but to preserve balance.* A species evolves to a point (ever shifting) where a healthy adult can evade its predators but others cannot. Should it become so "successful" that *all* its members could evade all predators it would endanger its food supply, and thus be in as much trouble as if it fell short of this point. The predator is the population czar for the species it preys upon. The lion protects the food supply of the antelope. Birds protect the food supply of caterpillars, who, in turn, prevent plants from exhausting the soil. Predator and prey are in a symbiotic relationship with one another. Each is as important to the other *as a species* as if they were in some sort of friendship-dependency. The individual, however, is completely trivial in all this, which, given our cultural indoctrination, is rather upsetting to us.

Humans lack predators, and have had to rely more on disease to perform this vital function for them. To our species, therefore, the germs that kill us are as valuable as the billions of benign ones that inhabit our bodies and perform various useful functions.

Animal predators prey not only on the weak and ailing, but also on the young. It is primarily the unprotected young that get caught, just as it is more often the unprotected human children who are borne off by predatory microbes. But failure to protect can come from inability as well as indifference. The poor and ill-fed have always died in disproportionate numbers, whether loved or not. Thus the effect of Western medicine has been primarily one of providing an artificial protection to the privileged unloved, a particularly unfortunate combination.

I have suggested that the patriarchal revolution, along with the duckling delusion and the medical tinkering that helped give rise to it, contributed to the creation of a prophet-minded culture —a culture dominated by the outsider mentality. These observations should not be viewed as justification for some kind of repressiveness. All groups need both to maintain structures and occasionally to alter them, to limit the (infinite) number of alternatives available at any moment and yet keep open possibilities that are not normally envisioned. These needs are inherently contradictory—there has never been and never will be a permanent solution. No living organism can survive without predictability, nor without flexibility. No group can survive without cohesion, nor without permeability. The continual renegotiation of these dilemmas is the foundation of social life.

Every viable organic entity must include an ordered base and an element of chaotic instability. These depend upon each other for their existence. There can be no swindlers if there is no trust. Yet trust would have no meaning without swindlers. To attempt the extermination of all swindling would be a gross error, as humanity has dimly recognized throughout most of history. On the other hand, to create an entire economy predicated on swindling, as we have done, is equally dangerous. One tries merely to keep the ratio low enough to permit predictability and high enough to prevent the population from lapsing into idiocy.

But how can we damp down the prophet conflagration without becoming even more repressive than we are? How can we maintain flexibility and restore connectedness at the same time? And does not the connectedness we have lost require a kind of blind adherence that is forever closed to those who have the sight given by self-consciousness? Can organicity coexist with awareness?

We imagine that we are more aware than our primitive forebears, but we are also *less* aware. We are painfully aware of our separateness, but utterly blind to our connectedness. We usually conceive of this blindness as a kind of liberation. The Horatio Alger version of Western history tells how an ignorant, dependent nobody freed himself from medieval embeddedness and became a free and powerful modern being, master of his own fate. The tale is a bit tarnished now and stands on the threshold of high camp, but perhaps it still needs to be pointed out seriously that another way of looking at the last seven centuries is in terms of humanity's increasing myopia about its relation to the rest of the world. We need, in other words, to become not less aware, but more aware. *Self-consciousness is not awareness, it is merely grasping one aspect of reality at the expense of another.* The "great" scientist, entrepreneur, artist, or writer imagines he or she is responding simply to individual goals. So, perhaps, does the hen who lays eggs by artificial light.

Parable 4

A man was hammering a nail and hit his thumb by mistake. The pain was so excruciating that he shouted and leaped about. The people nearby were full of admiration: "How beautifully he sings and dances," they said.

BECAUSE SHE'S THERE
or
SOCIAL CLIMBING
BEGINS AT HOME

He who loves his body more than dominion over the empire can be given the custody of the empire.

Lao Tzu

Chorus: Why has the queen gone, Oedipus, in wild grief rushing from us? . . .
Oedipus: Perhaps she is ashamed of my low birth . . .

Sophocles

It is customary to blame the isolated-nuclear-family system for many of America's social ills, despite the fact that it does exactly what it is supposed to do: socialize children to live in an individualistic society. To change it would be to change everything, and yet it is changing. Most of us will not live to see this transfiguration proceed any great distance, but if such things can be said to have a beginning, it has begun. I am speaking here, by the way, of real social change, not merely changes in intellectual fashion, such as are annually announced by academics and news commentators. Real social change is like geological change, while media-defined social change—the kind that makes one feel, in 1974, that 1968 belonged to a different era—is like the loose dirt daily blown about by the afternoon wind, subsiding in a slightly different place.

In the last chapter I tried to trace some of the more recent sources of Western social pathology, such as the culture of prophets and the duckling delusion. The transmission belt for these phenomena, as for most social processes, is the family. For while the family by no means transmits all of our culture from one generation to the next, it does transmit what is most elemental: the way feelings and close relationships are dealt with. Television, school, and other institutions may talk of these things and teach the child how to conceptualize them, but this is only as important as words like "balance," "wheel," "handlebar," and "falling off" are to someone trying to learn to ride a bicycle. Parents don't teach the culture, they *are* the culture. No matter what they do or how many child rearing manuals they read, they will transmit in spite of themselves the accepted cultural mode of mangling feelings and distorting relationships. This is not to say parents are helpless—only that they cannot disguise what they are, and that this is the only thing a child pays close attention to. The parents' insistence that a child *not* pay attention to this is what makes children schizophrenic.

The nuclear family is a social system with two castes—male and female—and two classes—adult and child. In the class system there is an avenue of social mobility, which is called growing up. In American families, the lower-class term for the higher class is, in fact, "grown-up," although the higher class itself uses the label "adult."

The adult class has certain privileges and powers. As in all class systems—since the family is the model for all class systems —the basic contract is one involving responsibility and the obligation to protect, in return for power, narcissistic rewards, and a disproportionate share of scarce resources. But, as I observed earlier, all such contracts are in part a protection racket: "If you do as I say I will protect you against my own wrath." It always seems like a terrible bargain, and yet is often accepted with pleasure by the oppressed, so repugnant is the burden of responsibility. If it were not for the extreme intensity of human dependency needs, political oppression would be a rare event.

What is unique to this prototypical class system is that social mobility is so complete. Almost every child who lives long enough becomes an adult. Furthermore, this mobility is not only expected but carefully prepared for: Each child is carefully indoctrinated into the behavior appropriate to her eventual initiation into the higher class.

This does not mean that other class systems have deviated in any essential way from the model. The adult class is constantly losing members, and any social class faced with the same problem of diminution behaves in exactly the same way—replenishing itself with energetic (if crude) new blood from the lower classes. Any ruling class that fails to do this is doomed.

Class behavior is learned in the nuclear family. By this I mean not only the specific behavior appropriate to one's social class, but also the underlying concept of social division, the whole minuet of interclass behavior, the fundamental contract between classes, and what it feels like to live in each one. This learning is not intellectual, but emotional and experiential. It is like learning to play baseball by simply being asked to play every position in turn. By the time the child reaches school she knows all about how class systems work, and while she may be naïve about the particular social class system of her own society and how she fits into it, the essential structure of all such systems is bred into her very bones by her family experiences.

One learns, for example, that those in the lower class are expected to be deferential to those above, and that when the highers boss them around they are not expected to be insulted or humiliated. The use of different terms of address (first name vs. Mr. and Mrs.) between members of different classes is also derived from the family, in which children are usually called by first names and parents by titles (such as "Mom" and "Dad") which call attention to their parental function. Control and allocation of resources is largely reserved to the higher class, which is then expected to protect and ensure some minimum provision for the child-serf class.

Class distinctions within the family tend gradually to decline over time, and each child ultimately graduates into the higher class (i.e., becomes adult). There is considerable variation in the timing of these changes ("You'll always be my baby" vs. "You're old enough to support yourself now"), but the rule holds. In this miniature two-class society proper social mobility behavior is learned by virtually every member of the lower class. All children know how to be social climbers, although they are seldom able to use this knowledge in the far less receptive outside world. Every child is expected to become an adult, but serfs are not expected to become nobles, and workers are not expected to become managers. There is a place for each child in the adult world, but most members of the lower social orders already have the only place they are likely to have—they are expected to "know their place." There is no vacuum for them to fill. Ordinarily, then, each individual is socially mobile within the family but not outside. Yet there are some individuals who use their mobility knowledge very aggressively outside the family, without any particular societal encouragement or demand for new blood. What motivates these people who do not "know their place"?

Family patterns vary a good deal from one society to another, and most of the prerogatives usually reserved to the parent are permitted the child in some society or other. There is one adult prerogative, however, that is clutched with particular intensity in virtually every society: the monopoly on sexual intercourse within the nuclear family. The family class system, in other words, is maintained by the incest taboo—the most fiercely endorsed taboo of our species. By the same token, since the nuclear family molds our social responses, it is highly unlikely that such a thing as a classless society could ever exist so long as there is an incest taboo.

Yet there are societies—small and simple, to be sure—in which social class as we know it does not exist. Stratification is by age only, so that it does not merely mimic the class system within the family but is a direct extension of it. The only superior beings are the elders, and everyone who lives eventually becomes one (in the absence of Western medicine anyone who lives to an advanced age is likely to be a rather superior specimen, psychically, physically—in wisdom as well as in status). This system thus retains the benign feature of the family itself, already mentioned: Everyone who lives out her life participates in both classes. Even more important, movement into the higher class does not necessitate separation from one's friends, all of whom are engaged in the same movement at roughly the same time.

Social class mobility, on the other hand, enables just a few individuals to make this transition alone, at the cost of rupturing most of their relationships. This is a sharp departure from the family model—as if the mobile individual were saying, "I alone am capable of achieving the status of adult."

Now some social tension arises in societies with fixed social strata—tension between the sense of movement *within* the nuclear family and the lack of movement outside it. This tension generates a variety of interesting beliefs—the notion of reincarnation and the idea of heaven, for example. Christian teachings exhibit the tension most strongly: "The last [poor] shall be first and the first [rich] shall be last," which is congruent with: "The children become adults, the adults grow old and die." If we take this as a kind of baseline for mobility strivings, then it becomes apparent that what the mobile individualist is seeking, from a familial perspective, is to become adult *ahead of his time*. Leaving his peers behind he wants to leap into adult status *contemporaneously* with his parents. In a word, he seeks to violate (but by no means to rescind—no radical he) the incest taboo. The prototypical social climber is Oedipus.

The myth of Oedipus itself reveals the importance of time. Oedipus is "out of sync" with his family, his period, his environment. Once it is discovered when, where, and to whom he belongs, he is like a wraith—no one knows what to do with him or how to relate to him. Much is always made of the duality of his family relationships (mother-and-wife, sister-and-daughter, brother-and-son); that is, he occupies not only his own family roles but *simultaneously* those of his father, whom he has killed in a fury of injured narcissism. Oedipus is a man who has o'er-leaped his proper time and thereby disrupted the flow of life; hence the plague that afflicts Thebes.

This leads us to the deeper meaning of the riddle put to him by the Sphinx: "What is that which has one voice and yet becomes four-footed and two-footed and three-footed?" By answering "Man," Oedipus wins his kingdom and his mother's bed, and is doomed to a lifetime of misery and horror (so much for success and living happily ever after). It is rather surprising that Oedipus' luckless predecessors had never heard the Sphinx's riddle, since it is found in some form or another in almost every part of the globe. An African version has it: "four legs in the morning, two at midday, and three in the evening," which keeps the proper time perspective. The Sphinx, however, slurs the temporal aspect and talks of "one voice," which is misleading, since the voice of an infant, a young adult, and an old man are hardly identical. Oedipus, however, *does* speak with one voice from two different stages of life.

This sense of temporal confusion appears in Sophocles' drama. It seems odd that the plague sent to Thebes as a consequence of Oedipus' crimes should appear only after he has been married to his mother long enough to have fully grown sons. In all these years, furthermore, Oedipus has learned nothing of his predecessor on the throne—seems hardly even to have heard of Laius or his murder. When Oedipus asks why the murder had never been investigated by the Thebans, he is told that the neglect was caused by their troubles with the Sphinx, who, however, died shortly after the murder. All the action of the drama seems predicated on the obviously false assumption that Oedipus is newly arrived in Thebes, newly married, and newly king. The time is out of joint, as it has to be for a man to be simultaneously son and husband.

This out-of-jointness is expressed in the plague visited on Thebes. Because Oedipus has gone out of sync with his environment he has polluted it. Plants are blighted, animals will not reproduce, women are barren. This should hold meaning for us for we are once again out of sync with our environment and the result is again a blight—albeit a more subtle one—which has left no living thing unaffected.

The impulse toward social mobility—that is, the individualistic migration from one class to a higher one—does not occur in the absence of powerful oedipal strivings. This is not to reduce a social phenomenon to a psychic one—one might just as easily view the oedipal situation as a mere subdivision of social-class dynamics. Both represent the violation of temporal and spatial harmony through the exercise of will. I suggested earlier that will was a concentration of energy necessary to bring an individual or part back into synchrony with the whole, or to force it *out* of synchrony with the whole. Individualistic social mobility and oedipal striving exemplify this process.

Before examining the mechanism through which this occurs I would like to say a little about oedipal culture. We use the term "oedipal" to describe adult responses governed by the childhood infatuation with the parent of the opposite sex. Now, according to Freud, time does not exist in the unconscious. Early images of a loving face, of exchanged tendernesses, of blissful feelings, of youthful and idealized parents—are preserved unchanged, uninfluenced by the reality of subsequent and less-pleasant images of family interaction. They form the raw material of romanticism in adult life. The overwhelming importance of the face in romantic ideation—as opposed to personality traits or bodily charms —suggests that some of these images may go back to infancy, when the face dominates the child's stimulus field.

This is not to say that all aspects of being in love are oedipal. Tenderness and sexual pleasure are powerful and reality-based components in their own right. It is the mystical, spiritualized, idealized feelings, the sense of enthrallment and destiny, that reveal the presence of incestuous undertones. Those who feel that sex without romanticism is meaningless are saying that sex must have an incestuous tinge to be enjoyable.

Romantic love also reveals its oedipal nature by its efforts to transcend consensual time. Romantic fantasies are either heavily nostalgic or seek escape into a different temporal realm. One popular form of nostalgia in early American films, for example, was the reappearance theme: The loved one is seen *not for the first time*. Often the lovers had been together at some earlier point but were parted, so their reunion is highly dramatic, particularly if some obstacle is present. *Casablanca* is the classic oedipal film of this type. Sometimes the loved one has only been experienced symbolically—in a photograph or painting (this occurs also in *The Arabian Nights*). In *Laura*, another forties classic, a detective becomes attached to a painting of the woman whose supposed murder he is investigating. When she later turns up he falls in love with her. The title song for the movie, a typical oedipal ballad, contains the lines: "She gave your very first kiss to you—but she's only a dream."

The theme of the familiar stranger, the meeting that is not the first meeting, reflects the fact that a stranger sometimes taps into a buried oedipal fantasy channel, allowing old longings to burst forth, often taking the individual quite by surprise. The *déja vu* so often associated with romantic love is in reality a *déja senti* experience, and its attached fantasy—the idea of "soulmates" —has an infantile origin. In the world of adult reality no two psyches fit together perfectly—human complexity being what it is—but the *feeling* of complete oneness with another person is given to almost everyone at moments during the first year of life, when one's needs are anticipated by the mothering one.

Some romantic fantasies seek, not the past, but a time out of time altogether. They express a yearning to be ripped out of the organic context in which each living thing has a temporal-spatial place of its own—child as child, adult as adult—and to find a new, mystical space-time in which generations fuse and those never-to-be-united finally *are* united. *A Portrait of Jenny, Peter Ibbetson*, the novels of E. R. Eddison, Nabokov, C. S. Lewis, and countless poems and science-fiction stories exemplify this theme. The escape from organic time into oedipal time is simply a more creative and willful form of nostalgia.

The fantasy of the time machine also expresses the wish to escape the boundaries of the life span. For some people, to become aware of the multiplicity of times and places is to experience one's own time and place as a prison. The joyousness that can only come from being completely present in one time and place is lost. The attention wanders, like that of a man at a party who imagines that the room holds somewhere a partner more interesting than the one with whom he is engaged, and ends by relating fully to no one. This wish, then, is the ego's wish not to die, the wish to build itself a monument—to smear itself all over the temporal-spatial landscape, like some proliferating science-fiction monster, for which, indeed, the human ego, with its infinite capacity for symbolic self-engorgement, is always the model.

While it would be ridiculous to speak of oedipal strivings as the "cause" of this hypertrophy of the ego, they provide important leverage in dislocating human beings from embeddedness in the real world. Earlier I used the term "oedipal culture," for just as there is a culture of children's games and jokes passed on from older to younger, virtually independent of adult society, and just as there are separate male and female cultures passed down within each sex, so, also, there is an oedipal culture passed down through the generations from mother to son-who-becomes-father, who in turn passes it to daughter-who-becomes-mother, and so on. It is a culture of nostalgia and dreams, of unrealizable yearnings, utterly detached from the everyday realities of family life, and this gossamer quality, far from signifying fragility, is what gives it its immortality and invulnerability.

Consider once again the socially mobile individual. Toffler points out that those who are most skillful at breaking off relationships are rewarded with success in our society. He cites studies showing that successful executives are unusually gifted at dissolving their early family ties, dissociating themselves from friendships that would be career liabilities, leaving the physical environment in which they grew up, sloughing off lower-status clubs, relatives, and acquaintances. Executives are even advised on techniques for withdrawing gracefully from these inconvenient ties.

At first glance this may seem like a contradiction: The upwardly mobile individual is gifted at sloughing family ties, yet his mobility is rooted in oedipal strivings. The contradiction is only apparent. The "successful" individual's ability to slough family ties is possible precisely because in that secret fantasy world he has never left home and never will. Once again, it is precisely the detachment and insulation of the oedipal culture from the realities of everyday life in the family that give it its peculiar invulnerability. The real mother can easily be left behind because the fantasy ideal is carried inside. It is the possession of that untarnished internal image that enables Peer Gynt to be a complete troll in his daily existence.

The role played by the father is also important in generating the oedipal impulse. Social mobility by definition requires that the son surpass the father (in a more subtle way this is true of all high achievement) and that the mother transfer from husband to son her status aspirations and security needs. (The women's movement demands that she transfer them to herself.) David McClelland, in his studies of achievement motivation, found that high achievers have mothers who are dominant and demanding, but not restrictive. Their fathers, on the other hand, tend to play an insignificant role in the family. He cites a study by Abegglen of business leaders who rose from lower-class status: Most of their fathers were frequently away from home, or ill, or absent altogether. McClelland suggests that wars and seafaring increase the achievement level of societies by removing fathers from the home.

Successful men, then, are brought up by mothers who make certain they reject and transcend their fathers. The son in such a family is encouraged to break out of his temporal setting and become a being who belongs to no place and no time. He has hitched his wagon to a star and ceases to pay emotional heed to the here-and-now. He is out of synchrony with his environment, living only for achievements that will make him worthy of a maternal ideal that can only be possessed in some beyond-space outside of time. A rather bizarre notion when one considers it coldly, yet such individuals, whose lives are sacrificed to an almost hallucinatory vision, are accounted the most sane and superior beings in our society (except, perhaps, by those closest to them).

The family dynamic of the socially mobile male is captured in the tale of Jack and the Beanstalk. A boy lives alone with his mother. They are poor, and he is doing a most inadequate job of trying to fill the gap created by the absence of an adult male. He is not overly bright and trades the family cow, virtually their only food source, to a stranger for a handful of worthless beans. The mother, in rage and despair, flings the beans out the window, cursing the fate that gave her such a naïve and incompetent booby for a son. At this point reality is left behind and we are plunged into the world of magic, for if we can believe a sharp-dealing stranger who says his beans are enchanted, we can believe anything. The beanstalk fantasy is like a daydream concocted to salve the boy's wounded feelings. It is his manhood that his mother has treated with such contempt, and with an "I'll show her," up springs a gigantic beanstalk reaching to the sky. The boy climbs the stalk, steals wealth and potency from the fearsome giant (with the help of the giant's wife, naturally—what can a little boy do without Mother's support, and what can he *not* do *with* it?), escapes, cuts the giant down to size, and lives alone with his mother happily ever after.

In essence, this is a story of successful social mobility according to the McClelland pattern. The father is both absent and (in his giant form) completely rejected by the son. The mother is exclusively absorbed with the son, and makes stern demands on him for independent and responsible behavior. The son devotes his entire being to meeting these needs of his mother.

Beneath all voluntary postponement of gratification—all voluntary inhibition, suppression of feeling, commitment to a task—lies a kind of arrogance. Setting oneself above one's own bodily responses is an act of snobbery, of satanic pride. (Pride might even be defined as self-induced scarcity.) Pleasure-loving peoples are modest and unassuming by and large ("feeling good was good enough for me"). They are less given to rank-ordering people and things. Social climbing and spiritual climbing (which are merely two different expressions of the same impulse) hold no interest for them. What is it that creates such interest?

Alexander Lowen offers an answer: "An organism's natural striving for pleasure is normally suspended in only two situations: in the interest of survival *and for the sake of a greater pleasure.*" Since survival is not really at issue here, the second of Lowen's two situations seems the more interesting. It suggests that invidiousness, ambition, vanity, arrogance, endurance, jealousy, striving, spirituality, competitiveness, avarice, intellectuality, envy (all the qualities that make our country strong) spring from the perception that one pleasure is greater than another. Once pleasures are ranked, in other words, we have left pleasure behind.

Yet surely there is some ranking of pleasure within every organism. All organisms sense that some objects promise a greater quantity of pleasure than others, and are drawn to those that promise most. But what can we say of the capacity of many humans to relinquish an available pleasure for one that is not even remotely present? This ability is not automatically available to members of the species—it is merely a potentiality that can be activated by early experiences. The folklore of preindustrial peoples, for example, is full of moralizing tales in which a golden opportunity was lost because the hero or heroine responded to the seductions of a lesser but more proximate pleasure.

In non-stress situations, pleasure is an organizing principle. The pleasure centers of the brain determine which messages coming into the brain are to be given priority. Now, one way people establish gratification hierarchies is through the relative importance of the various other persons in their lives—whether they are roughly equal or highly unequal in their pleasure-giving potential. If we imagine all the "others" in a person's life arranged in rank order on a pleasure-giving continuum, the resulting gradient would be very flat for some individuals and very steep for others. For the flat-gradient individual, one person is about as likely to give pleasure as another. For the steep-gradient individual, on the other hand, one or two persons will hold a much higher pleasure potential than all others. Their loss will be severely felt and difficult to replace. Flat-gradient individuals tend to be impulsive and unable to postpone gratification, while steep-gradient people are planners, schemers, inhibitors.

A child who has many caretakers, many sources of love and nurturance, will tend to respond to each in terms of the gratification they actually provide. The child whose life is dominated by a single nurturer, on the other hand, must cope with a deficiency of options. The one source is so important that its loss would render all other sources meaningless. And even if the source is reliably present, one cannot guarantee a constant outpouring of love. Yet it seems better to wait for the love of the important source than to seek a substitute.

Insofar as a single individual in the life of a child provides (a) intense gratification and (b) far more gratification than any other person, the child will at times be able and willing to forego immediate pleasure because of her confidence in the availability of fuller and more complete gratification at a later time. A hurt child, for example, will sometimes shrug off reassuring caresses from other adults and run some distance to receive the same comfort from his own mother. We take this kind of behavior for granted, since mothers are initially at the zenith of most people's pleasure gradient, but there is wide variation in the extent of this peaking. Institutionalized children, for example, have extremely flat gradients—they are of necessity promiscuous in their affections. Middle-class America is at the opposite extreme, with the mother vastly overshadowing all other persons. Simple communities lie in between these two extremes, with many different adults (as well as older siblings) playing a large part in seeing to the child's basic needs and satisfactions. Anthropologists call this pattern "diffusion of nurturance."

Concentration of nurturance in the mother, which tends to occur in the isolated nuclear family of today, engenders oedipal motivation. By this I mean simply that mental connections involving the concept "mother" retain inordinately high priority throughout life. They promise the "greater pleasure" for the sake of which the organism's natural striving for pleasure is suspended. The more extreme this concentration—the steeper the pleasure gradient—the longer gratification will be willingly postponed, in some cases indefinitely.

An old flat-gradient adage says: A bird in the hand is worth two in the bush. But is it worth a hundred? At some point the postponement will begin to seem worthwhile. The adage also stresses the value of tangibility. Flat-gradient individuals are highly earthbound (diffusion-of-nurturance societies, for example, show little inclination to romanticism in love affairs). They are not fascinated with obstacles and memories and fantasies—they want immediate pleasure. The steep-gradient individual, however, may find himself in a situation in which a *symbol* of the mothering one will outweigh the *reality* of some other pleasure-giving person. A person or situation that evokes an echo of the mother will outweigh one that does not. The Freudian idea of transference can be viewed in this light: The romantic lover has invested most of his love in the *symbol,* which can be attached to any real-life person who can trigger it. Eventually, reality may loosen the glue that holds the symbol and the person together, at which point he falls in love with someone else. What remains constant is the steep gradient. There is always One that is valued overwhelmingly over all others.

The process through which the romantic lover learns to invest in this symbol of the mother, rather than in the mother herself, is not complicated. If one person provides most of the child's pleasure it becomes extremely important to please that person—even to anticipate her wishes and preferences. The mother (for in most cases it *is* the mother) is incorporated by the child and becomes an internal force directing his emotional life.

There is nothing mysterious or magical about this. The mind is a complicated piece of circuitry that connects not real objects, but the representations of those objects and the individual's reponses to them. If a person loses a limb, the mental pathways associated with that limb do not immediately disappear—in fact the person for a long time tends to hallucinate the limb as still existing, so powerful are these representations. Similarly, when we lose loved ones we may behave in many ways as if they were still alive—our feelings, interests, and behavioral patterns may still be organized around their existence. What survives in ordinary oedipal motivation is not so much a desire for incest with the mother as an internal pattern of emotional responses—a readiness to put all one's emotional eggs in one symbolic basket. Behaviorally, this may display itself as intense monogamous attachment or extreme fickleness or any gradation in between—since the key to oedipal motivation is its lack of attachment to reality one cannot discern it by reference to its objects alone. One may fall in love once in a lifetime or every day; what is symptomatic of oedipal motivation is the intensity of that feeling—its tendency to blot out all other relationships so long as it is attached to a given person. It is also revealed by the ability to invest that love in symbols—mementos of the loved one, memories, fantasies of the future.

But the best index of all is the ability to defer pleasure. This may or may not be apparent in the everyday erotic life of the individual, but it will appear somewhere as a powerful force in the personality. People who show a strong tendency to plan, to strive earnestly toward far-distant and symbolic goals, to hold strong internalized values that are not responsive to context ("inner-directed" people, in Riesman's terms) are oedipally motivated, in the sense of having a steep-gradient mental apparatus.

This leads to many paradoxes. The word "romantic" tends to suggest wispy poets or the Brontë sisters. One would never dream of applying the term to captains of industry or political leaders, many of whom would scoff at overt expressions of romanticism. Yet the man who devotes his existence to fulfilling a maternal wish, renouncing immediate pleasures for ever-receding achievement goals, has romanticism rooted in every fiber. He foregoes everyday pleasures because he is after bigger game. But what *is* that greater pleasure? Power, wealth, fame, success do not produce ecstasy, but only the thin and pallid sensation of ego-satisfaction or pride-of-mastery. The "greater pleasure"—total and unconditional gratification by the mothering one—is illusory and anachronistic. The time is out of joint for oedipal personalities because they are out of joint with the time—still engaged in the mechanical fulfillment of a design programmed into them in infancy. Their interest in the here-and-now is largely limited to those pieces of reality that can be incorporated into the program. Very little arouses interest for its own sake.

In a study of successful Americans—business and government leaders, professionals, and artists—Cuber and Harroff found that for a majority of their subjects sex was "almost non-existent, something to be stifled," or a source of fear and avoidance. Unable to give or receive gratification, sex was merely a matter of tension release. They "performed" it, as a necessary "nuisance," with a "minimum of fanfare"—"like any other body function . . . it needs attention from time to time."

This is well to remember in relation to occasional public figures who are portrayed—publicly or in private rumor—as highly erotic. Sexual "conquests" may feed an ego or enhance one's status. Brief sexual encounters may drain off surplus tension in the manner Cuber and Harroff describe. Some may even manage to carve out a few more extended erotic interludes from their busy lives. But by and large, a successful public career is not compatible with leisurely and gratifying love-making. There are only so many hours in a day, after all, and strong involvement in a love relationship—even a marital one—will ultimately impinge upon career activities ("he's neglecting his work for this affair"). Should the careerist choose love he would cease to be a careerist.

Cuber and Harroff, commenting on the heavy emotional price their careerists have paid for their success, observe that many of them have been "able to inhibit the sexual side of their nature without visibly jeopardizing their mental health." It never occurs to them to question the relation of success itself to mental health —mental health is always defined by the values of the culture and career success is our most cherished virtue. Yet one need only walk down a city street to become aware of the hideous toll of human suffering—emotional, physical, mental, social—that these successful careerists have produced in the course of denying their own humanity. For when a careerist throttles his humanity in the service of achievement, what kind of a world can he build except one in which humanity is throttled?

America was formed on the principle that movement is excruciatingly slow when people move together—maintaining all their intricate and delicate interrelationships at every step of the way, stopping to repair any ruptures that might develop from the jarring motion, and nourishing a sensitivity to their natural surroundings. This snail's pace has been good enough for Nature, but a man, with his brief life span, is preoccupied with changes that are quick and visible and will serve as a monument to his ephemeral ego, so like a shrew or a piranha in its combined puniness and voracity. To get somewhere quickly, the American way is to take nothing and no one.

In the same fashion, oedipal motivation fosters intellectual learning of a narrow mechanical sort, but makes complex or emotional learning more difficult. The commitment to a symbolic goal alerts the individual to any message that can be enlisted in the service of that goal, but blinds him to messages that seem irrelevant to that goal, or call it into question, or place it in a larger balanced context. Our social sickness, like all sickness, is a state of imbalance. Our technological hypertrophy was achieved not in spite of or alongside of, but *because* of our social decay. We traded social integration for mechanical power, casually trashing the most exquisitely complex social organisms—built up slowly over generations. The technological advances of the past two hundred years are fondly imagined to have come free, or to have been paid for. They have not been paid for. Their cost in human unpleasure is incalculable—human beings, and, indeed, all living things, will still be paying the price for hundreds of years. What we have lost cannot simply be plugged in later on when we finally get to some technological Land of Oz and start to look around for the rewards. It is lost forever. Many of our social responses and organic sensitivities are already so blunted that we may become incapable of living in co-operative communities in another generation or so. It is not only that these qualities are disappearing at an accelerative rate, but that the conditions that nourish their emergence are now almost impossible to re-create.

I have argued that wisdom and understanding—the appreciation of totalities and interrelationships—are impeded by the steep-gradient structure. For the less one's emotional interest is invested in the here-and-now, the less fully one can grow from experience. If we wish to enhance the type of intelligence that I.Q. tests measure, then clearly we should design a society like middle-class America, in which oedipal motivation is exaggerated. If, on the other hand, we wish to enhance wisdom and understanding, we should seek precisely the opposite arrangement: diffusion-of-nurturance communities that will produce flat-gradient personalities.

Reality and Guilt

Perhaps this will become clearer if we look at another steep-gradient attribute: guilt. Guilt is highly valued as a mechanism for social control in mobile societies since it does not depend (like shame, punishment, social disapproval, or community constraint) on the presence of a stable social unit. An individual can feel guilty anywhere or anytime. Guilt is usually said to derive from "love-oriented" techniques of child rearing: Since the loss of love is the most terrible threat the child experiences, she internalizes the values and wishes of the parent so as to be able to anticipate and forestall parental displeasure. Guilt is a signal, like anxiety, that continuation on the same course will produce a disaster—in this case, the loss of parental love (and, as the child grows up and makes these wishes and values her own, the loss of self-love, self-respect). But love must be concentrated overwhelmingly in a single source for its loss to constitute such a disaster. Internalized private parental (as opposed to community) values are largely a function of concentrated parenting, and are, hence, a steep-gradient product.

Concentrated parenting allows parental displeasure to supersede all other forms of reality as a potential source of threat. The flat-gradient child will give more heed to a threat to her survival than to the threat of any one individual rejecting her. Not so the steep-gradient child. Just as culture can create substitute realities, so can the family—simply on a more individualistic basis. A steep pleasure gradient seduces the individual into substituting a parent-world for the real one. In this imaginary parent-world, good behavior and benign intent are rewarded, even when no parents are around. In the real world, whoever is so insensitive to the environment as to walk on thin ice will fall through, no matter how well-behaved they may have been. The steep-gradient individual's awareness of this becomes blurred. The whole world becomes a familial stage. Relationships become defined in obligatory terms, so that people imagine that the erotic interest of a partner can be earned through good behavior or coerced through indebtedness. Life is conducted on the principle of accumulating guilt coupons: "If I suffer enough, I will ultimately be rewarded." Or, to give it its more contemporary form: "If I cleave to the right values, am true to myself, the world will reward me." This guilt-based parent-world is obviously important to the development of mechanical insensitivity to feedback—of single-track intelligence rather than wisdom.

Achievement, Specialization, and Power

Achievement is always a specialization—the hypertrophy of some characteristics at the expense of others. It always involves an imbalance in the totality of the individual psyche. There is nothing wrong with this imbalance in itself—it makes for variety and entertainment in human affairs—so long as balancing occurs over time or across the community. In every group people accept narrow and warped self-definitions (clown, cynic, old reliable, sexpot, taskmaster, and so on) as the price of entry, and group members love nothing more than to narrate events about each other that confirm these caricatures. The individuals themselves even derive pleasure from having much of their humanity squeezed out of them at the door—their eccentricity is, after all, what secures their membership. A group of fully human and balanced individuals could change membership every day and never notice the difference. Limitedness serves to dramatize mutual interdependence, reminding everyone that they cannot survive without each one since none is whole. This is a lie, of course, since everyone is potentially whole; and groups do survive membership changes if they are gradual enough for the survivors to adjust and modify their caricatures. But it is a useful and necessary lie, and indeed, if we focus on this issue of proper timing (as we should), it is even a kind of truth.

The real lie begins when people become permanently trapped in their caricatures even outside a group context. In our society, for example, most positions of eminence are filled competitively, and hence require a permanently intense and narrow motivation. Success is achieved by becoming a machine—an engine without a governor, singlemindedly devoted to winning competitions and aggrandizing the ego. But it is important for followers to fantasize that these fragile beings on whom they depend are motivated by something other than pure narcissism. Hence the frequency with which American political leaders profess their humility—the one trait that by definition they cannot possibly possess.

Leaders obviously have a profound need for power, and my emphasis on the pathology of their motivation is tied to this. But power is of two kinds, which we might call positive and negative. Negative power is the ability to control, force, imprison, invade, terrify, and kill others. This is the common meaning assigned to the term, and when I use it without a modifier this is usually what I mean. Those who have a great deal of this kind of power, like the President of the United States and other major heads of state, are able to kill with relative impunity. Oppressed peoples who seek more "power to the people" want at least enough of this kind of power to keep from being killed, to remove the impunity, to create a "balance of power." A balance of negative power is two men with guns pointed at each other's heads. Calling it negative is not to moralize but to emphasize its static quality. When it is in balance nothing can happen—a state of zero is its high point. When out of balance someone sooner or later is killed or brutalized.

Positive power is the ability to influence others, to arouse love and respect, and to get one's needs met—without pressure and in a socially naked and unadorned state, devoid of status, position, or other weaponry. Western peoples rarely use the term in this sense, although it is more common in other cultures. We all know people who possess positive power to a high degree—they are simply people who were truly and unambivalently loved as children. They give and receive with equal facility.

I call this kind of power "positive" because it begins rather than ends at zero, and is dynamic when in balance. That is to say, two people with equal positive power will both gain love and respect, will both succeed in influencing the other, will both get their needs met. They will not be locked in a stand-off but will develop through their interaction.

The need for negative power is expressive of the lack of positive power. The less positive power one has, the more negative power one needs. But negative power does not feed, nor can it create. One cannot obtain love with it, nor respect for oneself (as opposed to one's status or weaponry). Hence the quest is doomed to failure. He who pursues negative power is in a pathological condition.

Some individuals with a modicum of positive power are unaware of the significance of this gift and pursue negative power anyway: We refer to them as charismatic leaders, and they seem the most benighted of all—like someone who shouts into a microphone even though his voice is already being amplified.

Leaders and successful achievers have highly developed wills, which is useful in times of crisis. But for these people every moment of every day is a time of crisis. Hence they tend to *create* crises around them—altering reality in such a way as to lend an air of authenticity to their underlying world view. Their willful behavior tends to drag everyone into the same state of desperation they themselves are energized to overcome.

It is the especially needy person who must *ensure* getting those needs met. The quest for power or eminence is less a forward than a backward search—an effort to re-establish the dominance of the infant, whose wish is his parents' command. As Bateson points out: "A command can closely resemble a cry for help," and Freud was fond of talking about "His Majesty the Baby." Part of the follower role is to prop up the leader and meet his overwhelming needs for attention, recognition, and service. Followers can do this either because their own needs are less urgent and they can get them met without going to all that trouble, or else because they lack the will that would enable them to erect this mammoth insurance system. That is to say, they either had their needs met early by many persons, or never had them met by anyone and lack any faith that such gratification will ever be forthcoming.

This raises a question that may have occurred to many readers: If dominant mothers and inconspicuous fathers produce high achievers, why haven't urban ghettos generated a great flock of black Carnegies, Edisons, and so on? Should not blacks from poor families with absent fathers turn out to be steep-gradient individuals?

The answer to this is complex. First, it is simply not possible, despite their desire, for most mothers in conditions of acute poverty to provide enough gratification for a steep-gradient structure to emerge. Child rearing tends to be a catch-as-catch-can affair —the child now a dearly beloved, now an oppressive burden. Of necessity, furthermore, it must often be shared. This is true of all acutely poor groups. It is, after all, only a very few who manage to rise out of their social class at any one time. Ambitious mothers who can concentrate their attention on a child to the extent that permits high but conditional gratification are in short supply among the grossly poor. Hunger and danger are highly corrosive of such concentration.

Second, some steep-gradient individuals simply become overwhelmed by maternal needs and are unable to function at all. McClelland observes that while fathers are generally trivial in the lives of high achievers, they are usually around during the very earliest years—long enough to provide some sort of balance in the family setting until the child is old enough to absorb the maternal overload. McClelland also notes that most high achievers find some kind of substitute male to serve as model for them. In the absence of some stabilizing force of this kind, steep-gradient males simply develop the kind of impulsive, grandiose, touchy narcissism that characterizes most warrior societies.

Finally, we must recognize that our notions of what constitutes a "high achiever" are highly class-bound. There is no qualitative difference in achievement terms between a robber baron of the nineteenth century and a heroin wholesaler in the twentieth. Some kinds of exploitation are legitimized by the state while others are not. Underworld success often demands greater skill, adroitness, business acumen, and administrative genius than "legitimate" business, and there are many high achievers in the ghetto that will die unknown and unrecognized.

Women, Mobility, and Achievement

Thus far I have talked about mobility and achievement as if they were something that only concerned men. I have talked of mothers and sons, but said nothing of fathers and daughters. What has been said, however, may help explain why women have been so secondary in the cultures of the past three millennia, and why they will be so primary in those to come.

In patriarchal societies women achieve social mobility only through men. They can either use their sexuality to good advantage—marrying someone of a higher class or becoming a successful courtesan—or they can rise through their sons. That is to say, they can prostitute either themselves or their offspring.

There have, of course, been exceptions—women who have overcome massive cultural resistance to achieve fame in some field of endeavor. While systematic data are difficult to come by, my impression is that with women, as with men, a high achievement drive is often associated with a powerful attachment to the parent of the opposite sex.

It is rarely, however, that a father is the first, most intense, or most reliable source of nurturance for a child. This means that, for women, the main source of gratification and the object of oedipal fantasy are not one and the same. This experience creates a profound difference between the psychic structures of men and women—a difference I believe to have far more powerful consequences than differences in anatomy or copulatory role.

Both sexes begin life with the same primary gratifier: the mother. When they reach the "oedipal age" of three to six years, however, the little boy is talking about marrying Mother when he grows up, while the little girl is talking about marrying Father —he is multiplying his attachment while she is dividing hers. A highly oedipal boy, therefore, has a steeper pleasure gradient than a highly oedipal girl. The difficulty that many creative women have in "getting it together"—in translating their abilities into a coherent career—may not be solely a function of the heavy negative cultural conditioning about achievement they have received. It may also owe something to the fact that their flatter pleasure gradient does not permit so heavy an investment in some sort of ultimate symbolic gratifier. Men who are high achievers are unconflicted because there is nothing in the original family picture to arouse conflict: The father is rejected and dismissed, the mother is all. It is much more difficult to reject and dismiss a mother. Since fathers are typically less central in child care, the girl who makes a heavy oedipal investment is taking a huge risk and stands to lose more than she gains. Boys take far less risk when they embark on the oedipal journey.

This is not to say that the difference acts only to make life easier for boys. Their emotional tasks are simply of a different sort. Little girls have to make a difficult leap of faith during this oedipal phase—have to divide their deepest affection and attach some of it to a relatively ephemeral object. Little boys, on the other hand, must divide *themselves*—must somehow relinquish their dependent attachment to the mother while at the same time retaining her as an object of oedipal fantasy. This is perhaps the origin of the masculine tendency to compartmentalize sexuality—to be more willing to divest it of loving and affectionate meaning. Boys are trained very early to reject and suppress the core of their emotional and interpersonal being—initially, their needs for mothering. They thereby become experts at filtering feelings—at allowing one feeling expression while blocking others normally associated with it. They have the difficult task of altering their relation to the mother while retaining their primary attachment to her. They thus lose what little girls are able to retain: a sense of continuity—a capacity to accept and cherish the idyllic memories of infant dependency. The mother-daughter relationship may often be fraught with tension and competition, particularly in adolescence, but in stable patriarchal societies it tends to be the strongest, closest, and the least conflicted, on the average, of the four parent-child pairs.

These different early experiences, then, suggest that while women will tend to be virtuosi in taking emotional and interpersonal risks, men will tend to be virtuosi in exercising emotional and interpersonal control. Men will be less willing to be vulnerable, to risk involvement and commitment in relationships, to get hurt, to let it all hang out. They will make a greater demand for interpersonal safety in their heterosexual relationships— wanting partners who are docile, affectionate, devoted, faithful, and unchallenging. Women, on the other hand, are more willing to live dangerously in their deepest relationships, more able to invest their love in partners who are distant, cold, and inconstant. This ability is learned early: As Ashley Montague points out, fathers provide far fewer gratifying tactile and security-giving experiences to their children than do mothers.

These differences should diminish rapidly over the next fifty years in response to the revolutionary changes gradually being brought about by the women's movement. It is important that the changes are being introduced at every point in the system—a necessary process if real change is to occur. Mothers are encouraged to de-intensify their child rearing activities, fathers to increase theirs, women to assume more sexual freedom and self-assertion, men to become more vulnerable and emotionally uninhibited, and parents to treat children in ways less differentiated by sex.

The greater emphasis on emotional compartmentalization by men contributes mightily to their ability to exclude feelings from direct consideration in task activities, and hence to their tendency to create machinelike and inhumane environments. It also accords with David Bakan's ideas about the relative importance of what he calls "agency" and "communion" in men and women. Bakan uses the term *agency* to describe the tendency of an organism to maintain its separate existence, *communion* to refer to its participation in some larger organism. Separation, self-armoring, aggrandizement, mastery, and repression are aspects of agency: union, openness, co-operation, and expression are aspects of communion. Bakan argues that agency is more pronounced in men, communion in women. Unfortunately, he seems to assume that this difference is biological, on the basis of some embarrassingly simple-minded psychological studies showing that girls prefer dolls while boys prefer trucks, and so on—that sex-role training, in other words, has been successful. Viewing such differences as biological is a little like saying that people who live in the mountains have a gene that makes them good climbers, or that coastal dwellers are biologically drawn to boats, or that civilized peoples are constitutionally attracted to plumbing facilities. The same psychologists who through painstaking research discover that men and women have different interests, are careful to buy different toys for their male and female children, and evince visible anxiety when the "wrong" ones are chosen.

The tendency toward agency in men is a function of a steeper pleasure gradient: Separation and detachment are made possible in men by the ability to invest in symbolic objects rather than real ones. Similarly, the greater "field-dependence" of women reflects their greater immersion in the dance of life, and the need of men to maintain internal consistency in the face of emotional dependency on a single gratification source. Field-independence is usually regarded with implicit admiration, and it certainly has its uses, but it also vastly facilitates mechanical responsivity. The same may be said of the more rigid homeostatic mechanisms found in men—their lower physiological responsiveness to environmental effects. Bakan suggests that "there is more harmony between the body and environment for the female and less necessity for acting on the environment."

Bakan makes much of the greater social responsivity and connectedness of women, and we may recall Toffler's remark that women are more reluctant than men to slough relationships after a move. People with flatter gradients develop their relational networks experientially, by living in the present. Ultimately they find themselves in a balanced system, with a variety of friends, relatives, and lovers each providing somewhat specialized emotional satisfactions. They are rooted in reality. Those with steeper gradients have more of their emotional life bound up in symbols of the Gratifying One. When such a symbol looms into their field of vision they are often willing to slough their entire relational network in favor of this illusion. Emotionally, with all his planning, scheming, striving, and long-range goals, the person with a steeper gradient is less reality-based. He can invest intensely in a relationship only so long as it symbolizes the One to him, or can be exploited in the service of his oedipal goals. When this ceases to be true he can withdraw from it almost as if it never existed.

If it is true that women tend to have flatter pleasure gradients than men, the impact of the women's movement on Western culture will be profound. Women are oppressed to some extent in all civilized societies. But Western culture is *founded* on the oppression of women and of the values associated with them: wholeness, continuity, communion, humanism, feelings, the body, connectedness, harmony. In Eastern cultures, women have often been even more powerless and constrained, but a higher value has been placed on their sphere—they have been viewed as having a more central role in the basic round of life. The women's movement emerged in the West when the social significance of women in the culture had reached its lowest point in history—when women were excluded from valued occupations, isolated from each other, frequently uprooted by their mobile spouses, and even had their domestic tasks reduced to triviality by technology. This process, whereby the intensification of some social form leads directly to its opposite, I call *social eversion.* We will encounter it again in a later chapter.

Two Routes to Status Change

There are two different routes that can be followed in moving from a lower to a higher class. One can move individually, dissociating himself from peers and entering the higher class as an individual, or one can change the status of the entire group or class. The first is variously called social mobility, social climbing, or bettering oneself, depending on the point of view. The second is called class warfare, revolution, or social evolution, depending on the circumstances in which it occurs. The first is an expression of agency, in Bakan's terms, since it increases separation, detachment, and atomization—the parvenu is integrated neither with his old group nor with the new one. The second is an expression of communion, for it seeks the collapse of social barriers. The first seems less violent in its effects, since it does not immediately disturb the social fabric; in the long run, however, the dissolving of connections that it occasions has the effect of producing instability and social chaos. The second method, conversely, is initially more convulsive, but the upheaval it produces yields social stability in the long run. What we call liberal reform has usually resulted in facilitating the first, or individualistic method. I observed earlier that the social critics of the fifties, in their attack on the somewhat deteriorated remnants of social responsivity left in our society, contributed not a little to the dissolution of connectedness and the further development of mechanistic behavior. Their approval of individualistic mobility—of the heroic deviant who rises above her peers is undisguised. What we call radical, on the other hand, usually involves an effort to bring about the second, or collective mode of change.

It is characteristic of those in the higher class, insofar as they are willing to tolerate any movement at all, to talk up the individualistic route. They stress the value of rising above the crowd, usually through education, emotional self-alienation, and aggressive striving. In this they are merely enunciating the oppressor-oppressed dynamic: only the strong and wily are fit to "protect" the oppressed. It is also characteristic of the earliest spokesmen of the oppressed to ape this view—to regard their role merely as one of enlarging the funnel through which their followers pass individually into the ranks of the oppressors. They exhort the oppressed to self-improvement and try to persuade the oppressors that the advantages of new energetic blood outweigh those of comfortable solidarity.

As oppressed groups become more sophisticated politically they increasingly reject this view and the leaders that represent it. They seek to rise as a group rather than individually. Instead of demanding equality—the opportunity to live up to the values of the oppressor class—they begin to assert the validity of their own values. The first feminist groups, for example, stressed voting rights and equal pay, and even today some groups seem largely concerned with making it possible for middle-class women to develop the same kind of careerist mentality that now afflicts middle-class men. The shift from the individual route to the collective one has expressed itself in a re-evaluation of the division of labor by sex and an attack on the masculine emphasis on agency. The difference in practice is a subtle one, since the reduction of agency in men necessitates an increase in agency in women, which the outsider might find difficult to distinguish from the equal-rights emphasis of the past.

The goal, however, is quite different. Women are in a position to bring to any activity a wholeness of which men are largely incapable, since the imposing specializations of men are achieved by severe emotional warping. If they follow the same path as men, women will merely join the ranks of the oppressors. Yet they cannot shun the specialities of men since that will make them dependent upon men and prolong both the oppression and the specialization. This is why such things as karate classes for women are far from the trivial matter they may seem to be: Nothing feeds oppression so well as the deep inner conviction of the oppressed that they are incapable of protecting themselves.

The difference, then, is internal. Women cannot and should not avoid becoming doctors, for example, but there is a danger, in accepting the peculiar initiation rites that men have developed for this profession, that they will thereby become the kind of doctors that most men are, and medicine will continue to be the ghastly deformity that men have made it. This is why consciousness raising is so important to liberation movements—the pathway along which the oppressed must walk is beset with a thousand pitfalls.

One important technique is to assess how oedipal one's motivation is. Since careerism for both sexes tends to hold oedipal meanings, a woman's ambition may be largely an oedipal rejection of her mother—the individualistic route, in other words. The extent to which she concerns herself with the fate of *all* women will indicate the extent to which she has maintained a balanced attachment to both parents. The same, of course, applies to men— it is the isolated achievers who reject the father altogether, and their achievements are correspondingly one-sided and inhumane. Wholeness of person necessitates an acceptance of our identity with all living things—to cast out or depersonalize anyone is to reject a part of ourselves and to dehumanize our environment.

Oedipus vs. Peter Pan

We began this chapter by looking at the family as the prototypical class system. I would like to end it by looking once again at youth as a subordinate class.

The counterculture in America has been pronounced dead by those who thought they invented it, but once again, we must not be distracted by media fads. Most of the people who discussed the counterculture did so in a manner that made it clear that they thought of it as a counter*society*, which, of course, it never was. The noisy manifestations have died away, but the values they dramatized continue lazily to diffuse through our culture. Oedipal motivation seems to be on the decline in America, despite the fact that many of the conditions that foster it are still present.

Those who still have it sometimes accuse those who lack it of not growing up, and when we look at the family as a class system the truth of this accusation becomes apparent. Not to grow up is a cultural secession. Oedipal culture is dying because people show a decreased interest in joining its dominant class.

This suggests a modification of my statement about the collective route to status change: Oppressed classes do not typically move as a group *into* the dominant class in a revolutionary situation; they create a *new* dominant class, parallel to and replacing the old one, which atrophies.

The adults in a society are in a position, as a dominant class, to define what it means to be an adult and what it means to be a child. That is why the word "mature" has always been such a bludgeon in the hands of adults. Yet that power to define is conspicuously weaker than it once was, while self-definition by the young as a class has grown stronger. This has certainly not been a matter of political consciousness. It was in fact the growth of the isolated oedipal family that created the conditions leading to its demise—a good example of social eversion.

Both processes began early: as individual families became more autonomous, children became more insulated from the adult community. Philippe Ariès argues that in medieval times children were treated simply as unfinished adults. They were not dressed differently from adults or given any special attention. Beginning with the Renaissance, and increasingly in the sixteenth and seventeenth centuries, interest began to be shown in the special characteristics of childhood life. Children began to be dressed in special garments (the first children's costume was simply what everyone had worn a century previous) and games originally enjoyed by both children and adults began to be defined solely as children's pastimes—as they remain to this day. At the same time the idea that children were innocent and needed to be shielded from sexuality began to gain currency, and special concern about the child's health and moral development began to appear. Schools began to be institutions especially designed for children, who were increasingly segregated from adults and grouped by age. Discipline was gradually extended to embrace the entire life of the child and exclude him from adult liberties.

But while children were being isolated from the corruptions of adult life and becoming immersed in their own, the family was at the same time becoming isolated from the community—becoming an autonomous unit. The idea of privacy evolved in the eighteenth century—one could no longer call on people without warning, and houses evolved rooms with specialized functions, so that society could be more easily kept at bay. "Until the end of the seventeenth century," remarks Ariès, "nobody was ever left alone." People now began to have private rooms, and the family began to narrow to include only parents and children. The eighteenth century was also the era in which children began to be forced to sleep alone, to be weaned and toilet trained early, and otherwise to be subjected to the kind of discipline that was taken for granted by 1900. In summary, children were, as Ariès puts it, "quarantined" from adult life by family and school so that they could be molded by conscious policy.

The miniaturization of the family and the quarantining of children have both gone much further since the eighteenth century. And while children have been increasingly exposed to the overpowering psychic assault of the small oedipal family, they have at the same time been increasingly protected from the realities of adult life, and immersed in narrowly age-graded cultures of their own. This has meant that the oedipal children fostered by the modern middle-class family could increasingly avoid moving into the adult class at all, but could remain instead in a world of their own making. They could be oedipal *children,* relieving them of the necessity of becoming oedipal adults.

Ariès points out several times the social identity between children and the lower social orders. When children began to wear a distinctive costume it was not merely an archaic one, it was also what the lower classes wore. When certain games were relegated to children, they were also relegated to the peasantry. As children were culturally separated from their elders, the rich were culturally separated from the poor. In both cases "class consciousness" has created cultural changes whose effects are only beginning to be felt.

Parable 5

A Japanese soldier named Soichi Yokoi found himself on
the island of Guam when it was occupied by American forces.
Faithful to the code of the army, which prohibited surrender,
he and a group of comrades took to the jungle and hid
themselves in caves. Twenty years passed, and his comrades
all died or were captured. The emperor had long since
surrendered, but Yokoi remained faithful. For eight more
years he stayed in hiding, completely alone. Finally, thirty-one
years after leaving his native land, he was discovered and
returned to Japan to find it completely transformed. He
apologized for disgracing the emperor.

DESIGNING THE LEAD
BALLOON
or
THE DESCENT
TO THE FUTURE

> *It is the way of heaven to take from what
> has in excess in order to make good what
> is deficient. The way of man is other-
> wise. It takes from those who are in
> want in order to offer this to those who
> already have more than enough.*
>
> **Lao Tzu**
>
> *The impure and the organic are inter-
> changeable conceptions.*
>
> **C. S. Lewis**

Western peoples are very mixed up about social change. They
tend to believe that it only takes place through conscious public
policy, when in fact the changes that really matter are occurring
by tiny increments every time someone buys something or builds
something. They also imagine that major social changes can be
achieved simply by deciding to make them. As a result, one
simultaneously hears excited pronouncements that change is perpetual and accelerating, and discouraged complaints that nothing
really changes at all.

It is my belief that our efforts to solve social problems have generally created more social misery and injustice than the evils against which these efforts were directed. Americans approach social change with the thoughtfulness of a slot machine addict, throwing laws and administrative orders into the political process like quarters. This is not to make the traditional demand for more planning, which usually means making the same insensitive decisions on a more gigantic scale.

What follows is directed not so much at those who are currently making a mess of our world, but at those who want to correct this condition by making a new mess of their own. It has not been sufficiently emphasized that the miseries from which people now suffer in the Western world were largely brought about by people who were convinced they were making the world a better, safer, and happier place. To assume, without the deepest self-examination, that any bold new program now under consideration would fare any differently is not only arrogant but stupid. The men who had the bright idea of wiping out the mosquito by drenching the world with poison should have known better, but we, after all, have the additional advantage of that fatal experience.

This is not an argument against change, but an attempt to generate some degree of thoughtfulness about it. I would like in this chapter to discuss what I feel to be some profound misconceptions about change that are shared by radicals, liberals, and conservatives alike.

Change and Stress

The first misconception is that it is possible to have change without stress. We are constantly told how adaptable human beings are—how culture has freed us from our bodies so that we can swing with anything that scientific tinkering, governmental tyranny, or intellectual fashion might see fit to inflict upon us.

It is true that humans are adaptable, but that adaptability is finite. It is also true that adaptation is stressful. Indeed, one of the consequences of our overtaxed adaptability is that it is even stressful to adapt to a happier condition when some misery to which we have become accustomed has been removed. Toffler points out that the body responds to novelty with massive physiological mobilization—the "orientation response," marked by a heavy adrenalin output. As change becomes chronic so also does the orientation response, with consequent damage to the organism. This is another example of an emergency mechanism becoming chronic, with the usual destructive consequences.

One of the better-kept secrets of medical science (it doesn't sell pills) is that the major cause of disease is change. People who live in stable environments with adequate nutrition have generally good health, while those who, like ourselves, are subject to constantly shifting living contexts tend to be more sickly. Furthermore, as Toffler has now brought to public attention, there is a direct correlation between the number of major changes (residence, spouse, job, etc.) experienced by a person in a given period and the likelihood of his or her falling ill. Most important of all, this effect holds *even if the changes were desired*.

Change, in other words, has been found to be injurious to your health. Flowers and trees often die when they are transplanted, and so, at times, do animals and people. Travelers fall ill with undue frequency, even though they are free from ordinary pressures and presumably having a good time. Old people, for whom adaptation is more effortful, die with such rapidity upon being institutionalized that the geriatric wards of many state hospitals have been characterized as delayed-action gas chambers. It would seem that the blithe assumption of our culture that chronic change is a fit condition for human beings to live in needs reevaluation.

On the other hand, most people do survive. Doesn't this argue that we can, in fact, adapt successfully? This, of course, is Toffler's position. After amassing evidence to show the grinding impact of change on the human organism he simply shrugs his shoulders and says faster adaptation is necessary if the technological behemoth is to continue to receive its ever-expanding daily quota of human blood. Like some victory-crazed football coach, he would tape us up, shoot us full of Novocain, and hustle us back on the field.

It is with the psychic equivalent of Novocain that we do manage to adapt to change. By numbing ourselves to life, by distancing ourselves from our senses, by losing events in a haze of conceptualization, we escape the trauma of personal disruption. "People are people everywhere" is a valuable palliative for those who have lost the capacity really to know anyone. From a trans-continental jet it looks as if very little is happening down there. The viewpoint is the same for the suburban drunk, the tran-quilized housewife, the nodding junkie. Whatever means is used, the principle is the same: Change only affects you if you are *here*. If you can get far enough off to conceptualize prechange and postchange as the same thing, you are free from the burden of adaptation.

But whether we numb ourselves to it or allow ourselves to be ground up in it, whether we initiate it or just experience it, whether we desire it or dread it, massive environmental change—social or technological, popular or authoritarian, radical or plutocratic—is stressful and brutalizing to the human organism.

The Futility of Positive Programs

The second misconception is that the social system in which we live is static and empty—a motionless container that must be filled with plans, programs, and energy. Energy is indeed re-quired to change *direction*, but this is not the same thing as say-ing there is now an energy vacuum. The American way is always to *add* something, to start something, to create new activities. Yet vast amounts of energy are already being poured into activities and institutions that already exist, and it usually seems burdensome to supplement all this with something new. Seldom does anyone consider the energy relation between what already exists and what is to be added. If the rich are stealing from the poor, we start a program to compensate the poor. If people are rotting in large custodial mental hospitals, we create some small model treatment centers. The word "model" is very big in our action vocabulary—model cities, model schools, model programs. The concept is a sensible one, but somehow the models never seem to catch on—perhaps because no one pays attention to what keeps so much energy bound up in the old ways.

Since we think of social change as adding something, the issue of cost is always raised—how much will a new program cost? But if change is viewed as redirecting energy rather than taking on a new task, the cost issue becomes less relevant. It is said, for example, that we cannot afford better schools, communities, health care, and so on. But what we can afford least of all is to allow some people to become very rich. This is our most expensive social program: To make it possible, we have spent billions upon billions of dollars, allowed our air and water to become polluted, our environment to become ugly, our cities to deteriorate, our health care to become third-rate, created untold poverty, misery, sickness, suffering, chaos, disorder, and mass murder. We nonetheless managed to afford it.

Most of our social problems would be better solved by negative action than positive action; that is to say, they would cease to exist were we to stop rewarding people for creating them. Our national policy has always been to subsidize the rich and ambitious in various ways: Currently, for example, we provide incentives to those who exploit and brutalize the environment—developers, loggers, highway contractors, oil companies, manufacturers. We soften risks, give tax relief, offer inducements to do what is already highly lucrative. We have given oil companies, through depletion allowances and import quotas, for example, billions of dollars to despoil the environment, maintain inefficient practices, engage in expensive and dishonest advertising (what an oil company spends to change its name would meet a fair-sized city's welfare budget for a year), and preserve the archaic view that they are in the oil business rather than the energy business. The fact that a corporation is taking some risks in order to make a huge profit seems an inadequate reason for giving them charity. It is one thing to pay for a needed service, quite another to guarantee excessive wealth to those doing a mediocre job of supplying it. Faltering industries can be put on a non-profit basis if what they provide is really essential. For while the increasing inefficiency of the mails is sometimes attributed to the fact that it is a government agency, this argument founders on the fact that telephone service has deteriorated even more dramatically in the past decade, despite constant rate increases and fat dividends to shareholders. Furthermore, although the U. S. Mail is itself non-profit, it has provided profits to others through the category of third-class mail, the elimination of which, for profit-making corporations, would do much to improve service.

We worry about overpopulation—particularly of Americans, since the deleterious impact of a single American on the environment is many times greater than that of a Third World person. Yet our tax system rewards us for having children. Similarly, we complain that developers are rapidly bulldozing away all the beautiful open spaces, creating ugly tracts of separated houses surrounded by useless strips of cropped grass. Yet we give tax relief to the property owner.

Anyone can multiply examples—I have mentioned only financial ones—but it scarcely needs a bevy of facts to support the notion that people don't commit transparently foolish acts without incentives. Whatever abuses we find around us are encouraged by us in some way or another, and it makes sense to find out why.

We like to think that a social change begins with a blueprint in our head—that we *initiate* a process of change. This is ignorant and megalomaniacal. When we decide on a course of action we are also *responding* to some change that has already occurred. We are saying that it hurts us and we want to avoid that hurt. Mechanical thinking and the Protestant Ethic have blinded us to the fact that we are links in a continuous feedback chain. We imagine that we are always beginning anew with our bold new programs, and that is the principal reason they fail.

Social Judo, or When the Right is Right

The third delusion about social change is that desirable reforms can be brought about when those who oppose them are either outvoted or re-educated as to what their best interests are. The pomposity of the left is so extravagant on this point that it is worth remembering that most of the evils the left now rails against were first attacked by dyed-in-the-wool conservatives. The histories and biographies on which we are raised present Heroes of Progress overcoming obstinate Obstacles to Progress. With each passing year, however, the conservative grumblings of the Obstacles become harder and harder to differentiate from the arguments of contemporary radicals. The reactionary of yesterday is the visionary of tomorrow.

Those who espouse the idea of linear progress cannot tolerate this kind of cyclical manifestation. Confronted with the statements of men and women who tried to halt the ravages of technology fifty years ago, they dismiss them as having a different meaning or as being right for the wrong reasons. But this is just intellectual snobbery—they were exactly the same reasons, at a time when those reasons were not yet fashionable.

Reactionaries have been railing against technological blight for decades. They have consistently opposed centralized governmental power and the hypertrophy of the executive branch of our government. They have attacked bureaucratization, sneered at the naïve belief in progress, complained that the acceleration in the rate of change was destructive of human values. It is only a decade or so since a concern with ecological issues was dismissed by liberals and radicals as a quaint reactionary preoccupation. Early opponents of Pasteur and the germ theory of disease —regarded for a half century or more as men without vision— sound strangely modern now that that theory has outlived its utility.

Or consider an issue more recently passé: fluoridation—a liberal's cause par excellence. A scientific dictum is embodied in chemical form and applied on a mass basis to a population for its own good. Those who opposed this process were derided as archaic and paranoid—dental health and mental health stood side by side against the forces of dark ignorance. Today, numbed by so many more serious intrusions of the bureaucratic mentality, it seems difficult to recall what the hubbub was all about, but the forces of darkness appear in retrospect to have had a somewhat deeper ecological and political consciousness than their heavenly opponents.

But let us not shrink from contemporary debates. Conservatives today are opposed both to gun control and to unilateral disarmament. For taking these positions they are deemed benighted and violent, but it must be admitted that the positions are at least consistent. Taken together they imply that, given the existence of weapons, the more equally distributed they are, the better. Although I would much prefer that all weaponry be abolished, I regard this position as incontestable.

Having guns so widely available in a disturbed population such as ours makes life extremely unsafe. Yet even a violent and crazy populace should not be disarmed while subject to an even crazier overweaponed government over which it has little if any control. Were I not familiar with the peculiar inability of liberals to relate single issues to broader contexts I would be amazed at their readiness to jettison one of the pillars of the Bill of Rights. Note that the demand for gun control only became widespread when guns previously reserved for fratricide began to be turned against public figures. Every state wishes insofar as possible to maintain a monopoly on murder and violence, but by and large the more it succeeds in doing so the worse things are for its people. The liberals are quite correct in feeling that the power of life and death should not be given to every individual—that if it is given at all, it should be to the entire community. But an authoritarian government is not a community, and it is an unfortunate paradox that the very individualism that invariably spawns such governments often seems to be the only protection against them. Such protection is illusory, since individualism means in practice that everyone stands alone against the centralized co-ordinating force that individualism makes necessary. Still, until something better is formed it is all we have. To reserve all weapons to those in uniform is to abandon the penultimate pretense of democracy. A man in uniform has made himself the instrument of another man's personal power—to what ends he cannot know. He and all those who wear that uniform are concentrated extensions of that power, and hence far more dangerous than a single lunatic with a rifle.

Nor can the conservative preoccupation with competitive power positions abroad be lightly dismissed. The history of human societies is one in which humane, happy, and healthy communities have continually been gobbled up or wiped out by competitive, surly, and emotionally deprived ones, and should we ever evolve from the latter to the former we might suffer the same fate unless the rest of the armed world evolves at the same rate. I do not wish to slide over the fact, however, that this preoccupation is a powerful deterrent to *anyone's* evolving in this direction and hence maximizes the chances of species destruction.

Many will feel these observations are frivolous—a high school exercise in tolerance. Any certified intellectual could put together a host of examples to show that conservatives taking these positions are motivated by less lofty considerations than those I have put forth. Nevertheless, when any large number of people espouse an ideological position and defend it with fervor they are championing a human need shared not only by themselves but by their opponents, who are thereby spared the trouble of paying attention to it in themselves. Anyone seeking social change who ignores such needs will probably fail, and anyone who seeks a more humane world will not achieve it by working for the suppression of such needs.

Radicals, for example, tend often to be compulsively counter-phobic about change, denying their own needs for security, dependency, and stability. They adopt the stance of the fearless adventurer into the unknown—unawed by the dangers that lie ahead and contemptuous of those who tremble and hesitate. It is my impression that when their own needs for stability are too strongly repressed they reappear in their ideology in the form of rigidity. In other words, if I am going to challenge and alter all that exists I will seek my security in the perfection and inalterability of my theory. It is perhaps this more than anything that accounts for the splintering that afflicts movements on the left.

These views are influenced by many years spent leading encounter groups, where I have observed that those who push hardest for an "intense" experience in the group are often the most resistant to it when it happens, while those who seem timid and defensive at the outset sometimes achieve the most profound changes. The emotional conservative in a group allows others to talk a braver game than they feel. In my group experience every position taken, however repellent, irrelevant, or obstructive it may seem at the time, is rooted in feelings that are shared, less consciously, by other group members. Such feelings are ignored at great cost. Real movement occurs when the false emotional division of labor is relinquished in favor of a recognition of (1) the legitimacy of all feelings, (2) the conflicts present within each person, and (3) the realistic differences between people in the way these conflicts are internally arranged. Steam-rollering and compromise can then be abandoned in favor of synthesis—for while basic human feelings and needs are few and simple, social arrangements for their expression and fulfillment are many and complex.

One of the human needs given short shrift by radicals is the need for order, routine, and predictability in daily life. So important is this need that many people can live out their lives in an uninteresting, draining, and oppressive daily grind and still retain a modicum of happiness, while others can live in a perpetual holiday, constantly exposed to exciting new experiences, and be miserable. The traditional schoolroom was created by people who paid no attention to human needs—aside from war it has perhaps been the single most brutalizing influence on Western culture—but those who recognize this have often reacted by creating a school milieu that disregards those few human needs the traditional schoolroom, with its ritualism, its predictability, and its utter freedom from responsibility, *does* satisfy.

The importance of order becomes apparent during periods of civil strife. The initial impact of what is loosely called a "revolutionary situation" is a sense of liberation and excitement—resembling the explosiveness with which children exit from an authoritarian school building. Radicals often mistake this festive air for some kind of permanent breakthrough and are discouraged when it evaporates after a few weeks and there is massive popular support for the re-establishment of social order. Yet we are surrounded by evidence that people are willing to sacrifice almost anything for order, despite their immense enjoyment of periods of release. Even though social order serves primarily the rich—protecting their favored position—the poor seem to want it just as badly. Nor are counterculture people immune from this need, although they are often not attuned to it. Civil disorders simply fit *their* routines better than those of the straight world. When these routines are disturbed for any extended period they react in the same way. As Bateson points out, one person's order constitutes a form of disorder for everyone else, since no one likes to arrange the world in precisely the same way.

The need for order is what makes protest actions so powerful—people are often willing to make some concessions to restore routine. To accept the usual polarized version of these events, however, is to miss most of what is happening. Both sides want order, and both sides want liberation from the constraints that oppress them, but each asserts only one side of this ambivalence, leaving it to their opponents to express the other. Each also believes firmly in the simplicity of its public stance. Underneath, however, there are extraordinary paradoxes. Victory for the protestors depends upon their having a higher tolerance for disorder than their opponents, but it often turns out that they lose precisely because a large segment of the psyche of the establishment is covertly on their side. To the extent the authorities secretly enjoy the liberating sense of crisis and chaos, they will be able to sit it out until the protestors themselves feel a need to return to their routine activities, and the protest may thereby fail. This happened at times during some of the campus confrontations of the 1960s. In other words, the secret enjoyment of disorder leads to a heightened ability to oppose disorder as a weapon.

Another paradox arises when the authorities, driven by a mixture of terrified and fascinated feelings about disorder, use disorder in the form of a violent mob of armed and uniformed men to "restore order," which it usually fails to do (not surprisingly, considering the confused motivation). Protestors are often shocked by this violation of their own sense of order. The demand for the removal of police or guardsmen is itself a demand for the restoration of order.

The simplicity of polarized value positions thus masks an intricate knot of covert emotional alliances. The statement, "I want A, not B, they want B, not A", usually means, "I know they want B more than I want it, and I can count so fully on their pushing it that I am unaware of my own less urgent need for it. At the same time, since I cannot see their need for A at all I must emphasize it at all times." This process is called distributing the ambivalence and is most conspicuous in married couples, who find it almost impossible to keep sight of the complexity of their own needs and feelings in the face of the inevitable drift toward emotional specialization.

Most of us are brought up to imagine that our spontaneous physical and emotional reactions are private and unique—not linked to other people. Our individualistic beliefs thus ensure that all such reactions are in fact *not* spontaneous but contaminated with egoism. Since people are born interdependent (William Condon of Boston University has shown with slow-motion film that the body movements of people in conversation are normally in perfect synchrony, although this is not visible to the naked eye) everyone is accustomed to (and depends upon) having some of his or her feelings and needs expressed by others. To look inside for every need or feeling is therefore likely to produce erroneous assumptions. Some of our own basic needs will be most fully expressed by other people.

None of us express our needs and feelings in an uncontaminated way—they are warped by narcissism, ideology, will, guilt, defensiveness, rationalization, and the sheer complexity of the pathways to expression that we have forged through all this resistance. A man may be able to find sexual satisfaction only by strangling old ladies or masturbating on a dandelion: We can identify with his sexual desire but not with the tortuous pathway to which his ego has confined him; and if he seeks to justify his behavior in terms of spontaneity, he can only expect us to laugh in his face. We are all poor judges of our own spontaneity. What feels "natural" may be only habitual, or merely a new pathway only slightly less circuitous than the old one.

None of this has anything do do with tolerance. Tolerance implies a lack of connection between opposing views and a wilful effort to soften that opposition. It is therefore as self-alienated as slavery, and can lead only to institutions that are indifferent to human feeling. Significant change must involve a fusion of opposites—not a compromise between antithetical positions, but a response that meets the human needs underlying both positions, since such needs are—with widely varying intensities—universal. This is by no means simple—anyone who offers to interpret the "real" needs underlying a given position is simply arrogant. Only those who hold the position themselves can profitably engage in such a quest.

Social miseries arise from gross imbalances in the distribution of energy throughout the social organism. We need to develop the social equivalent of acupuncture—a sense of how to stimulate and balance natural forces in society. Most efforts at social change pay very little attention to questions of energy—assuming that if enough money or anger can be brought to bear on the issue, change will occur. Yet change means the rechanneling of energy, and it does no good at all to view the *status quo* as a block of wood to be carved or burned. The *status quo* is an intricate and dynamic process—its points of stasis are *loci* where opposing forces have immobilized each other. Instead of continually trying to mobilize new energy, it would be more useful to unlock or take advantage of what is already present.

One example of an existing energy channel is the media. The media are motivated to expose, interest, and excite. They cannot avoid trying to do this. Radicals with an appreciation of this energy flow have ridden it with considerable success. Another such channel is advertising. Corporations are heavily invested in creating public good will: If there is a virtue anywhere in the popular consciousness, they want to be the first to claim it. This has greatly annoyed traditional radicals who speak of co-optation. Every large corporation, for example, now claims to be socially conscious and ecologically aware. Most of their statements are utterly deceptive, but this is the way it always begins. When a public lie dances on the stage, the truth is waiting in the wings. For such statements carry a double message: "I am ecologically minded" also says "It is important and virtuous to be ecologically minded." Corporations will ultimately impale themselves on these messages, being forced by competitive pressure to make them more and more convincing. At the same time the public is habituated to the importance of the claimed virtues, and an *expectation* is created that corporations should take responsibility for social issues. To fret over the deceptiveness of these early claims overlooks the importance of the chain of events they set in motion.

If energy is bound up in opposing positions, a vast pool of energy will be released when these opposing thrusts are united. Freud once suggested that if one wished to discover the nature of a hidden impulse, one had only to frame the question in negative form ("What does the dream clearly *not* mean?" "What is the *least* likely thing . . ."). The impulse, he said, is striving outward toward expression, while an inhibition, with equal force, is pushing it back inward; by adding the word "not," the energy of the inhibiting force is suddenly united to the force toward expression. Both are pushing in the same direction and the answer pops right out. Similarly, social change often occurs through a kind of political judo, in which the energy locked in opposing viewpoints is released through an acceptance of the emotional validity within each.

Blueprinting

The fourth common illusion about social change is that it occurs through some sort of cognitive process—a problem is isolated and diagnosed, a prescription is written, a course of treatment designed and executed. When a group of people come together to discuss a social crisis they often have in common only the distress they feel about it. Yet this shared feeling is the first thing that is discarded, so that they can "analyze the problem objectively." Since they have omitted the most important piece of data, and the only common ground they have, they tend to come up with solutions that are not only off the mark, but as destructive of human values as the social distress that brought them together in the first place.

The term "problem" itself reflects a faulty epistemology. It implies that the social environment is static, that those who are trying to deal with it are outside and above it—looking down on it like a math student looks down on a piece of paper. It also implies that the "solution" represents a cognitive beginning—an initiated action rather than an emotional reaction to what has already happened. This is all illusion and self-deception—we do not initiate social programs, we react to our experience, which alters as we do so. Furthermore, we are not and cannot be outside our social "problems." We are inside them—they are the medium in which we swim. Yet this self-deception has consequences, because insofar as we attempt to ignore our own feelings our "solutions" are bleached of humanity. The bureaucratized environment of which we so often complain has largely been created by our treating social crises as if we did not participate in them.

When Toffler rails against the "irrationalism" of the newer trends in our culture it is this kind of schizoid self-deception that he is protecting. Any departure from the railroad-track mentality that claims the future must in every respect be more alienated from the past than the present is stigmatized as a "revulsion against intelligence." Toffler apparently identifies intelligence with Newtonian physics, eighteenth-century rationalism and the pigeonhole departmentalism of the academics. He wants education, for example, to have a "consistent direction and a logical starting point," as if learning began anywhere or went in a straight line. He attacks all departures from conventional scientism as "garish," "sick," and "prescientific," and asks questions like, "What kind of cultural life *should* a great city of the future enjoy," as if it were logical for human interests and desires to be programmed out of the head of some planning commission or "utopia factory." Toffler seems to imply that we must all eat Wonder Bread and shop in supermarkets to be freed from any taint of "nostalgia," "irrationality," or "acting out." But we should not be misled into mistaking arithmetical and compartmentalized modes of thought for intelligence. There is nothing more irrational than the notion that ignoring our own feelings and needs will by some convoluted magic create an environment that will gratify us.

Scientists and would-be scientists often speak, with puritanical pride, about "cold, dry, hard facts"—triumphantly asserting their bloodless world view. Since they never look at any soft, wet, warm facts it is hardly surprising that they have failed to produce any theories that deal effectively with living wholes.

Don't Look Back, the Future May Be Gaining on You

The fifth misconception is that social change is linear. The statement that history never repeats itself has a certain validity, but so does the claim that there is nothing new under the sun. The fundamental relationships between parts, between parts and wholes, between organisms, and between organisms and environment fluctuate within a relatively modest range around a more or less constant norm. On the other hand, every specific arrangement of energy is unique, and the history of our planet has seen the continual proliferation of such arrangements. The bulldozer is not a shovel, and a detergent with a "new formula" may indeed be a new combination, however irrelevant or useless. There is no point in trying to maintain that time merely revolves endlessly, but there is also no point in arguing that the universe moves rigidly in one direction on a fixed track. We have gotten ourselves into a lot of trouble by treating the past as so much garbage, to be cast on a junk heap like the torn pages of a calendar with the days crossed off. A viable ecology requires that the past be recycled too.

There is much we can use back there. Every era is in part a corrective for the distortions of the previous one, but it also contains its own distortions. The railroad-track theory is dangerous in that it implies that if we pursue the future frantically enough, we can escape the irreconcilable opposites around which social systems are formed. Somewhere in the future, it is imagined, we will be able simultaneously to maximize security and surprise, community and privacy, variety and constancy, and everyone will be both equal and better than everyone else.

Our past is a part of us. Who is to say we cannot have it? "You can't go back" simply means "you have to stay on these rails." But human beings are not linear—what has been is as deeply us as what will or might be. Technology and intellectual fashion have pushed people into accepting smaller and smaller temporal fragments of themselves until there is not enough left to form a whole human being. The result of this has been another social eversion—the embracing of passionately nostalgic revivals and religions that allow people to reincorporate the entire universe into their temporally shrunken personalities. Our history is a living part of our being—a reservoir from which to draw nourishment and creativity.

Toffler himself grudgingly admits that continuity is "not necessarily 'reactionary,'" but views the need for such continuity as an unfortunate human limitation, like the need for sleep, for which the machinery of industrialism must occasionally make allowance—presumably until humans can be replaced by some more malleable species. It is inconceivable to him (and he is representative of most *status quo* spokesmen in this regard) that the future might contain any element once rejected by the industrial revolution, yet history is full of such revivals. Toffler's future is merely a linear extrapolation of the century that ended in 1960. Any deviation from that course is a "reversion" and a "rejection of the future." Toffler cannot see that the ideas and trends he dismisses as "reversionism" are simply building the foundation for a different future than he imagines. It is a little like someone of the coal-and-steam era attacking the proponents of electrical power as reversionists because they sought to generate electric power from falling water.

The most dangerous idea imaginable for an individual, group, society, or species is that the past contains no worthwhile arrangements—that the direction one is currently taking is the best of all possible directions, now and forever. Even biological evolution contains some major reversals. Our own biological ancestors found that at one time it was useful to take to the trees, while at another time it was useful to come down out of them again.

Toffler is saying we must climb higher and higher in the trees of technocracy because that is the direction we started in, and hence that is where "the future" lies. Others are nevertheless beginning to climb down. If *they* turn out to be the future, they will have been profoundly changed by their arboreal sojourn—in this sense, there is no going back. There is no reason to assume, however, that the year 2100 will resemble 1975 any more than it will resemble 1800. I suspect that it will have a good deal less hardware than today: Hardware already begins to seem a little unsophisticated in the light of the growing emphasis on relational processes in virtually every domain of human endeavor.

Power and Energy

The sixth misconception about social change is that in order to bring it about one must obtain power. This assumes, first, that what I have called negative power is a neutral force, and second, that social change originates in power centers. Both of these assumptions are false.

The worst evils of our political system come from the centralization of power, irrespective of who holds it. It is the most naïve kind of hero-villain thinking to imagine that a new face will change a system. The major organizations in our society have seen dozens of incumbents pass through their top positions without greatly affecting the oppressiveness of their fundamental patterning. The centralization of power is rooted in paranoid motivation—to imagine that anything benign or lovely could flourish in such an environment is as illusory as the perpetual-motion machine.

Consider the power concentrated in the hands of the President of the United States. It is the power, ultimately, to decide the life or death of every living person. To give such power to a single man or group of men is to court catastrophe. Even a paragon of virtue (and what sort of virtue would pursue such evil power?) could scarcely avoid blundering eventually, simply because he would be unable to keep abreast of the enormous volume of information required to act wisely. Concentration of power means that the locus of decision making is farther and farther removed from the locus of its consequences—that decisions are based on less and less information and are more and more cut off from feedback. The President may be well-informed in an absolute sense, but relative to his arena of responsibility, he is the most ill-informed man in the United States. Fortunately, this same concentration of power contains a self-corrective. In a complex social system the power of the power-glutton is limited by the narrowness and simplicity of his own world view—reinforced by the paucity of information available to him. The more dictatorial he is, the more likely he is to lose touch with the dynamic complexity of the world around him and destroy himself. Authoritarianism, as noted above, works well only in stable, homogeneous systems. Furthermore, power is symbolic, like stock market values. The minute anyone begins to doubt the power of a leader it begins to shrink.

The desire for negative power derives, as we have seen, from fear and mistrust of others—from the feeling that the world's gratifications will not be freely given, shared, or even exchanged, but must be coerced. Alexander Lowen suggests that the only people who can "handle power constructively" are those who have been "fulfilled in childhood and know how to enjoy life." But such people would not want or seek negative power. Anyone who would willingly make the kind of sacrifices required to become President of the United States must necessarily be afflicted with the need to coerce in a particularly virulent form. Such a man is precisely the person to whom such power should not be given. The power to blow up the world cannot be entrusted to anyone sick enough to seek it.

In the last analysis negative power rests on the threat of destruction. One cannot gain power by threatening to create. Anyone can create—props are not required, nor any coercion. Nor does one generally expect innovation or creativity to emerge from centers of power, which are fundamentally conservative in nature—concerned with control, with hanging on, with grasping. Those motivated to seek power tend to mistrust spontaneity, flux, creation—to believe only in what can be controlled, ensured, compelled. They are insensitive to the regenerative processes that occur in nature. They trust, in themselves, only their own defensive structure and learned skills; in others they trust only the tendency of most humans to be impressed by the canopy of status and the accouterments of power. Therefore, although they cannot innovate, it is of desperate importance to them that they stay on top of, abreast of, change. They ride the horse but cannot make it go. Government is largely a negative force—it can regulate, it can maintain, it can destroy.

But can a man who would actively seek the power of the Presidency refrain from using it under stress? If he achieves it, is he likely to tolerate restraints on it—either internally, in the form of decentralization, or externally, in the form of disarmament? International politics as it now exists grinds up millions of healthy individuals in order that the sickest ones can play a kind of chess game. Arthur Janov suggests that it is self-alienation that enables political leaders to discuss mass killing without qualms. Death is not a tragedy for those who cannot feel life. Since they themselves are dead internally, the actual death of others is unreal rather than horrifying.

A male bureaucrat once argued that women should not hold positions of responsibility because of the emotional instabilities associated with menopause, but I would rather take my chances with such a woman than with an ordinary power-hungry male. It seems astonishing that we fear menopausal lability more than the icy pathology that allows a man to order massive destruction and the killing and mutilation of hundreds of thousands of people merely to avoid being called weak, or to win points in a game of international chicken. The lust for power is the most dangerous of all sexual perversions, and the compartmentalized rationalism that often accompanies it is no cause for reassurance. The worst horrors in history have been perpetrated by "sensible," "practical" males "taking the necessary steps" to beat some symbolic opponent to a symbolic goal. Consider how much cold intelligence has been expended on a foreign policy that at bottom is founded on a kind of mad-bomber strategy ("Don't come near me or we all go up!"). René Dubos observes that Captain Ahab was a highly practical whaler: "All my means are sane; my motives and objects mad." The same might be said of Henry Kissinger, who was once quoted as saying that "power is the ultimate aphrodisiac."

These symbolic goals are generally disguised as life-or-death survival issues, but the passage of time always reveals their hollowness. In retrospect it seems to make very little difference to the daily lives of most individuals whether one group or another owns a piece of real estate or controls a governmental apparatus.

One would scarcely do better than chance in trying to guess who had "won" or "lost" a war from the subsequent fortunes of the combatants.

History is vastly misleading, in any case, since it is overwhelmingly, even today, a narration of the vicissitudes of, relationships among, and disturbances created by those inflamed with a passion for wealth, power, and fame. Attempts are made to write social history, but the medium itself interferes with this. Just as archaeology cannot altogether transcend the fact that it is based on human garbage, so history, which is a study of records, cannot transcend the fact that it is based on the products of those maddened by dreams of immortality—those who wish to "make their mark on history." Those who have lived for life itself are lost to record; for that which is green and healthy passes, only the detritus of the death avoiders remains. History is a kind of Marat/Sade of the human race—a diary kept by narcissists, about narcissists, and largely for narcissists. As such, it is useful to the man in power, for it lends credibility to his attempts to convince the populace that his frantic pursuit of symbolic, narcissistic goals represents some real effort on behalf of the people.

Since only madmen are attracted to positions of great power, and since such people are too infatuated to diffuse and decentralize that power, how can we keep them from holding it? How can we give power to those capable of detoxifying it? An obvious although patently unpopular solution would be to choose public officials through some sort of lottery system, such as we now use to hire killers who will not volunteer for the task. The Athenians used such a method, and while it had its problems, most of them could be attributed to the prevalence of precisely the kind of egregious vanity that made it a desirable system in the first place. In the long run it is generally more useful for the person who occupies a given role to feel comfortable in it, but this depends upon power being diffused to the point where the poison is present in small enough doses to be absorbed by the average human.

The idealist who seeks high office to implement high-minded goals is thus engaged in a self-defeating effort. He who seeks such power is an enemy of the people, whatever his program. He will explain his motivation in terms of wanting to "have a real impact," but anyone who acts out of this kind of grandiosity thereby becomes part of the problem rather than part of the solution, since his behavior springs from and helps maintain the motivational core of the oppressive system in which we live.

Efforts to increase the power of a heretofore powerless group are another matter altogether, since they involve the diffusion of power, which should be the central goal of all political activity for the foreseeable future. Community organizing and public exposure of official arrogance are two of the key enterprises in this process. Power is built in large part on the concentration and manipulation of information and hence relies heavily on secrecy. "Top secret" or "highly classified" usually means, "exposure will weaken our power." The right of privacy cannot be allowed the government or any other organization in which comparable power is concentrated, since such privacy is always used by those in power to concentrate that power further. "Private" and "public" are supposed, after all, to be antithetical concepts.

The most important reason for eschewing positions of power is that social change rarely originates in power centers. Many people imagine that Washington, D.C., is "where the action is," but this is true only for power addicts. No major cultural or social innovation ever came out of the Washington political community, although many lesser ones were implemented there. Political leaders merely generalize changes that have arisen elsewhere in the society. The ideas on which new programs are based have usually been around for years. People immersed in government often seem a bit archaic—their information is screened by too many people absorbed with protecting their positions and maintaining secrecy. They are low on information pertaining to system changes, high on facts and figures plugged into rigid and antiquated frameworks. Change in America has come from technologists, businessmen, scientists, inventors, artists, musicians, blacks, street people, the media, and from day-to-day decisions made by millions of completely faceless individuals.

The proper metaphor for Washington and other power centers is the feudal castle. The inhabitants of such a castle had a purely negative function—they could sally forth and destroy, but otherwise led a parasitic existence. The castle had no energy of its own—all was drawn from the farmed lands around it. To attack the castle was absurd for anyone not driven by narcissistic motives, for all of its life lay outside. To take it was to take nothing. One could absorb all the external food and water sources and leave the castle to starve itself. The feudal lord could then sit inside and look out over "his" lands, but he would in fact have been rendered irrelevant.

Leaders do not make change, everyone does. We have been engaged for so long in dreaming of ourselves as agents of change that we have failed in the role of reactor. People are the nerve endings of social systems. If they are stupid enough stoically to bear the pain such a system inflicts upon them, the system will go right on inflicting it. Social mechanisms are mindless, undirected. Insofar as they are deprived of information about human needs and responses, they will be inhumane.

Most Western societies are like people with no sense of pain—they blunder into horrible injuries because they have lost access to vital information from their peripheries. We are the numbed and atrophied nerve endings of our societies. We have been trained to smile politely when some social institution tramples upon us, and every time we do so we give it a lesson in inhumanity.

Parable 6

Once upon a time two poor men—one black, one white—
were traveling together, trying to reach a new and beautiful
land of which they had heard. After some time they met a
witch, who said to them, "Give me a piece of your flesh, and
I will make you wealthy. You will travel in style and ease."
The black man was not interested, but the white man agreed.
No sooner had he done as the witch asked than he was
beautifully dressed and mounted on a fine horse. He was vastly
pleased with the bargain and started to ride off. The black
man could not keep up with him on foot and this made the
white man angry. He scorned the black man's poor clothes, and
when he failed to keep pace he beat him with his crop. When
the black man threatened to leave him the white man bound
him and tied him to the horse and dragged him along on the
ground, for he was afraid to travel alone. This went on for
some time and the black man was badly injured and near
death. Then a change began to come over the white man. He
lost interest in the journey, took no pleasure from his surroundings, and seemed to derive his only satisfaction from comparing
himself to his comrade, whom he now treated as a servant.
He stopped in every village to display his wealth and acquire
more, by gambling or by swindling the inhabitants. Finally,
one day, he encountered another like himself, and trying to
cheat each other, they fell into a quarrel. Words led to blows,
blows to weapons, and both men perished in a gunfight. The
black man, scarred, but otherwise in good health, took the
white man's horse and continued his journey to the beautiful
land.

WATERMELON SEEDS AND THE WAYS OF CHANGE

> *Conceivably there was no alternative but*
> *to push further in the same direction, to wait*
> *for a neglected force, left in the rear, to fly*
> *forward again and recover ascendancy.*
>
> **Bellow**

> *Between yea and nay*
> *How much difference is there?*
>
> **Lao Tzu**

Much of what I have said may seem cause for unrelieved gloom. To fall into this gloom, however, is to exemplify the narcissistic pathology I have described. For gloom about the future depends upon making a linear extrapolation from the present. It assumes that Western culture will continue on its headlong course toward disaster, with nothing but human intelligence and enlightenment to slow it down—a pitiful defense at best. Prophets of doom tend to see themselves as sounding a desperate alarm in an effort to arouse people to a herculean exercise of will that will stave off the disaster; but I have argued that human will is the cause of, not the solution to, this crisis. To engage in linear extrapolation would make the prospect gloomy indeed.

But there is no need to do so. The future will not be a mere exaggeration of the present. A gloomy prognosis depends on the assumption that conscious human will has transcended the balance of nature and thrown it irretrievably out of kilter, so that man with his mechanical psyche can trample our entire ecosystem into oblivion. But what if this notion of the power of human will is simply another expression of our schizoid grandiosity? What if our conscious cerebrations are governed by a feedback loop too extensive for us to perceive? If humans are in fact incapable of transcending the ecological circuitry in which they are embedded, then the cause for gloom vanishes. Since we value ourselves only as thinking, willful actors, never as fleshly, feeling responders, we like to think of ourselves as intelligent voices crying in the wilderness ("If only I could make them all understand!"). This is simply the arrogance of individualism. If a thought occurs to me, at a given time in a given culture, about the defects and limitations of that culture, it is occurring to others as well, since it impinges on all of us in common ways, albeit to different degrees. Authors of books like this one are fond of imagining themselves to be the cause of future change. They dream of having themselves recorded in history books as having fostered some new trend (a fantasy encouraged by the historians' passion for punctuating history). But books are expressions, not causes, of change. Through them we alert each other that our heads are undergoing some alteration in response to the conditions around us and the feelings those conditions have engendered.

What I am suggesting is that nature *still* heals itself—that humans are still embedded in their ecosystem, despite their grandiose fantasies, and subject to its processes—that as our mechanical-mindedness reaches the danger point corrective processes begin to occur that alter our ways of thinking and acting.

I realize that this statement is almost blasphemous in an individualistic society that worships the idea of free will. Americans are extraordinarily fond of engaging in masochistic acts of various kinds to show that they are not governed by anything but their own free choice, which appears to mean that they are not attuned to their environment, other people, or their own bodies. They share the monotonous delusion that the human will does not have a uniform and predictable structure. Be that as it may, I regard the sudden emergence of ecological consciousness in this country—confused as it often is—as a system effect, no more willful than the march of the lemmings into the sea.

For all the suppression of feedback at a lower level, at a higher level the ecosystem is still functioning. God, in this sense, is not yet dead. Phenomena such as social eversion illustrate this functioning, as this chapter will attempt to show.

The Forms of Change

A straight line moving through a resistant medium becomes a sine wave. Rivers meander through flat meadows, a thin rod forms a loop when pushed against a wall. History is often portrayed in sine-wave images: rises and falls; Dark Ages and Renaissances; Classic, Romantic, Neo-Classic and Neo-Romantic eras.

From up close each rise or fall appears merely as a straightish line, but from a middle distance one is terribly aware of the curves. From still farther away the sine wave itself looks like a straight line. The rise of a great civilization then seems merely to be the concentration of culture, and a decline merely its diffusion, while the quantity and complexity of culture is continually increasing. The idea of linear progress is born.

This straight-line model works rather well if we use a quantitative measure of culture, such as the sheer number of artifacts or symbols per person. On the other hand, we have learned from long experience that a straight line often turns out merely to be a curve so flat that we are unable to recognize it as such. The axis of a sine curve may itself be a sine curve, for example. The truth captured by the old rise-and-fall model was that the components of culture do not change, but are merely recombined in an infinite variety of ways.

Yet these rearrangements are genuinely new and unprecedented. An adequate change model must capture both the static-bound-circular and the linear-open-unstable aspects of evolution. Human beings vocalize as do birds, organize as do ants, communicate symbolically as do bees, grasp as do apes, hunt as do cats, and so on; yet they do not merely repeat these traits—they are organized around an entirely new synthesis.

One problem with the linear model is that it obscures the layeredness of change—what Victor Gioscia calls "temporal stratification." The sailing vessel became obsolete before it achieved its technical zenith, as did the locomotive, radio, and film. Catholicism was in decline before it had gained full ascendancy, in the sense that Protestantism and various rationalistic philosophies began to emerge when the Church was finally succeeding in stamping out paganism. In a similar manner, the Protestant Ethic finally began to be internalized by much of the American working class during the post-World War II period, at which time the middle class began to question it. And as René Dubos points out, the middle of the eighteenth century brought not only the industrial revolution and the imposition of a vast armory of restrictive child-rearing techniques, but also an ardent enthusiasm for nature, "natural man," the return to bucolic simplicity, and so on. The belief that science would solve everything coincided with the belief that our departure from adaptive harmony with nature was the cause of all our troubles and diseases.

This layeredness makes one wonder whether any change is really occurring at all—whether the same ambivalences, the same dualities, are not merely being parceled out in different ways, or among different performers. But the fact that change is nothing more than a rearrangement detracts nothing from its significance. If we separate two parts of a whole, they will be different when re-fused, since their relationships with other wholes will have been altered by the separation. If they are changed as parts, they must be recombined differently. This is the principle underlying the prophet dynamic.

According to this perspective, any pattern, value, ideal, or behavioral tendency is always present in a culture at any time, along with its polar opposite. Only the relative emphasis given each pole and the ways of arranging their simultaneous expression tend to change. One pole is usually dominant, given overt expression, and highly valued; the other forced to express itself around the edges. Elaine Cumming discusses this process in terms of values and "anti-values," suggesting that "firmly held values seem always to be accompanied by contrasting, and even inimical, latent values" that are "available for conversion" into dominant ones. Furthermore, "the more loudly we proclaim a value, the more accessible to us must be some contrasting value." She points out, for example, that while we express our devotion to individualism by locating social pathology inside individual people, treating them as deviant cases no matter how many millions of them turn up, we enforce a collective life upon them in the form of prisons, hospitals, and institutional "homes." She also discusses other pairs of contrasting values such as equality vs. big government and openness vs. privacy, both of which we tend to find great difficulty in reconciling.

This rearrangement theory, then, sees change as merely the fluid patterns formed by the incessant variegated collisions between irreconcilable but equally necessary opposites. Its most important advantage over the linear progress theory is that it allows us to realize that a straight line is not necessarily the quickest path between two points—we can often get to a value most quickly by rebounding off its polar opposite. Not recognizing the opposites within us is what leads to our linear errors. For the expression of either of a pair of opposite impulses will unlock an ambivalent stasis, leading to the expression of the remaining one, and the freeing of bound and neutralized energy. This is why the venting of diffuse hostility is so often a preliminary phase of primitive fertility rituals. By the same token, the shortest road to an understanding of the fringes of the universe may be via the microscope rather than the telescope.

It may even have been useful for our civilization to have been on the wrong track all these centuries, although I am mistrustful of such panglossianism, which tends to blunt our responsivity where it is most needed. One could argue that the development of the schizoid male culture—naturally selected as long as there were many cultures in competition—may turn out to have been the fastest route to the emergence of its mutated opposite, essential now that aggression is no longer of any survival value. It has certainly hastened the development of a global culture, although one can imagine less risky routes. By this way of thinking, science might be encouraged to "make it bigger" and blow itself up. Art has followed this route, using art for art's sake as a kind of self-destruct mechanism. Detaching art from its social and cultural roots and making it pure led naturally to the realization that any event can be an art form as much as any other since all definitions of art are culturally derived. As everything becomes art, art becomes nothing, and pure science may follow the same route. Even secrecy has its value from this perspective, since it is an inherent part of the prophet dynamic—insulation allows independent evolution so that when exposure does come what is exposed has meaning and impact. Unrelieved truth is ultimately entropic.

These speculations, however, are a bit removed from our immediate concerns—pertinent examples of the Columbian strategy of going west to reach the East can be found closer at hand. In Chapter 2 I pointed out that although liberation movements tend to begin with demands for equal treatment, the oppressed group eventually transcends this goal and begins to recognize and affirm its unique superiorities. This affirmation is quite in keeping with the rearrangement theory of change. Yet the liberal, consistency phase of liberation, in which equality is stressed, may exert important leverage in this process. Let me use a rather trivial example to stand for a hundred others. Thirty years ago, when middle-class blacks were almost invisible to the dominant culture, most whites experienced the sight of a black man in a suit and tie as something incongruous. They felt that blacks didn't belong in this kind of costume—that there was something inappropriate about clothing a black body in this buttoned-up pomposity. By the time they overcame this racist reaction many blacks themselves began to feel that such constricting garb should be relegated to whites—that free black bodies belonged in free, expressive clothing. The third stage in the process was that many whites—especially young ones—began to experience the armored pomposity of suits and ties as unfit for *any* lively human body. The liberal phase, in other words, may be a necessary transition, since the application of the principle of consistency to pockets of variation serves to highlight absurdities in the dominant culture which are normally invisible because we are so used to them. *We become sensitized to the discomfort of a familiar cultural pattern by applying it to those for whom it seems unfamiliar.*

Thus consistency itself—the fullest expression of man's mechanical-mindedness—is transformed by natural social forces into something creative, new, and revitalizing. The human will fails of its goal, and humanity profits thereby. Our powerlessness to transcend the circuitry of the natural systems in which we participate—be they physical, biological, or cultural—is our greatest hope.

Social Eversion

The idea that social change is simply the rearrangement of polar opposites can lead to misconceptions. Cultures do not simply see-saw back and forth between individualism and collectivism, or centralization and decentralization, or specialization and fusion of roles, or openness and privacy, or equality and hierarchy, or thinking and feeling, or asceticism and hedonism. The multiplicity of such dimensions means that they can be recombined in an infinite variety of ways—and their expression allocated among different times, places, and categories of persons.

Similarly, the process of social eversion, in which a social pattern turns into its opposite by being pushed to an extreme, must be distinguished from the popular idea of the social pendulum, in which a trend begins to revert to a point of moderation when it has "gone too far." Superficial changes—changes in intellectual and artistic fashion, for example—are often accurately characterized by the pendulum metaphor. They represent movement within what a given culture regards as acceptable limits of variation. They provide a modicum of novelty in a fundamentally stable situation. Real social change, however (although it may first appear to be a pendulum effect), usually takes the form of social eversion.

Perhaps the most classic example of social eversion concerns an oft-noted by-product of the space program. Nothing could be more linear than the kind of scientific thinking that produced space exploration. It represents the extreme form of agency, of limitless narcissistic striving. Yet one major consequence of the space program is that it enabled masses of people to look back on our dwindling planet and reconceptualize it as "spaceship earth"—as a small, interdependent totality. Ecological consciousness on a mass scale thus sprang directly from the fullest expression of its precise opposite—a straight line creating its own curving.

Nor should we ignore the importance of narcissistic thinking itself in eliciting ecological consciousness. Many people have been

propelled into awareness by frightening stories of the consequences of human pollution. Such stories are often based on an
inflated idea of human power in relation to nature, but this con-
ceit may in the end prove timely. Thus human pomposity has
led directly to increased humility about planetary interdependence.

A more abstract example concerns our patterns of thought and
language. It is precisely our preoccupation with things rather
than processes, objects rather than relationships, digital rather
than analogic language, that led to the Platonic attitude toward
objects discussed in Chapter 2. This attitude, in turn, has made
our relationship to objects distant, detached, and unsatisfying. In
response to this dissatisfaction, we turn back to relationships with
other people—a more bilateral form of interrelation, and hence,
one in which the relationship itself is more likely to be the focus
of attention. Now the higher the ratio of living to non-living objects in our consciousness, the more our thinking and language
will tend to be analogic—the more prominent will be the iconic
and kinesic elements in communication. Note once again that it
is precisely through pushing the digital, thing-orientation to an
extreme that its opposite re-emerges.

The information explosion provides a similar example. As
digital knowledge expands, specialization increases and learning
becomes compartmentalized. Academics become potato sorters,
who know nothing about relationships since these all lie outside
their increasingly circumscribed fields. Yet the fields themselves
eventually become so elaborated that it is impossible even to
keep up with one's own, now so narrow as to have become irrelevant to any significant reality. This leads in turn to increasing
withdrawal of interest from digital learning altogether, and a
growing concern with relational understanding and wisdom.

The linear, constricted frame of science, furthermore, has not
prevented the emergence, within that frame, of two events that
threaten to alter it. The first was the psychedelic movement
which, it must be remembered, began in the laboratories of chem-
ists engaged in routine work. The second is the current upsurge
in psychic research, triggered largely by military interest in telepathy. Both events have created widespread interest in expanding
our root definitions of reality (most scientists, alas, are still trudg-

ing along with Newton under one arm and John Locke under the other).

Overpopulation provides still another example. Crowding tends to break down the stable, nourishing, and comfortable bonds that gratify people and make them willing to assume responsibility for children. The loss of this gratification leads to pleasure-*seeking* —to a hedonistic life style in which children seem a burden. As this mood spreads, the birth rate tends to taper off.

For one final example of social eversion we might take the isolated nuclear family with its heavy emotional overload—tending to destroy all efforts at maintaining tolerable emotional distances between family members. The implosion of needs—formerly satisfied in the extended family and the larger community—into the nuclear family has created a kind of behavioral sink within it. This is not a matter of spatial closeness: middle-class Americans today are probably less crowded within their homes than any people in history. It is rather the lack of emotional alternatives —the forcing, in other words, of a steep pleasure gradient on the young—that has produced the sense of emotional overload. This results in a longing for privacy and a phobic feeling about society, for society is recreated in fantasy in the image of overpossessive, smothering parents.

At the same time, the defective awareness of our interconnectedness with others in the community generates loneliness and fear. Both of these feelings—loneliness and the need for privacy—are endemic to a steep-gradient population, in which stable relationships are impossible, and yet personal boundaries cannot be maintained. The reverse is true in a flat-gradient system, in which every individual has a large number of stable medium-intensity ties.

As these feelings escalate, two things happen. First, long-term marriage relationships become increasingly difficult to maintain, and the divorce rate climbs. Second, the oedipal family inflates narcissistic, invidious, and competitive motivation in children. At first these trends exaggerate the pathological conditions that created them: With divorce, mothers are thrown back into even more intense relationships with sons, who grow up to be even more compulsive careerists. Eventually, however, the competitive motivation spills over onto women, who seek a larger role in the more prestigious occupational world. This triggers the women's movement which, as noted earlier, attacks the oedipal family on all fronts. Meanwhile, serial monogamy combined with working mothers deintensifies the mother-child relationship and leads to flatter pleasure gradients in the next generation.

All these examples of social eversion suggest that it is virtually impossible, *if the raw materials are at hand,* to avoid creating what is needed to balance a system, so great is the internal pressure for that creation to emerge.

Trunks in the Attic of Culture

Nature is miserly. It rarely discards any process that ever worked. This is equally true of social systems, and is one reason, paradoxically, why rapid social change can sometimes occur. A society does not suddenly change into something different—it merely begins to emphasize what was once deemphasized, to approve what was once devalued.

Social change seldom assumes a direction that is altogether undefined ahead of time. Most Americans, for example, are aware that their society is becoming less preoccupied with achievement, less future-oriented, more hedonistic, and so on. This is hardly astounding, since the signs are all around them. What *is* interesting is that people already have a sense of what it is they are approaching. People who have never lived in a hedonistic culture nevertheless have an idea about what it is and how it works, and whether they would like it or not.

We take this phenomenon for granted, but it has profound implications. It suggests the possibility that the elements of all cultural arrangements are latent in every cultural system, or at least every healthy one.

For maximum flexibility, the subparts of a system will each maintain the potentiality for all the possible behaviors that could flow from any part of the system. Many cultures, for example, have established certain special days (The Feast of Fools, Mardi Gras) during which the customary rules of the society are set aside. Not only are sexual restrictions violated, but also rules governing status and deference. Those in authority are derided, masters wait upon servants, the most lowly are raised to be king or queen for a day—all rules are turned topsy-turvy.

Such customs should not be thought of merely as a vacation from everyday social constraints. Often the conventions surrounding the inverted mores are as elaborate and constricting as the everyday ones. What these festivals do is keep alive the capacity to use social and behavioral muscles that are not ordinarily exercised. The meek try on arrogance, the arrogant meekness, and so on. Knowledge of behavior opposite to one's normal social role is kept alive. Ordinary complementarities and specializations are transcended, facilitating the possibility of rearranging social roles should this ever become necessary. Like mutations, these customs provide a hedge against change, and hence are much less wasteful and frivolous than they seem at first glance. They also serve to reduce what Bateson calls "schismogenesis"—the progressive differentiation of a society into alienated subgroups, with a concomitant narrowing of the personalities of their members.

These feasts are simply one of many mechanisms through which cultures increase their potentiality for variation. Societies seem to hoard their cultural possessions as if knowing that one of them might some day turn out to be useful again. Mythology and folklore, for example, are full of outdated culture patterns kept alive by dramatization. Universities, when the humanities dominated them, also played the role of cultural attic. Young people learned a lot by messing about in them and playing games. Unfortunately, adults tend always to move in on this kind of activity, afraid that the children will learn too much too fast (just as they sometimes did in the family attic). They put up compartments and try to force them to group the available information in familiar and traditional ways. This has become more exaggerated since the natural and social sciences became ascendant and turned the universities into trade schools. Academic departments and professional schools are to education what the Little League is to play.

This tension between the need to limit and funnel information and the need to keep options open is fundamental to all social systems. It is the same tension that produces the prophet dynamic, and arises at the biological level as well, as Bateson points out. In the wild, the population of a given species "functions as a storehouse of genotypic possibilities." Farmers and breeders, however, like professors, seek to limit the number of such possibilities so as to guarantee a uniform and predictable product in their domesticated species. Bateson, following the biologist, Simmonds, argues the need to maintain this storehouse of variability by fostering enclaves of unselected populations. Such enclaves, designed to offset the ultimately debilitating effect of deliberately selective breeding, would serve exactly the same purpose as free learning settings in a university, in which students do not need to march through a preordained mechanical hierarchy of learning stages, from "elementary" to "advanced." The breeders and professors seek to limit the amount of information going into the system—the breeder for fear an animal will appear with a head too big or insufficiently pointed, the professor for fear a student will ingest an idea before she is "ready" for it. This is necessary to ensure control and maximize production along understood lines, but it progressively destroys the possibility of altering those lines. Even Toffler, in his headlong pursuit of yesterday's future, recognizes this, and favors the preservation of "slow-paced communities" as a form of "mental and social insurance," in case the larger society makes some catastrophic error.

Oddly enough, however, free choice itself can be a principle which limits information, as I noted earlier in connection with arranged marriages. Since personal motivation is always present as a variable, the removal of all *other* bases for selection means that the system will be deprived of a great number of serendipitous rearrangements.

Deviance and Containment

The major way societies store information that is out of keeping with their dominant cultural themes is through the handling of what sociologists call "deviant behavior"—behavior that is disapproved, scorned, and usually punished by the community or its representatives. Sociologists worry a lot about deviant behavior and its control, and some of their puzzlement derives from the curious fact that when the entire focus of a community's energies seems to be the complete eradication of some bit of deviant behavior it nevertheless manages to persist. How can we account for society's impotence in such cases? There seems to be some sort of ambivalence in social systems that prevents the attack on deviance from achieving its logical consummation.

Michel Foucault, for example, describes how madmen in the fifteenth century were often given into the hands of sailors who carried them to distant cities, where they collected in large numbers and were often imprisoned. Although these people were considered a menace wherever they were found, considerable trouble was taken to see to their transportation and to house and feed them. We certainly cannot argue that dedication to humane values or merciful sentiments restrained the townspeople from simply doing away with them—men in those times, just as now, were quite willing to slaughter their fellows over a difference of opinion or a few coins. Yet they seemed in this case to be in the grip of some hesitation—some deeply rooted doubt.

It may be objected that madmen have traditionally carried a sacred aura that provided certain immunity from attack. This is true, and exemplifies the thesis advanced here. These madmen, however, were not viewed as pseudo-shamans and allowed to wander freely in the community—they were regarded as dangerous and were subjected to exile or imprisonment. But they were kept alive. It is as if the townspeople doubted whether they might not lose some potential resource if they were to destroy them entirely.

One sees this ambivalence and doubt in many settings. I have often been impressed with the energy that small groups will sometimes expend trying to accommodate troublesome individuals—willing at times to become completely paralyzed rather than lose a single obstreperous member. In one experimental study of groups the researchers found that although the deviant member is usually disliked, "it would be quite unfortunate to assume that he is therefore isolated from the group or repudiated by it: an accurate sociogram would have the deviant individual encircled by the interlocking sociometric preferences, sheltered by the group structure."

At the community level, deviant behavior is often both expressed and counteracted in relative secrecy, as if society's representatives assumed, not that visible deviance would unite the community in outraged solidarity, as some sociologists have suggested, but that it would contaminate and infect them. In such cases, it seems proper to say that societies respond to deviance as if they wanted to insulate it, to minimize it, to quarantine it, but to preserve it—in other words to *contain* it.

This ambivalence, this hesitation altogether to destroy the deviant trend, is at bottom just what it looks like—doubt that the reprehended or scorned behavior may not prove at some future date to embody a hidden but valuable resource of some kind. The "containment" of deviance is another hedge against social change. The contained deviant trend is like a cadre or a museum's archives or a germ culture or a zoo. In it are contained the seeds of a potential future orthodoxy—as few as possible, but a few.

This is not to imply that there is some deep wisdom in social systems, sagely recognizing the ambiguities of the future beneath the spurious certainties of the present. Societies are blind and witless automatons, forever blundering into destruction and decay. The containment mechanism is as crude and inefficient as is mutation at the biological level. In both cases random variation is maintained at great expense in preference to a more perfect system from which there is no escape.

Perfect adaptation produces almost certain obsolescence. Any self-maintaining mechanism must have a certain amount of error built into it. As Lewis Mumford said long ago, only imperfect systems, full of self-contradictions, have the capacity to survive. The reason that societies today tend to contain deviance rather than expunging it is that those societies are the survivors. Social systems that have survived are magpies and pack rats. They have attics full of alternative themes, values, and behavior patterns that no longer play any active role in the society. These are preserved not only in myth and ritual and folklore, but also in subcultural pockets and stylized individual roles. Of what relevance is Jesus Christ or Billy the Kid or Achilles in a modern industrial society like ours? Of what use a hermit in a gregarious community, a transvestite in a warrior tribe? Of what value are the insane? Foucault suggests that the invention of the mental hospital served the function of preserving the fantastic in hidden reservoirs—keeping alive, during the classical age, buried images that could be "transmitted intact from the sixteenth to the nineteenth century."

Madness involves a dissolution of structures and boundaries. The mad live outside the structural frame that society imposes. They are adrift in a turbulent and unbound sea. But that same sea is a reservoir, containing all the elements from which a social system can be constructed. If they are out of touch with the building, they are uniquely *in* touch with its components. They are thus both to be feared and to be treasured. They know both less and more than others.

The torch of culture does not tend to stay in the same hands for very long—those who are committed to the existing patterns tend to be by-passed by the less "cultured" who leapfrog, as it were, into a new golden age. Each torch holder imagines that his rude, uncultured neighbor can achieve grace only by traversing an imitative path, and is always amazed to find himself outdistanced in a direction he had never even considered. How could a nation of burghers ever surpass one of noble warriors, except by becoming noble warriors? How could Africa ever surpass Western nations, except by becoming Westernized? How can black Americans amount to anything except by becoming just like middle-class whites? But the lessons of history suggest that it is by *not* becoming like the dominant group that significant cultural advances occur.

White liberals used to believe that the stereotype of the warm and earthy black—singing and dancing, living in the present, enjoying bodily pleasures to the fullest—either had no behavioral foundation at all or was an unfortunate compensatory adaptation to centuries of slavery and oppression. I would like to suggest that this behavioral configuration—let us call it the watermelon pattern—was not so much an adaptation to oppression (although no doubt it was to some extent) as oppression was an unconscious adaptation to the watermelon pattern. Once the economic basis for the oppression of blacks had disappeared, blacks were oppressed in part to contain the watermelon pattern: to insulate it, quarantine it, disparage it, discourage it, and keep it alive. While blacks are kept from reaping the fruits of the Protestant Ethic, they were also preserved from its infection and internal rot.

The watermelon pattern was a return ticket in case the Protestant Ethic turned out to be a swindle, and now that the industrial era is about to take up its eternal position as a horrible and aberrant moment in human history, the ticket is redeemable. In times of change it is those who are most whole, least warped by elaborate custom and the degradation of impulse, who are in the best position to innovate creatively.

For the past decade blacks, Indians, and women have all been engaged in bringing neglected treasures out of the basement of our culture, trying to revitalize a sclerotic society. Blacks were the first to recognize this mission. They were intellectual pioneers—showing other oppressed groups how oppression worked and how to transcend it. The assertion "black is beautiful" was a profound cultural invention, as evidenced by the speed with which it diffused to other oppressed groups. For to achieve self-respect when one is a member of a despised minority is virtually impossible—like creating something from nothing. A significant foothold appeared during the early civil rights movement when white liberals went south full of condescension and ended by displaying a certain amount of envy and admiration toward black culture. Racism is like a magic spell—it has to be perfectly maintained to have the proper demoralizing effect on the recipient. One leak and the spell is broken. The mirror of reality replaces the enchanted mirror and the sleeper awakes from her dream of self-hatred. No matter how hard one tries, it is impossible to maintain self-respect in the absence of any validation from the outside. But with the tiniest fragment of such validation blacks rapidly built themselves a strong ideology of mutual respect and cultural assertion.

The black experience opened the eyes of other groups who had endured containment: women, Amerindians, Chicanos, prisoners, mental patients, high school students. All but one of these groups experienced containment in a very physical sense—being enclosed in ghettos, reservations, or institutions. This enclosure serves a double function: For the present, the deviant culture cannot infect the prevailing dominant one, but at the same time it cannot be engulfed and destroyed by it. Oppression and isolation keep it weak, isolated, and intact. Hence the moment at which the oppressed group breaks out of its confinement is a matter of very delicate timing—will the cultural seed which has been preserved in isolation flower amid the rot of the old dominant culture, or will the dominant culture (to mix metaphors a bit) smother it with antibodies? Much of the endless political debate that goes on in oppressed groups revolves around this difficult issue. To some extent it can be said that if the dominant culture is not sick, sclerotic, in decay, the question will never come up—the containment will be successful no matter what. Vigorous oppression based on deluded moral conviction is an almost insuperable weapon, especially against a minority. But if oppression begins to falter, if the illusion of superiority and righteousness starts to crumble, the vitality of the contained deviant culture will burst its chains. This does not mean that the argument over timing is meaningless. If cultures are to be blended (which is what always happens ultimately, even in war or revolution), timing will determine the extent to which the deviant culture plays a major or minor role in the new synthesis. This was the essence of the question of black separatism. To follow the integration route would have been to condemn blacks to an infinitesimal role in the synthesized culture. To preserve voluntarily the very containment that had previously been involuntary was to ensure that the new synthesis, whenever it came, would be a lot blacker.

Even in the oppressed condition there are variations in the degree to which a deviant culture can be preserved intact. A reservation allows more than a ghetto, and a ghetto far more than a prison or mental hospital. Institutions of confinement, as Erving Goffman has observed, have their own built-in culture, which is essentially that of the concentration camp—authoritarian, bureaucratic, infantilizing, and sado-masochistic. About all that is preserved in such institutions is whatever cultural variations people took into them individually. In that sense they are less efficient cultural attics, and their use betokens less vigor and elasticity in the society that places heavy reliance on them. A society that effectively contains a deviant culture by oppressing it without attempting to break it up and dissolve it must at least be acknowledged to be healthy and vital, however repulsive. The Nazi regime revealed its brittleness when concentration camps began to be used on a large scale, and the later attempt to annihilate an entire deviant population betrayed its total non-viability and imminent collapse.

Women are the one oppressed group in America that have not been contained geographically. Since women are not a minority, to have confined them together would have been to sound the instantaneous death knell of the dominant white male culture. Patriarchal cultures have always been petrified about large gatherings of women. The containment of women, therefore, has necessitated the construction of millions of individualized psychic prisons, euphemistically called homes. Women were subjugated by placing them under a loose form of house arrest. The phrase, "he can't even keep his woman at home," used to be a customary way of disparaging a man's domestic competence—virility rested on one's skills as a jailer. *Divide et impera.*

Even though kept apart from each other, women have shared a culture derived from certain common experiences: oppression, exclusion from the sources of power in society, and relative non-commitment (usually stigmatized as "feminine intuition") to mechanical modes of thought. Their emergence as a group has been vastly hampered by the illusion that they already participate in the dominant culture. Consciousness-raising among women has stressed unity and the awareness that they share a vital culture alien to masculine compartmentalism and inhibition.

The likelihood of a deviant culture being contained is a function of how sharply it contrasts with the dominant culture. Black culture is diametrically opposed to the Protestant Ethic of inhibition, frigidity, and miserliness. Feminine culture is antithetical to the male culture of feeling-suppression, schizoid rationalism, and mechanical action. Most Amerindian cultures in one way or another oppose the Western emphasis on individualism, parts-over-wholes, and the exploitation of the environment, favoring instead a view of nature as a balanced whole in which humans play an equal rather than stellar role. It is my impression, furthermore, that those Amerindian cultures most antithetical to our own, like the pueblo cultures, have been better preserved than those (like the plains cultures) more similar to ours.

The fact that so many new and contrasting strains are now being fed into our culture is a sign both of its illness and its vitality, just as a high blood count shows both that an organism is sick and that it is responding vigorously. Rome, during its long decline, exhibited the same eager appetite for alien and deviant traditions, and although it never corrected its self-destructive commitment to massive inequality of wealth and other addictions, this receptivity certainly prolonged its existence. The same phenomenon is visible now, especially the fascination with Eastern thought and new religions. If it leads to a fundamental restructuring of the culture, we may fare better than our ancient predecessor.

There is hope in the emergence of ecological thinking in America. Modern ethnography in the West began to flourish in the beginning of the twentieth century, just as pure non-Western cultures were evaporating from the globe. This in itself betrayed a vigorous pack-rat response on the part of a number of Western societies, but the awareness of totally disparate ways of viewing the world was for a long time the privilege of a few anthropologists. Today every civilized bookstore in the country has a section reserved for books about Amerindian cultures and ecology, and recognition of the rich cultural heritage that the white invaders of America destroyed is growing geometrically. Most important of all, it is increasingly recognized that the absorption of this heritage is not an esoteric recreation, but a necessary step to survival.

Before leaving the topic of containment, a word needs to be said about technique. I have mentioned oppression and isolation, but perhaps the most important of all is the technique of negative definition, described by Ronald Laing in connection with family dynamics.

Laing points out that parents often fix a child in a deviant family role by sending two messages: (1) You *should* be X, but (2) you *are* Y. He observes that the second message is inherently more powerful than the first—that a child can be made to feel guilty by being told "you should be more responsible," but that the statement "You are irresponsible" is irresistible—a covert instruction that carries its own justification within it ("You can be no different because this is what you *are*"). The conscious intent of the parent is to change the behavior, but the unconscious intent is to fix it permanently, and this is, in fact, what the behavior achieves. To define a trait as negative, and simultaneously to insist that it is an intrinsic part of someone's character is to ensure the subservience of that person and the persistence of that trait. This is precisely what containment seeks to achieve, and hence this technique is an essential part of the containment dynamic. "You *should* work and strive, but you *are* lazy and shiftless" was the message through which the watermelon pattern was both negated and preserved.

Neither message need be explicitly communicated in words. The containment of feminine culture in our own society is to some extent implicit. Consider, for example, the impact of current attitudes about housewives' time. Whereas men in their occupations are accustomed to placing some sort of value on their time and that of other men, the assumption is usually made that the time of housewives has no value. Many women are willing to spend an entire day rushing from one store to another in an effort to save a few dollars—work that yields them far less than the legal minimum wage. This attitude is inculcated by the masculine occupational world. For while men schedule appointments with each other—a way of showing mutual respect for the value of each other's time—housewives are expected to operate without schedules. Repairmen, telephone installers, deliverymen, and so on, have been successful in refusing to constrict their own convenience by making scheduled appointments with housewives, who are expected to wait at home until the workman arrives. Nothing could convey more powerfully the low esteem in which the role of housewife is held than this disregard of daily scheduling needs. The lowliest flunky in the masculine occupational hierarchy is given temporal superiority over every non-working woman. The twin message, "You *should* be doing something useful, but you *are* useless," has not been lost upon the non-working woman, who is wont to say, "I'm just a housewife." What is preserved by this containment is an antidote to the narrow and ultimately meaningless utilitarianism of the male world, in which only that which is quantitatively measurable is accorded value.

Our discussion of deviant cultures suggests a danger, albeit a rather remote one. Should all oppressed groups achieve liberation and the world arrive at some sort of unified culture, would not vital cultural patterns be forever lost?

The danger is real, however unlikely it may seem at present. Some vague presentiment of this reality probably contributes to the increasing preoccupation with finding new forms of life elsewhere in the universe. But it should be emphasized again that the containment of deviant groups is not the only means through which societies preserve alternatives. Myth, folklore, drama, and literary fantasies also serve this function. The centrality of Charlie Chaplin in the culture of the 20's and 30's in our own society exemplifies this mechanism. Chaplin's tramp personified the antithesis of all the prevailing values of that culture—values such as ambition, striving, courage, stoicism, toughness, directness, postponement of gratification, dignity, and "manliness." He was a monument to responsivity in a culture rapidly expunging every vestige of it in everyday life.

It is by no means clear why or when a social system suddenly becomes vulnerable to these encapsulated antitheses—why the cell walls suddenly give way and allow the deviant trend to flood through the society and transform it. Clearly some hunger, some lack, some fatigue with the artificial absurdities of existing arrangements makes it possible, but the process is rather unclear.

We call such moments crises. We define an event as a crisis when our ordinary routines cease to make sense. Thus the more meaningless our routines seem in the first place the more a crisis is likely to occur. A crisis lasts (that is, is defined as such) until all the various routines begin once again to make sense. It may seem impossible to go to work and absurd to wash the dishes when a loved one has just died, and in a functioning community other people usually move in to fill the gap, breaking their own routines to perform necessary functions for the bereft. But ultimately a sense that "life must go on" returns—the flood waters recede, the family member returns from the hospital, the dead are relinquished—and routines are taken up again.

Often, however, the routines are changed, incorporating the larger context made visible by the crisis. The coronary patient reserves his energies for enriching rather than emotionally depleting experiences, the devastated city rebuilds with an eye to beauty. Crisis often allows the suppressed and despised parts of a system a chance to infuse new life into it—to give it a second chance, like the one the dream of Marley's ghost gave to Ebenezer Scrooge.

Parable 7

Every spring a trader from Ispahan came to town. He was a clever and energetic man and each year brought quantities of useless and defective merchandise which he unloaded at considerable profit. After a few years the townspeople got wise to the trader, and when he reappeared the following year they attacked and beat him and destroyed his merchandise. The canny trader, however, was determined not to lose this lucrative market and came again the next year disguised as a beardless Egyptian. Although the townspeople had generalized their caution to some extent, the trader's visit was a successful one, and he repeated the maneuver the following year. This time his disguise was penetrated, however, and he was again beaten and relieved of his remaining wares.

From that day on, the stubborn trader appeared each spring in a new disguise. Sometimes he took the role of an old man, sometimes that of a woman; sometimes he was a Hindu, sometimes a Turk. He assumed many postures, many accents, and became an increasingly gifted mimic. Each year he devoted more care to planning his visit to the town —designing his costume, perfecting his accent, gait, idiosyncrasies, and so on. Since the town was a favorite of transient and unscrupulous traders, it was easy for him to lose himself in the throng.

The townspeople, meanwhile, kept a sharp eye out for the trader, whom they regarded as a special enemy. As the years went by they involved themselves more and more in anticipating his visits. Each spring they held meetings to discuss ways of penetrating his incognito, which was all the more difficult as no one could any longer remember what he had originally looked like. They tried to find common denominators in his multi-faceted behavior. They chose scouts to observe all incoming traders and take note of any that seemed suspicious. Eventually they began offering prizes to anyone who could detect the trader. This led to wholesale

molestation of traders, and the townspeople were forced to
make rules for the contest that would protect the innocent.
The prize would be offered only to one who could discover
the trader without touching him, and there were heavy
penalties for selecting the wrong man. With this the situation
became stabilized, for while exposing the trader was now
the major spring recreation of the town, the rules of the
contest made it extremely difficult to bring about.

Thus it went on for many years. Some years the trader
was successful, sometimes the townspeople. The trader
viewed the situation in terms of his own ingenuity, his
perseverance in the face of occasional severe beatings, and
his ability often to outwit an entire town devoted to exposing
him. While he never became rich, he lived very comfortably,
and was able to accumulate a sizeable nest egg on the
profits of his more successful excursions to the town.

The townspeople viewed the situation in terms of the
excellent organization they had created to forestall the trader.
They were pleased with the determination and co-operation
they had shown, and were gratified that often they were
able to detect the trader's imposture, despite his almost
superhuman skill at disguise. The organizational network that
they evolved to achieve this goal served them well whenever
they were threatened by danger from fire, flood, or war, and
the town had a long and modestly prosperous existence.

After several decades, the trader died. By this time,
however, the spring ritual of anticipating his visit had become
an elaborate and enthusiastic enterprise, and it was necessary
to induct townspeople into the vacant role. Each year
thereafter some of them would disguise themselves as
traders and mingle among the true outsiders. Any who were
successful in remaining undetected for the duration of the
Fair divided the prize formerly given to successful detectors.
After the prize was awarded there was a huge celebration.

Today, a century later, the Festival of the Trader is still
the biggest holiday of the town. Amid the delight of the
celebration no one remembers the fierce struggle from
which it arose.

Chronicles of Noga

THE BROKEN CIRCUIT

> *There'll always be a Carthage.*
>
> **Hannibal**

> *I am here because of you, and you are*
> *here because of me.*
>
> **Mulla Nasrudin**

It is quite possible that humanity may prove to be a dead end like the dinosaur—too big (with its technological extensions) and too stupid (with its relational insensitivity) to participate felicitously in the dance of life. Apparently this is not the first time that extinction has threatened human beings, however, and they have yet managed to survive and prosper on the strength of a certain flexibility and craftiness, and a profound inability to commit themselves heartily to a specific presence in nature.

Whether survival or extinction is humanity's destiny simply depends upon whether the self-corrective processes described in the last chapter turn out to include or exclude our species. Western culture seems to be engaged in a frantic effort to heal itself, while at the same instant it is hurling itself toward global destruction at an accelerating rate. Let us be levelheaded in our apocalyptic visions, however: "Global destruction," "ecological catastrophe," "nuclear holocaust," and all the other terms of warning connote a degree of finality for which there is no realistic referent. None of the plausible global disasters presently envisioned would extinguish all life on the planet, although most of them would pretty well annihilate mammalian species. By and large, to talk of a dead planet is mere hyperbole. Whatever happens, there will probably be an ecology of some sort—perhaps centered around little slugs that consume and break down hydrocarbons.

Nature, then, will heal itself, either because the species that became so noisily diseased will also heal itself, or because that species will destroy itself and permit alternative forms of life to flower with greater joy and grace. Assuming a godlike, abstract posture, one could advocate with equal reasonableness throwing our energies in the direction of self-cure, or fulfilling our self-destructive destiny with as much verve as possible.

But we are not gods, we are humans, and we do not live in the abstract, although the key representatives of our technocracy seem to *exist* in it, rushing jerkily through their own time in a kind of mechanical stupor, as if they did not recognize it. We are humans, and not to attempt to revive our humanity and heal our own sickness would be as pretentious and silly as all our other efforts to be other than who we are.

Furthermore, self-healing processes are already emerging in Western culture, and everything we do in our lives, however trivial, adds energy either to these processes or to our previous linear course.

With the best will and most sophisticated political consciousness in the world, we might manage to devote about 10 per cent of our waking hours to a deliberate attempt to cure the diseased system in which we live, while unconsciously and automatically spending the other 90 per cent feeding and supporting its pathology. There is no point despairing over this or wasting time in guilty conscience-examining, which seldom leads to anything vibrant or healthful. When awareness of our position among these conflicting forces passes from the cognitive to the emotional level—from concept to bodily sensitivity—we can rely upon our own visceral sensations and those of others to negotiate this difficult terrain more creatively and less effortfully.

Western culture, like the schizoid personality structure, is built upon broken feedback circuitry. Responsivity is blocked and in its place is inserted a programmed instruction from an internal conceptual apparatus. In place of feedback from others the individualistically programmed person inserts self-feedback. In place of increasingly fine mutual tuning each individual mechanically obeys his own program, following his own closed circuitry until he spins himself into oblivion. The program is truly his own in the sense that the culture provides a limited selection of ideological instructions and the individual is free to put together his own unique combination. What he is *not* free to do is to disobey the instruction to respond in a mechanistic fashion, perceive nonmechanical forms of transpersonal linkage, or recognize that he has been instructed to be "free" (i.e., mechanical). This is typical of the mystification techniques discussed by Laing and Bateson in relation to the families of schizophrenics.

But no matter what our culture trains us to believe—no matter what we tell each other—we *are* connected with one another. The only thing that changes is how we are connected: organically, mechanically, symbolically, consciously, unconsciously, bodily, verbally, or whatever. Our culture attempts to break the emotional connections between people and substitute bureaucratic ones. By training us to blind ourselves to our fundamental interdependence—feeding us instead the myth that we are isolated particles trying to find a way to come together—we are led to invest our feelings, needs, and desires in abstract goals and institutions, believing all the while that in so doing we are independent of one another. Our culture is like a con man who persuades us to cheat those close to us of their due, and to invest instead in ourselves. He, of course, shows us how to do this, and lives off the proceeds. We are still connected, but now through the con man. He mocks our conformity to persons and tells us to do our own thing, leaving co-ordination to more and more remote and impersonal mechanisms, understood by fewer and fewer people with more and more concentrated negative power. Knowing that coherence is intrinsic to life itself, and that accommodational responses are a part of our human birthright, he rejoices as increasingly impersonal forces—authorities instead of intimate groups, bureaucracies instead of authorities, machines instead of bureaucracies, ideological symbols instead of machines—wag these accommodating instincts, and tells us this progression is in the direction of perfect freedom.

I have already described the evolution of modern humanity's circuit-breaking proclivities. It might also be useful to examine the way in which circuit-breaking is learned at the individual level. We are born into a symbiotic relationship with another human being. Our heartbeats and body motions are in synchrony with hers. This bond must be loosened if the child is to achieve psychic and physical health, and the capacity for sensitive attunement must be extended to include many other people. But that capacity itself need not atrophy, and in most non-Western societies does not. How is that interpersonal attunement shattered, so that the gap left can be filled with rules, procedures, slogans, force, regulation, and philosophy?

Ashley Montague points out a number of ways. At birth the infant in our society is usually isolated almost immediately from the mother and placed in a roofless cage. Often its tactile sensitivity is further dulled by bottle feeding. This is useful training for mastery and for relating to machines: Since the reactions of the bottle are less complex and far more predictable than those of the breast, the infant learns that fundamental needs are satisfied by manipulating inert and unresponsive objects, rather than by interacting in a mutually adaptive attunement with another organism as complex as itself. In most "primitive" societies, furthermore, the infant is constantly held or carried, thus demanding a complex mutual adjustment of movement and position. In most Western cultures tactile sensitivity is also muted by clothing. Even in the few situations where touching is freely allowed, the development of interpersonal sensitivity is limited: "Margaret Mead has pointed out how the attention of the American baby is directed away from the personal relationship to his mother by toys which are introduced into his tub." (Montague.) This, like the bottle, is good training for life in a hardware society. It helps account for our tendency to put our energies into simple mechanical problems that can be "solved" once and for all, ignoring the complex issues that require constant adaptation and readjustment and reduce all our elegant once-and-for-all solutions to trivial irrelevance. Scientific and social scientific research, social legislation, and the approach of American Presidents to the Vietnam War all seem rooted in this bathtub experience. Inanimate objects are so much easier to "handle" and we are so poorly equipped to relate to organisms as complex as ourselves that it is tempting to confuse one with the other.

In addition to all this obligatory lack of contact there is an ideological conviction that a child must "learn to be by herself." Few non-Western societies have invented such a rule. Why must the child learn to be by herself? To prepare for urban living, or for old age? Perhaps, but also so that she can learn to relate to inanimate objects that are easily controlled, and take her instruction from mass dispensers—doctors, television, educational toys, and so on—instead of learning directly by trial-and-error interaction with other organisms.

One of the most powerful techniques ever designed for circuit-breaking in infancy was scheduled feeding. The unresponsiveness to human need that characterizes our social institutions today probably owes something to the fact that they are designed, maintained, and led by people exposed to this form of training. In scheduled feeding the cycle of hunger-cry-feed-hold-sleep is broken by the mother, who inserts the concept of mechanical time, feeding the child according to machine time instead of biological time. The unfortunate impact of this procedure on the infant's well-being has long been recognized, but it is worth noting that it can also be hard on the mother. Scheduling might be convenient for her in some ways, but she is often forced to listen to increasingly intense screaming until the clock rolls around and to negate her own spontaneous yearning to feed, nourish, and comfort the crying infant.

It is usually assumed that the more contemporary emphasis on demand feeding is a complete negation of the effects of scheduling. But from the mother's viewpoint this is not really the case. Instead of being enslaved to the clock she is enslaved to the infant's cry—either way she is supposed to ignore her own internal responses in deference to a mechanical principle. Under the demand system the child's cry is not a phatic communication triggering an emotional need to respond, but is rather a signal with a fixed symbolic meaning. Instead of cry→desire to soothe, we have cry→interpretation (hunger)→automatic requirement of feeding. Parents will thus be circuit-breakers whichever set of mechanical instructions governs their behavior. Both tend to breed insensitivity in children.

The same pitfall emerges with other child-rearing instructions in the early Spockian tradition, despite Spock's frequent admonitions to "trust one's instincts." In the first place, our "spontaneous" impulses are by now far too numbed and polluted to put much trust in, and even if they were not, a book full of instructions and causal connections would soon overwhelm them. A child-rearing manual may be a necessary evil in a society that lacks stable child-rearing communities, but it is rather difficult to be attuned to a child with a book in one's hand and a head full of goals. The manual is for the mother what the bathtub toys are for the child. If the mother manages to sensitize herself to the child, she usually loses contact with her own feelings and needs, and vice versa. My impression of the products of Spockian child rearing is that as a group they are more tuned in to their own viscera than are their predecessors, but even less sensitive to the needs and demands of others—a sensitivity denied them by parents who stifled their own needs in favor of producing "healthy" offspring. It is not the content of the formula that breaks the circuit, but the instructional form in and of itself.

It would of course be absurd to condemn circuit-breaking as an undiluted evil. There are times when the postponement of gratification, the blocking of feeling, the cutting off of communication, desensitization to one's environment, and so on, are valuable and even necessary to survival. But circuits are more easily broken than reconnected, and all circuit-breaking carries within it the danger of escalation spirals that are difficult to halt. Our civilization has reached a point where many channels of awareness have almost entirely atrophied. The most body-centered and "sensorily awakened" American can never match the level of sensitivity that primitive hunters and gatherers possess all their lives. But one cannot possibly retain such sensitivity in an urban environment and live. We cannot be fully attuned in a hopelessly discordant environment, but it is perilous to remain too long out of touch with that environment, or ourselves, or each other.

Attunement

This is the moment, in books of this kind, where one is supposed to offer concrete suggestions for some sort of action. "Enough diagnosis, time for prescription." I do not know why this is so—why books of social analysis should ape the format of a market research report or an engineer's memorandum. The recommendations that are made always seem fatuous to me—either so vague and general as to be implicit in the analysis itself, or so concrete and trivial that one could have offered them without going through any of the analysis. I want to state here that I intend to violate the traditional form: I have no suggestions to offer. I have described a way of being and its pathological consequences. This implies that some sort of reversal of this way of being—this attitude of mind—would be helpful, but how one arrives at it cannot be prescribed but only discovered. To say otherwise would be to announce that I have only been kidding all along. There can be no mechanical prescription for demechanization—any person, armed with some piece of awareness that I hope has been reinforced by this book, can begin to experiment with his or her own circuitry in whatever sphere—personal, political, or occupational—suggests itself.

Any change based on the kind of thinking that needs words like "blueprint" and "implementation" is not change at all but an extension of the problem. Nothing benign will arise without alterations in mind set, and given a more responsive mind set almost any activity would begin to constitute real change. It is characteristic of Americans to ask, "What shall we do?" but the question is wrong. Humanization will not come from doing any specific thing, but rather from doing whatever we do with a different orientation. "What?" is not a question that ever leads to wisdom.

The question, "What shall we do?" is also a self-alienated one, implying that we are unmotivated, unfeeling objects—suitable only for being manipulated by instruction for task purposes, like robots. The same attitude appears in the oft-heard and rather chilling phrase, "we must find ways of *motivating* them . . ." —as if people didn't have motives of their own, but were empty husks waiting to be filled up with needs and desires by social workers, educators, and other people-processors. We tend to define our actions from the outside, in terms of "problems" divorced from any connection with ourselves: "What shall we do about pollution?" instead of, "I'm sick of having my air spoiled, and I want to confront the people who are doing it and make them stop."

The quest for an action formula also expresses a desire to control the future, and even though no formula has ever delivered such control, the act of seeking it requires us to detach ourselves from our environment. Becoming attuned, on the other hand, means taking the risk that commitment always brings. If you commit yourself to a boat, it may sink; if you do not, you will never sink—but never sail either. Becoming attuned means committing one's fate to nature and allowing the possibility of death— the possibility that an environmental change might dissolve everything. In reality, of course, we take this chance anyway, despite all our bizarre security operations. The only way to avoid death is not to be alive in the first place. The only way to avoid the loss of love is never to love. And the only way to avoid obsolescence is never to finish anything. All of these solutions are rife in our society, where we talk a lot about risk-taking but do everything in our power to avoid it. When we assert the importance of flexibility, it is because we fear that we don't have it. What we *call* flexibility usually turns out to be detachment, noncommitment. Our talk of flexibility is nothing more than timidity: we know things are constantly in flux out there, and we tell each other to keep our options open and never put more than one toe in the water. What we fear is that if we committed ourselves wholly to any fixed course of action and it proved awkward, we would not have within ourselves the flexibility to respond in a way that would save us. In this we are probably correct since what detachment produces is in fact rigidity. One learns to swim by swimming—and to respond to shifting pressures by staying in touch with them. Such attunement means greater risk and pain as well as greater joy.

Despite our cultural training, the need to be in a state of risk —to test one's harmony with nature—runs deep in the human psyche. It surfaces in the love of being frightened and exposed to real or imagined physical dangers—an important feature of amusement parks. It surfaces in the love of active and somewhat risky attunement sports like skiing and surfing, in which enjoyment and skill involve moving in a state of sensitive harmony with and adaptation to natural forces. It surfaces in the love of gambling, in which one tests one's harmoniousness with the abstruse order of the universe. It surfaces in "tempting fate."

Champions and virtuosi in every field define their successful performance in terms of two opposing and compartmentalized theories. One stresses control, mastery, self-discipline, and technique. The other stresses innate gifts, inspiration, being psychologically ready or "together," and being in some sort of mystical harmony with the environment. In our society we tend to lay primary stress on the mastery theory and relegate the other to the realm of superstition.

Victor Gioscia points out, however, that we see and hear because our sense organs are synchronized with certain wave frequencies in the environment. We tend to think of seeing and hearing, with all their amplifications, in mastery terms, but in fact we see and hear because we are in harmony with these tiny parts of the environment. One can view great achievements from the same perspective, for they clearly depend upon being in the right place at the right time with the right experience and the right state of mind—in special synchrony with the surroundings.

When I speak of the content of action being less important than the internal orientation with which it is carried out, I have something like this in mind. The attunement attitude is sensorily and viscerally open, receptive, and responsive—capable of altering direction in response to feedback from within and without.

Attunement assumes a motivated and energetic presence. People who "play it by ear" in our society often have no idea what it is they want, and enter the situation with the same emotional and sensory deadness as those who come in highly programmed. Attunement involves an active, focussed responsivity.

Its opposite, the mastery attitude, reveals itself by its overt or covert goal of ego aggrandizement. People often object to remarks such as I have just made that they fail to provide a means for making a large enough impact on the system. They want to leave their mark. But this impulse to grandiosity is what continually recreates the sickness around us. Social action founded in pomposity is part of the problem, not part of the solution. Middle-class radical action often begins with people sitting around trying to figure out how they can make the biggest killing in social change terms and hence leave a monument to themselves. This is sometimes masked by assuming an earnest attitude of social responsibility and global guilt, but this is just spiritual pride. It is the height of pretension to assume active personal responsibility for a whole class or nation, although one might wish, out of a feeling of internal revulsion, to dissociate oneself from and oppose the acts of that class or nation. Responsibility begins and ends with being a responsive nerve ending for every system to which one belongs.

This does not mean that everyone must abandon hope of meaningful change occurring in their lifetime beyond their immediate environment. Good news travels fast, and the media, for all their faults, are hungry for social novelty and do a fair job of spreading it. Anyone who manages to generate around herself a more benign environment will find others engaging in similar processes before long. If one is concerned about having this known as the Mary or John Doe Plan, and implemented on a mass scale, it will soon become a malignant environment for most other people; but if the knowledge diffuses organically the innovation will be modified in a thousand different ways as it spreads and no one will bother about credit for the idea.

The problem is more complicated for oppressed groups, who may find that creating a more benign local environment arouses hostility from representatives of the diseased system. This will force them at the very least into self-defense and probably into a certain amount of willful mobilization. This was the experience of the Black Panthers, for example. Such mobilization arises spontaneously out of the immediate experience of acute oppression, however, and is not to be compared with the James Bond effusions of middle-class ideologues. Attunement requires something different from each person, but it may at times imply diametrically opposite behavior for people of different classes.

Directions

I am engaged here in a rather ironic enterprise: attempting to encourage people I do not know, through a linear abstract medium, to alter their orientation to the world in a way that should induce them to reject my effort as mechanical and invalid. Bearing this inconsistency in mind, I would like to summarize those of my remarks that have obvious prescriptive implications. These are not "things to do," but directions that seem healthy—not processes to initiate, but trends already under way and available for new energy inputs.

(1) *Decentralization.* The diffusion of power was a central tenet of the new left ("small is beautiful, big is ugly"). The old left, of course, favored the opposite trend and welcomed the increasing concentration of power within a few large corporations on the grounds that this would make them all the riper for nationalization. This is sound enough as a strategy, but the idea that changing the formal ownership of a giant bureaucracy would affect the way it functions exemplifies the infatuation with symbols that afflicts rationalistic thought.

Diffusion of power, however, raises issues of co-ordination. Mass organizations create at least the illusion that they provide a system for co-ordinating the activities of large numbers of people. This is largely a hoax, as we can see by the chaos and incoherence in which we live. The illusion is contrived by leaving out of the process of co-ordination almost everything that matters to people and making a great show of precision about the rest. At the same time it must be acknowledged that co-ordination in a decentralized condition requires a far greater output of energy on the part of each person. In the long run this energy output will not be greater in any real sense, since (a) free and equal communication is far more exhilarating than straining oneself through the coercive funnel of an impersonal bureaucracy, and (b) nothing causes a greater energy drain than feelings of helplessness and powerlessness. But so long as the traditional systems exist to create such drains it will seem effortful to transcend them.

What diffusion of power means, then, is the withdrawal of energy and interest from vertical (mass, bureaucratic, authoritarian) channels of communication and the reinvestment of this energy in lateral channels.

At present, centralization and decentralization are going on simultaneously. In traditional spheres the bases of power and wealth are becoming continually narrower. At the same time local alternative institutions organized in explicit antipathy to their large-scale counterparts are quietly proliferating. This means that while traditional organizations are becoming larger and more powerful, they are beginning to lose their human fuel. It will probably be twenty years or more before this begins to have significant effects, and real change will no doubt be achieved only after some serious confrontations have occurred. These confrontations will at first seem unequal—the powerful, armed, and organized few against the weaponless, dispersed, and unorganized many—but dispersion can be a source of strength as well as weakness (you can't shoot down a cloud), and the power loci will have become ambivalent and subject to infiltration by human beings.

An important example of power diffusion is the development of rank-and-file police organizations. The fact that these groups tend to voice reactionary sentiments has distracted most observers from the system effects of such action. There is a kind of naïveté, fostered by intellectuals and the media, that gives undue weight to ideology, but it really matters very little what beliefs these men espouse. What matters is that they have given up their position of powerlessness and are beginning to question their role as hatchet men for the middle class, a role in which they run all the risks and receive none of the rewards. As they refuse to expose themselves to absurd dangers, other solutions will have to be found by the authorities to whom they have heretofore been unquestioningly obedient. Collective action in one's own behalf is the cause, not the result, of sociological wisdom.

(2) *Deceleration.* Democracy is impossible in America for the simple reason that people move around too much to form the kind of stable community bonds on which democracy is founded. Mobility cuts away every opportunity for people to lean on each other and forces them to depend upon vertical bureaucratic systems for their needs. How can a people frame their wishes in political terms when they don't know each other well enough to talk to each other? Instead, questions are framed, defined, and asked by specialists, and answered individually, if at all, by people who have no way to explore their relational implications. Democracy is only possible with some minimal degree of interpersonal coagulation.

To be in transit, furthermore, is not to be really living, since one is during that period detached from her surroundings, either by being physically walled off in a metal vehicle, or psychically, by virtue of her role as observer-outsider. In America we are in transit a good proportion of the time, and the wind rushing past our ears makes us unable to hear our own viscera, or one another's. Our ideology, furthermore, has made us feel that our longing for roots is shameful and must be stifled or shoved in some handy orifice.

There are limits, however, to human malleability, and even Americans are showing signs of resistance to the demand that they trash their roots and march about continually in exile from one another ("keep moving, no loitering"). Interest in the past is reawakening, and the word "ritual" has become a favorite, even if no one knows what it means. It will take much longer for mobility to decrease, for the worse our environment gets, the faster people will move about in it, leaving each place as soon as they have spoiled it. But sooner or later, when all environments have become equally uninhabitable, people will have to make a commitment to their surroundings, and not treat them like motel rooms. Like all great social changes, it starts with not being ashamed.

(3) *Depolarization.* During periods of crisis the forms of specialization that we have learned to accept as the natural order of things must often be dissolved. To achieve this, we are forced to recognize our own internal multiplicity and confusion, both individually and collectively. The charade of ayes and nays must give way to a sensing of the internal debates masked by external polarization.

Conflict is essential to life, as is confrontation to communication. Depolarization does not soften conflict—it sharpens it and makes it real, stripping away false issues and allowing confrontation to be dynamic rather than static and compartmentalized. Depolarization simply means freeing ourselves from the prison of cultural role assignments and expressing our full humanity.

Depolarization can never be permanent. There is pleasure in assuming and playing out specialized roles, just as there is in putting on costumes and participating in rituals. Adults as well as children take joy in pretense—in enacting the steps of a complex interpersonal minuet and doing it well. Life is more than emotional expression, and the binding of tension in elegant forms is of intrinsic value. When the old specializations have been flooded out, new ones will emerge, in order that energy can be concentrated in certain parts of the social system, to be released as needed. Unfortunately, this energy binding tends gradually to become rigid and blocked, and depolarization is a way of flushing out the system from time to time so that it can rearrange itself more gracefully.

The form of the rearrangement does not concern us. Cultures cannot be planned, nor are they ever logical. They need only be coherent. Contradictions can abound quite comfortably, as long as the cultural patterning insulates the contradictory behaviors from one another, in time, space, or relationship. These satisfactory contradictions are arrived at through trial and error. Attempts to apply logic and principle are invariably fatal, since they seek to destroy the very contradictions on which social health depends.

The most important form of depolarization in our society today is the attack on sex roles by the women's movement. The division of labor by sex became a dangerous form of social rigidity as work ceased to be localized and became increasingly divorced from daily living. When men and women work in a shared environment the division of labor by sex is a harmless piece of social complexity. But when the work of a man is totally detached from the world his wife and children live in, the same division of labor becomes sinister. This is particularly true when the detached activity has priority, as is the case in our society, where the producer is always given priority over the consumer. Homes are supposed to follow jobs instead of the other way around, and if the husband-producer makes the environment less habitable this is tolerated as a necessary part of his work. Communities are more habitable and more coherent when the work of both husband and wife is within them and relevant to them. When the wife withdraws inward into the home and the husband withdraws outward to an outside workplace, both become atomized. Furthermore, when the husband works in a setting detached from his emotional and interpersonal life, his activities as a producer will be uninformed by those concerns and hence inhumane. And if the wife, meanwhile, is devoting her energies to home and children, detached from larger social issues, she will rear children defective in social responsiveness. In other words, if the husband tries to deal with the system without reference to the home, and the wife tries to deal with the home without reference to the system, both will do a wretched job.

The depolarizations sought by the women's movement would flood out these compartments and restore a necessary piece of social circuitry.

(4) *Reconnection*. The heightening of bilateral communication is implicit in all of the preceding trends, but it merits separate attention. Reconnection is a subtle process. It cannot be achieved by an attack of gregariousness, nor the widespread implementation of encounter-group norms—fundamentally geared to a ships-that-pass-in-the-night culture such as we now have. When people's lives and experiences are shared to a degree that permits reliable awareness of one another's emotional location, reconnection will occur spontaneously.

To achieve this it will first be necessary to deracinate the narcissistic cancer that has implanted itself in the core of Western culture. This may seem impossible at first glance—what aspect of our culture is not founded on narcissistic motivation? One riffles in vain through the Yellow Pages of the mind.

Yet there are certain root sources of narcissistic energy that can be and are being undermined—sexism, the Protestant Ethic, and the oedipal family being perhaps the most important. Sexism and the oedipal family are under full assault by the women's movement, while the Protestant Ethic has already entered what promises to be a long convulsive decline.

Furthermore, it would be a mistake to assume, as many people do, that narcissism is a kind of natural baseline toward which human beings automatically gravitate if not trained to do otherwise. It is a mistake, furthermore, that is taught by the culture— the very kernel of the individualistic delusion. Animals co-operate and are attuned to one another, as do humans unless taught not to. If a passer-by on the street starts to fall, our instinctive response is to catch her. This can be observed physiologically and kinesically. If we have time to think, however, to remember our urban armor, to perceive that the faller is drunk and/or filthy, to imagine ourself getting involved in an unpleasant scene, and so on, we are quite capable of inhibiting the impulse and letting the faller collapse to the ground. The mistake we make is in assuming that it is the inhibition rather than the catching response that is "natural." We do, in fact, have a rich repertoire of reconnective impulses to draw upon, were we able to establish the conditions under which they could again be released.

All of this has a nostalgic ring. One thinks again of the simple community, for the loss of which our hearts mourn and our heads rejoice. But the simple community is not a viable goal. Even if we could, what would be the sense in returning to a form of life that has already proven itself hopelessly vulnerable to the disease that now afflicts us? We must find an alternative to village life—one that contains antibodies to narcissism. What gave the simple community both its joy and its weakness was its localism. A viable alternative must make provision for global communication, however local in spirit it might wish to be. Communication is the single area in which it still seems reasonable to talk with any enthusiasm about growth.

This growth is not of the kind the technocrats would seek, however. The emphasis in communication technology thus far has been largely one of "conquering distance," which is the same old narcissistic enterprise. Communication growth will be of value only insofar as it is a *relational* increase rather than a hardware increase. For relational growth we do not need to add anything, we need merely to connect better.

One of the usual responses to a crisis, for example, is a sharp amplification of communication. The number of people remains constant, as does the number of communication channels available and the amount of hardware. It is the utilization of available channels that is drastically increased. This is done most efficiently by people flocking together, but it may also involve an increase in people contacting each other individually in person or by telephone.

This is a highly appropriate response but its meaning is often misunderstood. Our mechanical world view leads us to exaggerate the extent to which this communication is directed toward finding a "solution" to the crisis. In coherent communities, the communication is largely directed toward finding out how everyone *feels* about the crisis, how it affects the total network of relationships, and how the community can cope with it with the least damage to that network. Otherwise, instead of rushing into the street, making many phone calls, or holding meetings, it would simply be a matter of notifying the person or persons most capable of dealing with the external event.

In modern communities this is increasingly done. One calls the police or fire department or ambulance or Red Cross and may not even talk to a neighbor about it. In the most extreme case people may even hide away and not respond, but this denotes total social breakdown. Ordinarily, even in urban settings, calling the crisis expert is accompanied by some clustering of people.

The heightened communication that crisis brings in vital communities is for the purpose of exploring the potential relational changes posed by the crisis. But the interrelationships in bureaucracies are mechanically defined and do not change in any case. This is why they are so ponderous and so monumentally ineffectual relative to the number of human hours invested in them. The language of bureaucracies is digital language—they can deal competently with an infinite number of discrete events by sorting and classifying, but almost by definition they have no mechanism whatever for dealing with the relationships among those events, and consequently break down whenever called upon to do this. When finally forced to confront a serious crisis, people in bureaucracies typically suspend the bureaucratic structure altogether and shift to an *ad hoc*, informal mode of organization.

Most people are able to make a threefold distinction between mental alertness, knowledge, and wisdom or understanding. The first concerns the rapidity with which new bits of data can be assimilated, the second the number of bits already assimilated, while the third refers to the capacity to appreciate complex interrelationships. The first has always been the province of the young, while the second and third have been traditionally reserved for the old. The knowledge sphere has now been reassigned to the young in response to the information explosion, and even wisdom is no longer attributed to the old. Since the old know so little about the new bits of data, it is assumed that they cannot very well discuss their interrelationships, although in fact the understanding of relationships transcends the content of those relationships, and hence the old have a fund of untapped wisdom which is wasted.

The old are rightly indignant at the elevation of youth. The young are as ignorant as ever about relational questions, and it must be profoundly irritating to hear accolades offered to people who are continually reinventing the wheel. Yet at the same time the old have only themselves to blame for this, since they have abdicated their proper realm in order to invade mechanical domains in which they have nothing special to contribute. Had they sustained their interest in relational matters they might have preserved their birthright. Now there are "experts" even in relational areas to which those seeking wisdom are referred, to their eternal discontent. For an expert cannot by definition have wisdom, since he only possesses information accumulated within a single compartment. He knows nothing of relationships—of "the larger interactive system . . . which, if disturbed, is likely to generate exponential curves of change" (Bateson)—and can only offer as a substitute the fatuities of his field.

An alternative to village life which would be non-cancerous and yet resistant to external cancerous influences would have to place an emphasis on relational thinking and relational language that is utterly foreign to most Westerners. We would have to start thinking in terms of networks and images rather than numbered boxes. Let me give two examples:

(a) When we become aware that a muscle is tense we try to relax that muscle. Following Western medical thinking, we approach the body one segment at a time, imagining that comfort will be achieved when we have tracked down each and every muscle and relaxed it. Escape from wire-taut rigidity is sought by collapsing into a state of corpselike flaccidity. Forcing ourselves into utter submission to gravity, however, is not necessarily a source of comfort. We feel good not when every muscle is flaccid, but when there is a balanced distribution of energy throughout the organism. Tension is not a matter of one malfunctioning part, but of a bad distribution of energy flow. A tense muscle in one part of the body usually means that others nearby are flabby and immobilized, so that the tense one is doing work for the others. Relief is as likely to come from activating the inert areas as from trying to immobilize the overworked ones.

(b) Political science is the study of various bad substitutes for organic relationships. Of necessity they all take as their premise the lack of adequate interpersonal communication. What could be more meaningless, for example, than a vote—a binary response considered apart from the role of the responder or the responder's relationships to all other responders? It is like asking all the cells in a fingernail to decide individually whether they are for or against red corpuscles. Yet the vote is supposedly the foundation of our own political system—we are indeed fortunate that the reality of politics is as far removed from this sort of thing as it is. One can count and classify cells for an eternity and still not have an organism. It is the relationships among units that determine their meaning, not the units themselves.

A perceptive young secretary in a university department once remarked that 80 per cent of her work was unnecessary and could be eliminated if there was any trust in the academic community. The same is true of the kinds of decisions that committees make and remake. Since no one is very intensely connected with anyone else, issues must be dealt with in terms of policy and precedent. Earnest voices are always raised to caution that precedents are being set, but a few months later it is hard for anyone to remember why they had ever wanted what they had legislated with such difficulty. Organizations live for years with procedures that came into being as an adaptation to the eccentricities or skills or incompetencies of a single person, long since departed. The truth is, it would take less time and be far more enjoyable if decisions were frankly treated in terms of personal needs and interpersonal relationships instead of pretending that only abstract principles were involved.

Institutions are like trees. The green living part consists of relationships between people. As these become habitual they leave a dead deposit in the form of structures and procedures. Like a tree trunk, the dead deposit grows continually larger, while the living matter clings to the outside of it. The dead tissue of the trunk is much easier to understand than the living tissue of the bark, and can be more easily dealt with in quantitative terms. It is easy to lose sight of where the life is because the tree still looks very imposing after it is completely dead.

Reconnection is a matter of remaining part of the bark instead of pretending to be a hunk of cellulose—of remembering that the splendid isolation of the human ego is a schizoid fantasy. Primitive peoples know that we are part of one another and of our environment. The primitive hunter begs pardon from the animals he kills because he recognizes their common immersion in an ecological whole. The hunter may err in behaving as if his act of courtesy would affect the animal population, but he would never make the gross error of behaving as if there were no relationship.

Distinctions

I have spoken about reconnection, about responding to internal sensations, about being a good social nerve ending, about recapturing primitive awareness. Such remarks are subject to heavy misinterpretation, since they call up associations to the familiar and useless categories with which we customarily define our experience. For academics this reflex will be irresistible, no matter how much explanation is given, but for those interested in ideas and difficult modes of perception I would like to offer some words of clarification and differentiation—to state what attunement and responsivity are *not*.

They do not imply passivity or fatalism. An organic response is a *response*. For oppressed groups, for example, it might well be social or political action of the usual kind: community organizing, boycotts, demonstrations, and so on. These may be done with varying degrees of attunement for, to repeat, it is less a matter of *what* than *how*. The more the communication takes place solely among those who already think alike, for example, the less it can be considered a force for health. Activity carried out in a mechanical, non-responsive way can be as numbing as passivity. Confrontation is almost always of value, but the best confrontation is one that is bilateral. Guerrilla theater, for example, is usually as much a one-way communication as a lecture and hence just about as effective. Successful confrontations are usually interactive, sometimes violently so.

Americans often feel a little uneasy if they are not engaged in frenetic activity, preferably of an uncomfortable and toilsome variety that betokens victory over their inner inertia. But everyone feels more active and hopeful at some times than others, and there is no particular virtue in futile struggling—a discouragement that is attended to usually lasts a shorter time than one that is not. On the other hand, nothing breeds a sense of helplessness and hopelessness like anger that finds no mode of expression whatever. To walk this tightrope requires great sensitivity.

They are not synonymous with "spontaneity." This is a particularly difficult distinction to make since I have placed so much emphasis on internal feeling states. I have suggested that one's own emotional state is usually a valid index of the functioning of the system in which one participates. I have further argued that one has an obligation—a duty, even—to express that emotional state in some form or another in order that the system can function in a healthy manner, since no system can operate humanely without adequate feedback. Does this not imply a kind of visceral despotism: that whatever I am feeling is real and valid and important and should be acted upon?

One could make a case for such pure impulsivity from a societal perspective, since it does insure a high level of emotional information for the system. Unfortunately, as we all know, it is ultimately fatal for the individual organism, and hence constitutes a kind of kamikaze approach to ecological well-being. Furthermore, since all social systems are structured to limit feedback to some extent, an unfocussed impulsive response, even if disastrous for the individual, may go unregistered by the system. Even a hurt child has brains enough not to waste her tears on empty space, but runs to find a parent before venting her unhappiness.

A more serious limitation on spontaneity lies in the fact that our own viscera are quite seriously corrupted by cultural learning and cannot be completely relied upon as a valid index even of our own emotional state, much less that of the system. All feelings have been tampered with, and tend to express themselves through roundabout channels. For some, the angry channel is constricted, and they tend to feel tearful when angry. For others, the tears channel is blocked and they tend to feel angry when hurt or sad. Others have headaches or stomach pains, and so on. Distress in general is a valid index that the system is hurting and hurtful, but great specificity is not to be sought. It may be true, as anti-psychoanalytic therapies maintain, that no one knows the truth about another's psyche, but it is also true, as the psychoanalysts maintain, that no one knows the truth about himself, either. It is pure pomposity to imagine that our expressed impulses have any more emotional validity than those of our uptight neighbors. Access to our own feelings is spurious in the absence of access to those of others.

"Spontaneity" in our culture tends still to be imbued with narcissistic goals. There is still much invidiousness in our play, much posing, much seeking after admiration and special status. The ideology of free expression is often used to sanctify recognition-seeking without discipline, which is the worst of both worlds for the audience, who must put up with the artist or performer's narcissism without getting anything back. As a friend put it, in response to the artistic effusions of college students: "They all want to have their shit cast in bronze."

They are not necessarily attained through personal development. Since socialization in Western culture makes it dangerous to trust one's own impulses with too great specificity, it might seem logical to devote one's efforts to self-cure, self-mastery, enlightenment, spiritual development, personal growth, or whatever. This position implies that if one achieves personal harmony, then harmony with nature will automatically follow, which is a little like saying that the best way to cement a friendship with a man is to have a love affair with his wife. It might be, of course, but then again it might not. Being attuned to someone is not the same as total identity with her. My own experience with those who have energetically sought internal harmony, with some sense of success, is that they have simply become detached —whether or not this was an explicit goal. And although they often *feel* in harmony with those around them this is usually illusory and unreciprocated. Their feeling of being attuned is merely that of going stoned to a beautiful movie—one is highly sensitized to, appreciative of, identified with others, but disengaged from them—observing and experiencing but not interacting. This is not to say that such a state cannot lead to attunement, for it sometimes does. But it is not the same thing as attunement, which requires an extra step, an external focus. And since the choice to turn inward is not random, that step is rarely made.

To become internally harmonious is to become disharmonious with one's past and cultural environment, since these are what created disharmony in the first place. There is no way to escape all this—it is all part of our being. One cannot become truly harmonious—inside and out—in a discordant world. One can only seek greater harmony within and without simultaneously.

A frequent delusion in this kind of effort is that the part of oneself that seeks internal harmony is one's own, while all the disharmony was somehow imposed from without. Similarly, middle-class Americans trying to overcome their personality difficulties tend to be deterministic about their problems, seeing them as inculcated by their parents and culture. Yet they imagine that their strengths—that with which they strive to overcome these problems—spring full-blown from their own wills, like Athene from the head of Zeus. But if hang-ups come from parents and society, so does the ability to overcome them. And if it is the self that is integrated and overcoming, it is also the self that is being integrated and overcome. And if the hang-ups are manifestations of society, *so is the self that integrates and cures.* We are part of all we experience, however repulsive it may seem, and without an outward focus all is illusion.

They do not imply conformity. Stressing the importance of reconnection is sometimes interpreted as advocating some kind of conformity or "fitting in," although in fact it demands the precise opposite. Avoiding a cybernetic connectedness with the environment by presenting a false conventional self to the world is a schizoid strategy. "Fitting in," furthermore, is a mechanical concept, appropriate to inanimate blocks of matter. It makes the absurd assumption that a one-way adaptation between two organisms is possible—an idea only an individualistic culture could invent. For at bottom conformity and egoism amount to exactly the same thing—an inability to be fully present and emotionally engaged with another person.

Attunement would require us to abandon our automatic tendency to suppress or ignore our visceral reactions to our surroundings. For to ignore, fail to respond to, or wall oneself off from the existing milieu is to maintain it. "Doing your own thing" usually turns out to be a mechanistic process of responding to observable messages from within and ignoring external feedback. Restoring connectedness means reacting—protesting when injured, expressing pleasure when pleased. The institutions we endure today are oppressive because they suffer from a shortage of feedback. They are not without blame for this, of course, since they insulate themselves from feedback as much as possible. But we need to overcome our learned deference to the inhuman and unresponsive projections of our mechanical egos—bureaucracies, machines, structures, statuses, degrees—and transfer this courtesy and consideration to human beings and other living things.

Sometimes humans act as agents of mechanical systems—presenting themselves as mere extensions of an organization or profession, subordinating themselves to their status, position, or some symbol of achieved mediocrity—an M.D. or Ph.D. To the degree that they act in this way they have renounced their humanity and cannot claim to be treated as human beings. Hence a retaliatory cycle is activated: In their "official capacity" they act in an inhumane way, but if we retaliate they feel that hurt at some level as human beings and become both more official (to protect themselves) and more inhumane (for revenge). This is unfortunate but should not lead us to misdirect our sympathies. We are obligated only to allow such persons a moment to reveal whether they will choose to be human or official—the moment they have chosen the latter their claim to have their human feelings considered must be disallowed, since they have opted out of human circuitry. If one wishes to try a conversion—to attempt to reach their humanity through the screen of their self-obliteration, this is a highly desirable enterprise but an ambitious one, fraught with emotional risk. It is important in such cases to maintain clear awareness that the respect and consideration are directed toward the person, not the structure. The only valid index of the accuracy of the effort is the degree to which it detaches the person *from* the structure.

People defend official behavior in terms of the necessity of "getting their job done." To reveal the emptiness of this statement it is only necessary to ask, in as large a way as possible, just what the "job" is. Is medical arrogance healing? Does academic nitpicking inculcate wisdom? Does police brutality protect the people? Do hospital procedures nurture the sick? Do phone company procedures facilitate communication?

One could easily spend her life in such confrontations, and a joyless life it would be: I certainly do not want to advocate walking about unarmed on a battlefield. Yet it is important to be aware that every act of self-restraint in relation to an inhumane structure constitutes positive feedback for that structure—a vote of confidence. Our definitions of "responsibility" have always placed a heavy emphasis on self-control, but "response-ability" means responsivity or it means nothing at all.

To be focussed only on one's own viscera, of course, is not

attunement. Never to accommodate is as mechanical as to accommodate all the time. I feel the need to accent the importance of disruption and protest in relation to mechanical structures because we are so subservient to them. Educated people have learned to say "sick" in place of "wicked" when confronted with individual life-styles and behavior patterns they dislike, but they routinely accept the most bizarre institutions with complete equanimity. In part this is due to an inability to see pathology in the powerful and successful—the achievement of high status is *ipso facto* regarded by psychiatrists, psychologists, and social workers as a criterion of mental health ("he is functioning well") while lack of interest in self-aggrandizement is "ego-weakness." National leaders in their official capacities at times exhibit behavior that would be considered frankly psychotic in one less eminent, and without arousing a ripple of alarm. But the inability to see institutions as pathological extends far beyond the blind acceptance of their representatives. We not only accept warped and brutal institutions as normal, but think nothing of employing psychiatrists and psychologists to persuade perfectly healthy people to adjust to them. Yet the inculcation of sado-masochistic attitudes in military training camps, of fascistic attitudes in high schools, and of feminine self-hatred in marriage is more crippling psychically for those who succeed in these patterns than for those who fail.

One final caution is necessary. If we stop ingratiating ourselves with our mechanical extensions, this should be an end in itself, not a way of making some comment about ourselves. Americans tend to seize any opportunity to prove their uniqueness and specialness, but if this is the motive, the enterprise becomes worse than useless—it actively nourishes the disease. Since we are all unique to begin with, the effort to *make* oneself unique is suspect. It attempts to deny a truth that Americans find particularly hard to swallow: Our differentness is not a personal achievement but a function of our participation in a larger entity. Diversity is created by groups—individuals would arrive at the same place without some kind of human support system, since they would then be entirely programmed by inner circuitry, which is more or less uniform. Connectedness involves a recognition that uniqueness is a collective product.

Epilogue

We are born into intimate mutual-feedback relationships with our environments, both human and non-human. Commitments to fantasy break this circuit. Signals are ignored, and behavior becomes mechanical, insensitive. The environment hurts me, but I am intent on a remote, fantastic goal, and I do not cry out but forge ahead. Machine that I have become, I hurt the environment and it cries out, but I cannot hear it, intent as I am on remote, fantastic goals. Indeed, there is a certain retributive justice to it: I torture the environment, it tortures me. A positive-feedback spiral is launched, for the more I make myself into a machine, the more I will tend to torture the environment, and the more the environment tortures me back, the more I need to make myself into a machine.

We have mocked primitive humans for imagining themselves to be one with nature. We "know" that we are separate from the environment. We have mastered it. Indeed, we have declared war on it, and we have won. We have defeated the air, crushed the sea, slaughtered the land, and stand alone in glorious victory, sick and gasping, like an infant who has triumphed over its mother.

All the errors and follies of magic, religion, and mystical traditions are outweighed by the one great wisdom they contain—the awareness of humanity's organic embeddedness in a complex natural system. And all the brilliant, sophisticated insights of Western rationalism are set at naught by the egregious delusion on which they rest—that of human autarchy.

The achievements of Western culture are materialized dreams, and since they were only made possible by the strangling of our feelings, they have increasingly materialized the evil in man—perverse brutality, whining arrogance, cruel obsessiveness, and devouring power-hunger. And when all these mangled impulses have been given physical form we will be unable to see the sky or the trees or any living thing, so inundated will we be by the machinery we have vomited up from our ulcerated insides.

To reclaim ourselves and our environment we need to drain energy from the narcissistic tumor that possesses us; to listen, sense, and be here; to retrieve what we have cast off, to repossess what we have projected onto others, to make whole what we have truncated; to move together in a reciprocal dance of integrity and grace. We keep searching for the stargate, but it is not hidden. Hovering delicately in the spaces between things, it has been there all the time.

Notes

page 1. Alexander Lowen, *Betrayal of the Body* (Collier Books, 1969), p. 231.

2., para. 4 Lowen, *Betrayal*, p. 116.

5., para. 2 Gregory Bateson, *Steps to an Ecology of Mind* (Ballantine Books, 1972); Norman O. Brown, *Life Against Death* (Vintage, 1959); David Bakan, *The Duality of Human Existence* (Beacon, 1966); William Irwin Thompson, *At the Edge of History* (Harper, 1972).

7. I am indebted to Bruno Beretta for this parable.

9. Bateson, *Steps*, p. 18.

11. Norman O. Brown, *Love's Body* (Random House, 1966), p. 147.

12., para. 4 Grace Stuart, *Narcissus* (Macmillan, 1955), p. 45.

16., para. 2 Ross V. Speck and Carolyn L. Attneave, *Family Networks* (Pantheon, 1973).

16–17. Kiyo Morimoto, "On Trying to Understand the Frustrations of Students" (Harvard University Bureau of Study Counsel, 1972). I also learned about choice from discussions with Fatima Mernissi.

18. Brown, *Love's Body*, p. 184.

20., para. 2 Norbert Wiener, *The Human Use of Human Beings* (Avon, 1967), pp. 129–41.

para. 3 Alvin Toffler, *Future Shock* (Bantam, 1970), pp. 197–215.

22., para. 2 Weston La Barre, *The Human Animal* (University of Chicago Press, 1954), p. 258.

para. 3 Sigmund Freud, "The 'Uncanny,'" in *Collected Papers*, Vol. IV (Hogarth, 1953), pp. 368–407.

23., para. 2 Henri Bergson, *Laughter, An Essay on the Meaning of the Comic* (Macmillan, 1911), pp. 8 ff., 37 ff.

24–25. From Fatima Mernissi.

page 28., para. 3 Toffler, *Future Shock*, pp. 359–64, 428–31, 449–52.

30., para. 1 Bateson, *Steps*, p. 433. What is said here about medicine applies equally well to our approach to social ailments. For malfunctioning part, simply read "party or parties responsible," and for germs read "outside agitators."

32., para. 2 René Dubos, *Mirage of Health* (Harper, 1959), pp. 1–52, 68–72, 80–108.

——, *Man, Medicine, and Environment* (Mentor, 1969), pp. 88–94, 106 ff.; Toffler, *Future Shock*, pp. 325–42.

para. 4 Irving K. Zola, "Medicine as an Institution of Social Control," *The Sociological Review*, 20 (November 1972), pp. 487–504; K. White, et al., "International Comparisons of Medical Care Utilization," *New England Journal of Medicine*, 277 (1967), pp. 516–22.

35. Sandra Levinson and Carol Brightman, *Venceremos Brigade* (Simon and Schuster, 1971), pp. 166–67.

37. Plato, *Phaedo*, 67; Lowen, *Betrayal*, p. 231; K. Kristofferson and F. Foster, *Me and Bobby McGee*.

38., para. 4 Donella H. Meadows, et al., *The Limits To Growth* (Signet, 1972).

38–39. Most of these growth figures are from Toffler, *Future Shock*, pp. 9–35.

39., para. 1 For animal activity, see Ashley Montague, *Touching* (Columbia University Press, 1971), pp. 15–25.

39., para. 2 Dubos, *Man, Medicine*, p. 97; David Bakan, *Disease, Pain and Sacrifice* (University of Chicago Press, 1968), pp. 19–31.

para. 4 Bakan, Ibid., p. 36.

40., para. 3 Toffler, *Future Shock*, pp. 35, 403, 412, 428–29, 458, 460, 468.

40–41. Leon J. Yarrow, "Separation from Parents During Early Childhood," in Martin L. Hoffman and Lois Wladis Hoffman (eds.) *Review of Child Development Research*, Vol. I (Russell Sage Foundation, 1964), pp. 89–136; Gerald Caplan, *Mental Health Aspects of Social Work in Public Health* (School of Social Welfare, University of California, Berkeley, 1955), pp. 123–33. For schizophrenia, see Bateson, *Steps*, pp. 201–27; R. D. Laing, *The Politics of the Family* (Pantheon, 1971); R. D. Laing and A. Esterson, *Sanity, Madness and the Family: Families of Schizophrenics* (Basic Books, 1970); Theodore Lidz, et al., *Schizophrenia and the Family* (International Universities Press, 1965).

41–42. Some readers will realize that I am discussing, in a brutally oversimplified fashion, the issue of universalism versus particularism. Cf. Talcott Parsons, *The Social System* (Free Press, 1951); Max Weber, *The Protestant Ethic and the Spirit of Capitalism* (Allen and Unwin, 1930). For the limitations of authoritarianism, see Warren Bennis and Philip Slater, *The Temporary Society* (Harper, 1968), Chaps. 1 and 3.

44., para. 3 Marshall McLuhan, *Understanding Media* (McGraw-Hill, 1964).

45., para. 4 R. D. Laing, *The Divided Self* (Pelican, 1965), pp. 80 ff., 139 ff.

46., para. 4 Ibid., p. 162.

47., para. 3 Philip Slater, *The Glory of Hera* (Beacon, 1968), Chap. 2; Bruno Bettelheim, *Symbolic Wounds* (Thames and Hudson, 1955).

48., para. 1 C. S. Lewis, *That Hideous Strength* (Macmillan, 1965), p. 46.

49–50. La Barre, *Human Animal*, pp. 258–59, 268.

50–51. Ibid., pp. 240 ff., 246, 260.

51., para. 1 This statement about social fictions is a paraphrase of W. I. Thomas' famous dictum about situations defined as real being real in their consequences. See W. I. Thomas and D. S. Thomas, *The Child in America* (Knopf, 1928), p. 572.

51., para. 2 La Barre, op. cit., pp. 267–68.

52., para. 1 Bateson, *Steps*, p. 434.

55., para. 3 Erich Fromm, *Man for Himself* (Rinehart, 1947); David Riesman, *The Lonely Crowd* (Anchor, 1950), and *Individualism Reconsidered* (Free Press, 1964); William H. Whyte, Jr., *The Organization Man* (Simon and Schuster, 1956); George Orwell, *1984* (Signet, 1961). For imprinting, see Lorenz, *King Solomon's Ring*, pp. 59–61.

56., para. 2 Fritz Perls, *Gestalt Therapy Verbatim* (Real People Press, 1969), p. 154. The Gestalt prayer (p. 4) involves the same lonely-but-brave scenario that has always been popular in protestant cultures, and can be seen as an updated version of the stiff upper lip. It mimics traditional American WASP independence training, and serves as delayed socialization for people with possessive and overprotective parents.

56–57. Marcia Millman, "Nightmare or Paradise?" *Social Change* (in press); Ray Bradbury, *Fahrenheit 451* (Ballantine, 1966); Aldous Huxley, *Brave New World* (Bantam,

1966); George Orwell, *1984* (Signet, 1961); Eugene Zamiatin, *We* (Dutton, 1952).

page 58., para. 3 Cf., e.g., The Performance Group, *Dionysus in 69*, ed. by Richard Schechner (Farrar, Straus, & Giroux, 1970).

58–59. Bakan, *Duality*, p. 89.

60., para. 1 Lowen, *Betrayal*, pp. 38–42.

para. 2 Ibid., pp. 42–43.

61., para. 2 Freud, *Civilization and Its Discontents* (Norton, 1961), p. 62. Lowen, op. cit., p. 257.

para. 3 Ibid., p. 258.

63., para. 2 Laing, *Divided Self*, p. 80.

para. 3 Ibid., pp. 80, 86, 95.

64., para. 2 Bakan, op. cit., p. 89.

para. 3 Laing, op. cit., p. 151.

para. 4 Ibid., pp. 142–43.

65. Ibid., pp. 144–45, 151, 158.

69. Lao Tzu, *Tao Te Ching*, trans. by D. C. Lau (Penguin, 1963), Book One, XIX; Idries Shah, *Wisdom of the Idiots* (Octagon, 1969), p. 13.

69., para. 1 Wiener, *Human Use*, p. 31.

70., para. 3 My book *Microcosm* (Wiley, 1966) is an elaborate description of this process.

72., para. 3 La Barre, *Human Animal*, p. 246.

74., para. 2 On human roles, see Bennis and Slater, *Temporary Society*, pp. 79–87.

77., para. 1 Toffler, *Future Shock*, p. 99.

77–78. William N. Stephens, *The Family in Cross-Cultural Perspective* (Holt, Rinehart and Winston, 1963), pp. 325–39.

78., para. 2 Bennis and Slater, *Temporary Society*, Chaps. 1–3.

80., para. 2 Sigmund Freud, *Totem and Taboo* (Norton, 1950).

para. 4 Stephens, *Family*, pp. 338–39; G. Rattray Taylor, *Sex in History* (Ballantine, 1954); Philip Slater, "Culture, Sexuality, and Narcissism," *Social Change* (in press).

81., para. 2 Weber, *Protestant Ethic*, pp. 121, 153–54.

para. 3 Philippe Ariès, *Centuries of Childhood* (Knopf, 1962), pp. 71–72.

84., para. 2 Notably Emile Durkheim, *The Division of Labor in Society* (Free Press, 1933).

87., para. 3 Slater, *Glory of Hera, passim.*

para. 5 H. R. Hays, *The Dangerous Sex* (Putnam, 1964), pp. 17–21.

88., para. 2 Bennis and Slater, *Temporary Society*, Chaps. 1 and 2.

90., para. 1 Slater, *Glory of Hera*, Chap. 1.

para. 3 Bateson, *Steps*, pp. 309–37.

91., para. 2 See, for example, Alice Ryerson, "Medical Advice on Child-rearing Practices: 1550–1900." Unpublished doctoral dissertation, Harvard University Graduate School of Education, 1960; Montague, *Touching*, pp. 122–26.

para. 3 Ibid., pp. 131–37.

para. 4 Ibid., pp. 126–31.

94., para. 3 David Riesman, *Individualism Reconsidered*, pp. 99–120.

95., para. 1 Richard Bach, *Jonathan Livingston Seagull* (Avon, 1970). Quotations from pp. 27, 29, 30, 41, 57, 58, 60, 61, 64, 65, 86, 88, 106, 112, 114, 120–21; Gary Shaw, *Meat on the Hoof* (St. Martin's Press, 1972); Philip Roth, *Our Gang* (Bantam, 1971).

96., para. 1 Dori Appel Slater points out that in the counter-culture the quest for internal mastery has largely replaced the worldly variety.

97., para. 3 Wilhelm Reich, *Character-Analysis* (Noonday Press, 1962), pp. 248 ff.

98., para. 2 Montague, Ibid., p. 82.

para. 4 Reich, Ibid.

100., para. 2 Theodore Rosebury, *Life on Man* (Viking, 1969).

para. 3 I am indebted to Jacqueline Larcombe Doyle for this observation.

105. Lao Tzu, *Tao Te Ching*, Book One, XIII; Sophocles, *Oepidus the King*, trans. by David Grene (University of Chicago Press, 1959), 1074–80.

106., para. 3 This discussion of the family as a class system describes a norm. There is of course considerable variation in actual behavior from group to group and family to family. The American middle-class family system is more "democratic" than any European type, just as its social class behavior is less formal. The structures, however, are identical in both cases.

109., para. 4 Apollodorus, III, 5, 8. See also the note on p. 347 of the Loeb Library edition.

110., para. 2 Sophocles, *Oed. Tyr.*, 1460–65.

para. 3 Ibid., 103–32.

111., para. 3 Compare the anti-oedipal Stephen Stills song a generation later: "If you can't be with the one you love, love the one you're with." Contemporary popular music shows a striking decline in oedipal romanticism. Even when relationships between young men and older women are portrayed the people involved are real rather than idealized—replete with wrinkles, hang-ups, and bad jokes, along with their more endearing qualities.

page 113., para. 2 Toffler, *Future Shock*, pp. 117–18.

para. 4 David McClelland, *The Achieving Society* (Van Nostrand, 1961), pp. 342, 345, 404–6. A Russian study, which I have not yet seen, purportedly finds that the fathers of "great men" are older than the average. If this is true, it would obviously fit the interpretation suggested here. Freud's own oedipal conflict was profoundly affected by his father's age.

115., para. 2 Alexander Lowen, *Pleasure* (Lancer, 1970), p. 85. Italics mine.

115–116. For a more extensive discussion of this principle, see "Prolegomena to a Psychoanalytic Theory of Aging and Death," in R. Kastenbaum (ed.), *New Thoughts on Old Age* (Springer, 1964), pp. 19–40.

118., para. 2 Riesman, *Lonely Crowd*, pp. 31 ff.

119., para. 2 John Cuber and Peggy Harroff, *Sex and the Significant Americans* (Pelican, 1965), pp. 172–75, 180.

para. 4 Ibid., p. 180.

124., para. 4 Bateson, *Steps*, p. 300.

125., para. 2 McClelland, Ibid., p. 405; Slater, *Glory of Hera*.

126., para. 4 Vivian Gornick, "The Next Great Moment in History Is Theirs," *The Village Voice*, November 27, 1969; Matina Horner, "Toward an Understanding of Achievement-Related Conflicts in Women," *Journal of Social Issues*, 28, 1972, pp. 157–75.

127., para. 2 Montague, *Touching*, pp. 272–74.

128., para. 2 Bakan, *Duality*, p. 15.

para. 3 Ibid., pp. 113–20, 122–24.

132., para. 3 Edward Devereux has suggested to me that it is the decline in parental role specialization that is responsible for the weakening of oedipal trends in our society.

133., para. 2 Philippe Ariès, *Centuries of Childhood*, pp. 33–34, 38–39, 50 ff.

para. 3 Ibid., pp. 47, 50–53, 57–58, 71, 100 ff., 130–33, 329–36, 369, 375, 398–400; Ryerson, "Medical Advice."

134., para. 3 Ariès, op. cit., pp. 59, 61, 92–93, 99, 314.

135. Adapted from a report in the Boston *Globe*, March 1972, by Crocker Snow, Jr.

137. Lao Tzu, *Tao Te Ching*, Book Two, LXXVII; C. S. Lewis, *Hideous Strength*, p. 173.

138–139. Toffler, *Future Shock*, pp. 334–36.

139., para. 2 See, e.g., Dubos, *Mirage of Health; Man, Medicine and Environment;* Toffler, op. cit., pp. 327–42.

139–140. Cf. Bakan, *Duality*, p. 88. For the most extensive and intelligent discussion of this relationship, see Victor Gioscia, *Time Forms* (Gordon and Breach, in press), from which this paragraph is derived.

143., para. 2 Dubos, *Mirage*, pp. 109–39.

146., para. 2 Bateson, *Steps*, p. 4.

147., para. 3 See Slater, "Social Bases of Personality," in Neil J. Smelser (ed.), *Sociology: An Introduction* (Wiley, 1973), Second Ed., pp. 612–24.

149., para. 2 Sigmund Freud, "Negation," in *Collected Papers*, Vol. V., pp. 181–85.

150–151. Toffler, op. cit., pp. 365, 405, 449–52, 460, 467, 480. Italics mine.

152., para. 3 Toffler, op. cit., pp. 360, 393, 428–31, 450–52, 474.

154., para. 2 Lowen, *Pleasure*, p. 108.

155., para. 2 Arthur Janov, *The Primal Scream* (Putnam, 1970), p. 146.

para. 3 René Dubos, *Mirage*, p. 228; *Time*, December 4, 1972, p. 39.

156., para. 2 Cf. Norman Brown, *Life Against Death*.

157., para. 3 China and Cuba may seem to be exceptions to this statement, but are in fact illustrations of it. Revolutions bring about change only insofar as they represent a *diffusion* of power. The innovations are *brought into* a new power center *collectively* and from outside by a disadvantaged group. The decrees of the revolutionary leader merely certify the diffusion of power. If they fail to do this, no real social change is involved and the leaders are considered to have "betrayed the revolution."

161. Saul Bellow, *Mr. Sammler's Planet* (Fawcett, 1971), p. 53; Lao Tzu, *Tao Te Ching*, Book One, XX.

164., para. 1 Gioscia, *Time Forms;* Dubos, *Mirage*, pp. 5–14.

164–165. Elaine Cumming, "Allocation of Care to the Mentally Ill, American Style," in Mayer N. Zald (ed.), *Organizing for Community Welfare* (Quadrangle, 1967).

168–169. Cf. Joseph Chilton Pearce, *The Crack in the Cosmic Egg* (Pocket, 1973); Sheila Ostrauder and Lynn Schroeder,

Psychic Discoveries Behind the Iron Curtain (Bantam, 1971).

page 169., para. 2 I am indebted to Jacqueline Larcombe Doyle for this example.

169–170. This paragraph is based on conversations with Jacqueline Larcombe Doyle.

171., para. 1 Bateson, *Steps*, p. 69.

171–172. Ibid., pp. 356–57.

172., para. 1 Toffler, op. cit., p. 391.

173., para. 1 Michel Foucault, *Madness and Civilization* (Mentor, 1967), pp. 18–31.

para. 3 Robert A. Dentler and Kai T. Erikson, "The Functions of Deviance in Groups," *Social Problems*, VII (fall, 1959), pp. 98–107, quoted in Lewis A. Coser, "Some Functions of Deviant Behavior and Normative Flexibility," *American Journal of Sociology*, 68, 1962, p. 175.

174., para. 3 Lewis Mumford, "The Fallacy of Systems," *Saturday Review*, October 1949; Foucault, op. cit., p. 170.

177., para. 2 Erving Goffman, *Asylums* (Anchor, 1961).

179., para. 3 R. D. Laing, *The Politics of the Family* (Pantheon, 1971), pp. 77–81.

185. Idries Shah, *The Exploits of the Incomparable Mulla Nasrudin* (Dutton, 1972), p. 16.

187., para. 2 Laing, op. cit., pp. 103–16; Bateson, op. cit., pp. 201–43.

188–189. Montague, *Touching*, pp. 65 ff., 230–55, and *passim*.

190., para. 2 Benjamin Spock, *The Common Sense Book of Baby and Child Care*, Rev. Ed. (Duell, Sloan, & Pearce, 1957), pp. 3–10, 48–49.

193., para. 3 Gioscia, *Time Forms*, p. 75.

195., para. 2 A fund of wisdom about the issues involved in size, collective life, and mass power can be found in a counter-culture pamphlet called *Methods of Organization for Collectives*, which can be obtained from *Anti-mass*, Box 31352, San Francisco, California 94114.

202., para. 1 Bateson, op. cit., p. 433.

INDEX

Exploitation
consequences of, 42
legitimate, 125
Extensions of man, technology and,
9–34
arrogant virtues, 26–27
autarchy, 17–18
automaton behavior, 22–23
boosters of, 33
"cannot be stopped" argument, 34
community network system, 15–16
control, 9–14
courage and perseverance, 23–26
genetic code, 19–21
health (Western medicine), 29–
33
impact on, 14–15
individuality, 18
interpersonal styles, 15, 17
mañana mentality, 27
medical thinking (as a machine),
22–23
personal choice, 16–17
rationalism, 33–34
variety among cultures, 27–29

Fahrenheit 451 (Bradbury), 56
Failure, 61–62
Fairy tales, 76, 92
"Fall" (Adam and Eve myth),
47–48
Familiar stranger, theme of, 111–12
Feedback, 22, 40, 46, 49, 142, 163,
187, 205, 211
ignoring, 23
linearity, 45
negative, 45, 52, 61, 62
Finger-tip control, 12–13
Flouridation, 143
Foster, F., 37
Foucault, Michel, 173, 174
Frankenstein (Shelley), 19
Frantic buying activity, 16
Free choice, 172

Freedom, 46, 48–50, 83
authoritarianism and, 55–56
as inherently illusory, 58
from instinct, 49–50
meaning of, 58
of the mind, 59
schizoid type of, 23
search for, 64
self-mystification of, 48–49
and will, 58–62
Freud, Sigmund, 22, 39, 61, 80,
111, 124, 149
Fromm, Eric, 55
Future, the, history and, 151–53

Garden of Eden myth, 46–48
Gatling, R. J., 9
Genovese, Kitty, 59
Gestalt therapy, 56, 74
Gioscia, Victor, 164, 193
Goffman, Erving, 177
Gotterdammerung fantasies, 65
Greek drama, 57
Group communication, 69–70
Guerrilla theater, 204
Guilt, 121–22
Gun control, 143–44

Hannibal, 185
Harmony, internal, 206–7
Harroff, Peggy, 119
Harvard Bureau of Study Counsel,
17
Hays, H. R., 87
Heaven, idea of, 109
Heimlich sensations, 22
Hermits, 56, 174
Hippocrates, 32
Hiroshima, bombing of, 23
Hitler, Adolf, 76
Household prophets, specialization
and, 83–86
Housewives' time, attitudes about,
179–80

Human, meaning of, 4
Human evolution, tempo of, 38–39

Ideology, 76, 144–45
  of free expression, 206
  of individualism, 55
Idries Shah, 69
Incest taboo, 108
Individualism, 44, 53, 55, 80, 144
  arrogance of, 162
  beginning of, 18
  manufacture of mutations, 75
  as a shell game, 82
  social mobility of, 130–31
Industrialism, 11
  mechanical *weltanschauung*, 19
Infantile omnipotence, fantasy of, 12
Influence, receptivity to, 53–54
Instinct, freedom from, 49–50
Intellectuals, skills taught to, 43–44
I. Q. tests, 120
Interpersonal sensitivity, development of, 188
Interpersonal style, marital selection,
  17
Isolated nuclear family, social eversion, 169. *See also* Nuclear
  family, social climbing and

Jack and the Beanstalk, 114
Janov, Arthur, 155
Jesus Christ, 174
Jonathan Livingston Seagull, 94–97

Karate classes for women, 131
Kingdoms, social forms of, 79–81
Kinship, 78–79
Kissinger, Henry, 155
Kristofferson, K., 37

La Barre, Weston, 22, 49–50, 51, 72
Labor, division of, 83–86, 145
  re-evaluation of, 131
  by sex, 198

value of, 84
Laing, Ronald, 45, 46, 59, 62, 63–
  64, 65, 179, 187
Language, 3–4, 85, 168
Lao Tzu, 69, 105, 137, 161
Laura (motion picture), 111
Lewis, C. S., 48, 112, 137
Liberation movements, demands of,
  166
Libido, 89
Limits to Growth, The (Club of
  Rome), 38
Linearity and principle, 43–45
  feedback, 45
  sense of unimpeded motion in, 44
Living by the clock, 60–61
Locke, John, 169
Lorenz, Konrad, 55
Love, 49, 98, 99, 116
  child's loss of, 121
  romantic, 111
Lowen, Alexander, 1, 2, 37, 60, 61,
  62, 115, 154

McClelland, David, 113, 114, 125
Machines, invention of, 22
Machismo ethics, 88
McLuhan, Marshall, 44
Madmen, attitude toward, 173
Man, meaning of, 4
Mañana mentality, 27
Marital selection, 17
Mass production, 63
Maternal behavior, 91
Matriarchy, 87
Mead, Margaret, 188
Mechanical responsivity, 53–57
  duckling myth, 94
Medicine, Western society, 29–33,
  108, 202
  advancement of, 32
  duckling myth and, 97–98, 99,
  100
  as a machine, 22–23

power factor in, 32–33
treatment of infants, 91
Mental hospitals, 57
Middle of the Night (motion picture), 17–18
Millman, Marcia, 57
Mind-body dualism, 59
Modernism, beginning of, 79
Money, being sensible about, 53
Monster films, theme of, 14
Montague, Ashley, 127, 188
Morality, objectification of, 54
Morimoto, Kiyo, 16–17
Mumford, Lewis, 174
Mutation pattern, 75–76, 92, 171

Nabokov, 112
Napoleon I, 28
Narcissism, 18, 25, 79, 80, 95, 156, 161, 167, 169, 199, 200, 212
and longing for immortality, 47
male commitment to, 89
of the prophet, 73–74
Nasrudin, Mulla, 185
Natural selection, 99–100
Nazi party, 177
Negative power, 123–24, 154–55
Neo-Classic era, 163
Neo-Romantic era, 163
Network system, community, 15–16
Newton, Isaac, 169
Nicholas II, Czar, 80
1984 (Orwell), 56
Nuclear family, social climbing and, 105–9
achievement, 122–29
specialization and power, 122–25
women and mobility, 125–29
behavior pattern, 107–8
castes and classes, 106
oedipal strivings, 109–13
parent prerogatives, 108
priorities of pleasure, 115–21

routes to status change, 130–32
sexual intercourse, 108
stratification by age, 108–9
successful executive (McClelland pattern), 113–14
tension within, 109
youth as subordinate class, 132–34
Nursing homes, 57
Nurturance, diffusion of, 116–17

Objectivity, 52
simple community, 41–42
Objects, utilitarian orientation to, 63
Oedipal strivings, 110–11, 112
careerism, 132
decline of, 132
Oedipus myth, 109–10
Oil depletion allowances, 141
Oppression, adaptation to, 175
Order, importance of, 146–47
Overpopulation, 169

Paranoid process, 10, 11, 49, 51, 59, 143
Part tasks, competence at, 83
Pasteur, Louis, 143
Patriarchal revolution, 86–92
competitiveness, 92
duckling myth and, 92–99
as recent phenomenon, 87
specialization, 87–88, 89, 90
Patriarchy, 4, 87
Peloponnesian War, 48
Perls, Fritz, 56
Personal choice, notion of, 16, 17
Personal involvement, 83
Peter Ibbetson, 112
Pharmacology, 31
Pills, side effects of, 31
Plato, 37
Platonism, 62
Pleasure
behavior based on, 60

in non-stress situations, 115–16
obtaining, 13
priorities, social climbing and, 115–21
sexual, 111
Poison, defined, 37
Police organizations, rank-and-file, 196
Political science, 202–3
Pollution, 141, 168
industrial, 11
psychic, 11, 50
technological, 10, 11
Population, growth of, 39
Portrait of Jenny, A, 112
Positive power, uses of, 123
Possessions, value attached to, 63
Power
achievement and specialization, 122–25
to allay anxiety, 51
balance of, 123
center of, rewards and, 42
diffusion of, 195–96
energy, social change and, 153–58
negative, 123–24, 154–55
positive, 123
presidential, 153–54
Pride, 115
Primal horde, myth of, 80
Prisons, 57
Progress, idea of, 3
Prophet dynamic, 69–101, 106, 161
autonomy, 74
division of labor, 83–86
duckling myth and, 92–99
individualistic delusion of, 73
narcissism, 73–74
parent system and, 71, 73
patriarchal revolution, 86–92
personality of, 72
physical autonomy of, 84, 86
Propaganda, "truth squad" approach to, 72

Protestant ethic, 142, 164, 175, 178, 199
Protestantism, 164
Psychedelic movement, 168
Psychic pollution, 11, 50
Psychic research, 168
Psychopathology, 22
Psychotics, 72
Punishment (for social errors), 62
Push-button control, 12–13

Racism, 176
Radical movements, 43
Rationalism, 33–34, 90, 150–51
compartmentalized, 155
schizoid process, 178
Reality, 12, 22, 50, 117, 168–69
despair and, 2–3
dictating, 61
guilt, social climbing and, 121–22
proving one's, 65
Reappearance theme, 111
Reciprocal gift giving, 12–13
Recycling, requirements of, 11
Referral agencies, 57
Reformation, 81
Reich, Wilhelm, 98
Reincarnation, 109
Rembrandt, 48
Renaissance, 133, 163
Reversionism, 152
Riesman, David, 55, 118
Romanticism, 117, 118, 163
Romantic love, 111, 117
Rome (ancient), 178
Roth, Philip, 95
Rudolph the Red-Nosed Reindeer, 92, 93, 95
Rules of society, feast days putting aside, 170–71

Schismogenesis, 171

Schizoid process, 22, 23, 31, 40,
    45–53, 89, 150, 187, 203
  Adam and Eve myth, 46–48
  conceptual systems, 51–53
  emergence of culture, 50–51
  freedom, 48–50
  living by the clock, 60–61
  susceptibility to response, 59
  use of will power, 60
Science fiction, 11–12, 19–20, 112
  film themes, 14
Scientific medicine. *See* Medicine
    Western society
Security data banks, 11
Self-consciousness, 101, 155, 191
Selye, 39
Sex roles, women's movement attack
    on, 198
Sexual conquests, 119
Sexual mores, changes in, 89–90
Sexual pleasure, 111
Shaw, Gary, 95
Simmonds, 172
Simple community, 200
  child's needs, 116
  collective behavior of, 77
  family crisis, 57
  kinship categories, 78–79
  leaders of, 77
  mass democracy and, 77, 78
  objectivity in, 41–42
  primeval bliss in, 27–28
  social control, 55
Social change, 3, 137–58
  American approach to, 138
  media-defined, 106
  misconceptions, 138–58
    cognitive process, 149–51
    futility of positive programs,
      140–42
    linear, 151–53
    power and energy, 153–58
    stress and, 138–40
    when right is right, 142–49

  pendulum effect, 167
  real, 105, 167
  ways of, 161–81
    deviance and containment,
      172–81
    and forms of, 163–67
    role of cultural attic, 170–72
    social eversion, 167–70
Social climbing, 71, 105–34
  achievement, specialization, and
    power, 122–25
  nuclear family, 105–9
    behavior pattern, 107–8
    castes and classes, 106
    parent prerogatives, 108
    sexual intercourse, 108
    stratification by age, 108–9
    tension within, 109
    youth as subordinate class, 132–
      34
  oedipal strivings, 109–13
  priorities of pleasure, 115–21
  reality and guilt, 121–22
  routes to status change, 130–32
  successful (McClelland pattern),
    113–14
  women, mobility, and achieve-
    ment, 125–29
Social division, concept of, 107
Social errors, 62
Social eversion, 129, 152–53
  examples of, 167–70
Social justice, search for, 41
Social metastasis, 37–66
  adaptation to bad environment, 40
  authoritarianism, 41–42
  cancer metaphor describing, 39–
    40
  drama and detachment, 57–58
  exploitation and brutality, 41–43
  freedom and will, 58–62
  linearity and principle, 43–45
  mechanical responsibility, 53–57
  population, 39

power factor, 42
schizoid process, 45–53, 59
social justice and, 41
technological culture, 62–66
Sophocles, 105
Soulmates, idea of, 111
South Vietnam, 29
Space exploration, 11–12, 167
Spatial closeness, 169
Speck, Ross, 16
Spock, Dr. Benjamin, 190
Spontaneity, 205–6
Status change, routes to, 130–32
Status quo, the, 56, 148, 152
Stephens, William, 77–78, 80
Stereotypic public personality, 72
Stress, change and, 138–40
Successful executives (McClelland pattern), 113–14
Suicidal despair, 3
Surrender signals, human beings 22–23
Swindlers, trust and, 100–1

Taylor, G. Rattray, 80
Technological culture, 62–66
  developments in, 65
  false-self system in, 64
  relationships within, 80
Technological development, war and, 14
Technological growth, competition and, 14
Technology, extensions of man and, 9–34
  arrogant virtues, 26–27
  autarchy, 17–18
  automaton behavior, 22–23
  boosters of, 33
  "cannot be stopped" argument, 34
  control, 9–14
  courage and perseverance, 23–26
  genetic code, 19–21

health (Western medicine), 29–33
  impact on, 14–15
  individuality, 18
  interpersonal styles, 15, 17
  mañana mentality, 27
  medical thinking (as a machine), 22–23
  network system, 14–15
  personal choice, 16–17
  rationalism, 33–34
  variety among cultures, 27–29
Telepathy, 168
Thompson, William, 5
Time machine fantasy, 112
Toffler, Alvin, 20, 21, 28, 34, 40, 76, 77, 82, 83, 113, 129, 138–39, 150, 152–53, 172
Tolerance, implications of, 148
Transference, Freudian idea of, 117
Trust, swindlers and, 100–1

Ugly duckling. *See* Duckling myth
Unheimlich sensations, 22
Unilateral disarmament, 143
U. S. Mail, 141
Unloved person, recognizing, 98–99

Venceremos Brigade (Cimino), 35
Vietnam War, 23, 28, 95, 189

Wars, 14, 48, 113
  of small tribes, 77
Washington political community, 157
We (Zamiatin), 244
Weber, Max, 81
Whyte, Jr., William H., 55
Wiener, Norbert, 20
Women
  consciousness raising, 177
  containment of, 177–78
  in Eastern cultures, 129

T.